GRACE
AND GRIT

GRACE
AND GRIT

My Fight for Equal Pay and Fairness
at Goodyear and Beyond

|||||||||||||||||||||||||||||||||||||||||||||||||||||||||||||||||||||||||||||||||||||||||||||||||||||||

Lilly Ledbetter

WITH LANIER SCOTT ISOM

THREE RIVERS PRESS
NEW YORK

Copyright © 2012 by Lilly Ledbetter

All rights reserved.
Published in the United States by Three Rivers Press,
an imprint of the Crown Publishing Group,
a division of Random House, Inc., New York.
www.crownpublishing.com

Three Rivers Press and the Tugboat design are
registered trademarks of Random House, Inc.

Originally published in hardcover and in slightly different form in the
United States by Crown Archetype, an imprint of the Crown Publishing
Group, a division of Random House, Inc., New York, in 2012.

Library of Congress Cataloging-in-Publication Data
Ledbetter, Lilly M.
Grace and grit: my fight for equal pay and fairness at Goodyear
and beyond / Lilly Ledbetter with Lanier Isom.—1st ed.
p. cm.
1. Sex discrimination against women—United States—
History—21st century. 2. Ledbetter, Lilly M. 3. Women—
United States—Biography. 4. Sex discrimination against
women—Law and legislation—United States. 5. Goodyear
Tire and Rubber Company. I. Isom, Lanier Scott. II. Title.
HQ1237.5.U6L43 2012
331.4'2153092—dc23
[B]   2011034579

ISBN 978-0-307-88794-8
eISBN 978-0-307-88793-1

Printed in the United States of America

BOOK DESIGN BY BARBARA STURMAN
PHOTOGRAPH ON PAGE 245: AP PHOTO/RON EDMONDS
COVER DESIGN BY NUPOOR GORDON
COVER PHOTOGRAPH BY JASON WALLIS

2 4 6 8 10 9 7 5 3 1

First Paperback Edition

CONTENTS

PROLOGUE

DURING MY time at Goodyear, I'd discovered many an anonymous note at work, some serious, some not. Once, a guy left a note on my car windshield asking me out. The next thing I knew, as I waited for my bacon-and-cheese biscuit in the drive-through at Hardee's on my way home, that fool came knocking on my window to see if I'd gotten his message. Another time, someone wrote, "My brother's married to a white woman. Would you go out with me?" At that time in Alabama—we're home to more civil rights struggles than anywhere in the country—you didn't see blacks and whites dating. I was slightly amused by that one. Other times, I found notes like the one warning me about another crew trying to take credit for my crew's production numbers by changing information in the computer, and the one telling me that excess scrap rubber on the floor was going to be blamed on my shift rather than the shift that actually caused the problem.

Over the span of twenty years at Goodyear, I'd probably gotten a dozen notes. Most of the time I figured they were from workers on the day shift, but I never knew exactly who wrote them. Whoever left the helpful notes, though, made it possible for me to survive situations that could have ended my career. No one else I knew of, neither management nor union workers, received notes like these, at least no one ever said so. I have to believe this was because I stood out in the crowd, to say the least, as one of only a handful of women managers at Goodyear.

THE DAY I discovered the note that changed the course of my life started like any other.

If you've never been to Alabama, you probably don't know that we have the prettiest springs in the world. Late that afternoon the pear trees were in full bloom and the cherry trees were starting to unveil their pink buds. I was driving to work as usual, heading west on the two-lane highway snaking through the rolling hills, only a couple of other cars on the road, probably people like me going to work at one of the plants in Gadsden.

All through my years at Goodyear, the highlight of my day was the ritual of going to work while most people were coming home. I loved seeing the sky's changing colors as evening fell and the endless headlights streaming toward Jacksonville while I traveled in the opposite direction, my Buick riding quiet and smooth. I always did like to travel my own road.

That afternoon before I left, my husband, Charles, kept following me around the house while I was getting ready, trying to convince me to stay home from work, to give my injured knee some rest—it had been about a week since my coworker had accidentally shut one of the hydraulic gates on me. I had a knot as big as a baseball on my knee, but I only had two more days until my appointment with the orthopedist and I was determined not to miss work.

But Charles was the type of person who borrowed worry. As

he stood behind me in the bathroom while I applied my mascara, he was downright mad, insisting I take his advice. He fussed about the fact I was lifting heavy Hummer tires, telling me I'd ruin my knee for good if I didn't listen to him. Recently retired from Fort McClellan, where he'd overseen housing on the army base, he was probably hoping I'd stick around to eat dinner with him and keep him company through the evening, watching an episode of his favorite show, *Law & Order*.

Even though Charles was well aware that Goodyear frowned on any absence from work, he just didn't understand how anxious I'd become lately. Over the previous year, rumors about layoffs and the plant shutting down had been flying around. Several batches of bad tires had gotten out the door, and I'd been blamed for one batch of four hundred that had been scrapped. Everyone, both managers and the union workers, was on edge.

Charles's haranguing wasn't helping my nerves, so when I about poked my eye with my mascara wand, I snapped at him to find something else to nitpick about. Then I locked him out of the bathroom to wrestle the support hose onto my good leg in peace. The next thing I knew, Charles hollered at me through the door that he was running down to McDonald's to buy me a chocolate milk shake for supper. I smiled thinking about him throwing on his jacket and shoes to hustle out the door. Charles was always in motion; he couldn't sit still if his life depended on it, not even to watch TV (unless *Law & Order* or the Atlanta Braves were on). The minute he got home from work, he'd make a pot of coffee and throw his laundry into the washing machine before he went out to rake some leaves or cut the grass. As long as he was straightening and fixing around the house, he was happy and his blue eyes sparkled.

A little while later I finally got out the door. I kissed Charles good-bye, milk shake in hand. It was impossible to stay mad at him for long. It was then, rushing down the walkway, that I heard the whippoorwill's call. Hurried as I was, I stopped still to listen. When I was a girl, if my grandmother Granny Mac heard a whippoorwill, she immediately took to bed. She swore someone was going to die. Standing in the driveway, listening to its haunting song, I tried to shrug off a child's sense of dread.

By the time I got past Jacksonville onto the old highway, I began to think about the job. I looked forward to this hour when I sorted through most of my problems. Passing churches and junkyards I'd driven by a thousand times, I couldn't help but think about how much I missed the tire room. Tire building was one of the toughest jobs at the plant. I'd loved the work and the old-timers, now in their fifties and sixties, who'd been building tires since they were teenagers, just like their fathers. I'd recently been transferred to quality control, where I just didn't feel like I belonged. The fact that my coworker, used to working solo, had slammed a hydraulic gate on my leg because he forgot that I was walking behind him, certainly seemed like a sign. And everybody knew my transfer had been a demotion, retaliation for speaking out about my supervisor's unfair performance evaluations.

As the miles melted behind me and I got closer to the plant, I remembered how I used to be able to leave behind worries about what was going on with the kids or Charles as I mused over the details that awaited me in the tire room. I'd run through the stock that needed prepping, how many men might not report to work, and the production schedule. By the time I checked in at the gates of the plant, I'd have sealed off my emotions, ready for work.

Now I could feel myself trying to clamp down on my worries about my new department. I knew that once I walked through those steel gates, I needed to carry my shoulders high like Hector, my ballroom dancing teacher, taught me, "reaching them toward my back pocket," as he put it. I took a deep breath and tapped my fingers on the steering wheel as I hummed my favorite tune, "Bad,

Bad Leroy Brown," picturing myself on the dance floor. That helped a little.

When I reached the plant that evening I was running late, and my knee throbbed. I stopped by my cubby in the small, empty office area upstairs across from the copying room to check my mail, as I'd done every day at Goodyear. I flipped through the company memos about the upcoming safety-training class and fliers about the next car collectors show being held in the parking lot, almost missing the torn piece of copy paper with black handwriting on it.

I read the scribbled words, and my heart jerked as if an electric jolt had coursed through my body. Though I stood perfectly still, I was churning inside. I quickly stuck the note in my pocket and hurried to the ladies' room, where I sat on the sofa trying to breathe. I hoped no one in the copy room had noticed me leave in such a hurry.

I'd never in my life gotten a note like this before. Someone had listed my name and those of the three other tire-room managers, with salaries next to each name. My salary was exactly correct, down to the dollar. Over the years, I'd worried about being paid less than the men who were doing the same work I was, but I didn't have any proof. I was like a wife nursing a nagging suspicion that her husband's having an affair, with no hard evidence. But now there it was in plain black ink, what I'd always feared: The other managers, all men, had been making more than I was.

A lot more.

Still reeling, I got up and started pacing the bathroom floor, wishing I'd stayed home with Charles, like he'd suggested. Then I stopped and pulled the crumpled paper from my pocket. The paper listed three men who'd started in 1979, the same year I did. The one woman on my original squadron of five was long gone, and over the years the few women who'd been promoted to management hadn't lasted. Now, in 1998, I was one of a few female area managers in the entire operation of about fourteen hundred people. I often wondered how the other women managers were making it, although I never got the opportunity to talk to them. The plant was so large, and I never socialized outside of work. It was always clear that I'd never be part of the boys' club—and that was just as well. It wasn't a club that I wanted to belong to. So I kept my boundaries clear.

The annoying low buzzing of the fluorescent lights in the ladies' room filled my ears as I squinted at the numbers. Maybe I was seeing things. Maybe this note was a serious mistake or a bad joke. But I knew in my gut that it wasn't. If you've ever hit an animal driving down the road, you know the sickening recognition the thudding sound sends through your body. I had that feeling in spades.

As I read those numbers again and again, I couldn't help but think how I'd started at Goodyear. Almost forty at the time, I was far from naïve: I'd known from the get-go that I'd have to work longer and smarter than the men in order to prove myself. But how in the world could I have been paid less all these years? The difference in salaries just didn't make sense.

I stood frozen, finally raising my eyes to the ceiling. I stared at the spread of brown water stains on the white ceiling tiles. Layers of thick gray dust coated the steel vent, and the outline of a dead roach rested directly above me in its fluorescent grave. I had to close my eyes. That was a mistake. Suddenly, a feeling of dread overwhelmed me, the same feeling I had when I went to sleep these days and dreamed about not being able to find my way out of the plant or about crazy gigantic tires chasing me. This was far worse.

After a few minutes, I knew I had to get it together or I'd really be late. That's when I felt the shame, the haunting humiliation deep in my bones. As the numbers kept looping through my mind, I couldn't shake the realization of how stupid I'd been to try so hard and think that it would pay off. I'd wanted so badly to win approval, and I had done so in the eyes of most of my coworkers, who valued my hard work and loyalty—and who gave it back to me.

But how dumb I'd been to think that this would counter the hostility surrounding me. How arrogant to think that I was the woman who had the strength to win at Goodyear. Those numbers said loud and clear that it didn't matter how hard I'd worked, how much I'd wanted to succeed and do the right thing: I'd been born the wrong sex, and that was that.

Unable to budge, I glanced at my watch and then stuffed the note into my pocket. I rubbed my face, trying to bury what was now nothing short of a sense of desperation. After I washed my hands, I stared at myself in the large mirror. On the outside, nothing about me had changed. But as surely as if I'd looked out a window and seen the sky turn an uncanny grayish pink and felt that strange stillness right before a funnel cloud forms, my horizon had transformed, my life had shifted, and a storm was headed my way.

CHAPTER 1

Possum Trot

||||||||||||||||||||||||||||||||||||||||||||||||||||||||||||||||||||||||||||||||||||||||||||||||||||||||||||||||

Have you heard of the
Nothing impossible possum
Whose faith and belief made
His dream to blossom?

—MARJORIE AINSBOROUGH DECKER,
The Christian Mother Goose Book of Nursery Rhymes

IF YOU grow up in Possum Trot, Alabama, you run across some rough characters from time to time. You might even be related to a few. In truth, the tough guys at Goodyear weren't a far cry from what I'd seen and heard in the fields picking cotton or in the barn helping milk the cows at Aunt Lucille's dairy farm.

I'll never forget the afternoon when my grandfather, Papa, decided he wanted to kill my dog, Buzz. Papa, who claimed to be part Irish, was so pale that he looked part ghost. I'm honestly not sure there was any good in him, but I can also say that he wasn't all that different from most of the other men around me.

I was only five the day Papa came after Buzz, but my memory of that afternoon is clear as day. I was playing tea party in the front yard, scooping up dirt with a broken teacup Granny Mac had given me, and Buzz was my honored guest. As I set down a cup in front of Buzz, I heard Papa hollering down the road. I looked back at the house, hoping to see that Mama was still right inside the screen door cooking supper, and that she'd hear the racket in time to come out and protect me and Buzz. She wasn't. As Papa's large figure approached us, my stomach clenched. He was carrying something; it looked like a hoe.

I'd never had a pet before, unless you count the rooster who used to follow me around. But one day Buzz had appeared out of nowhere. We immediately took to each other. He was a funny little dog, brown and white and black with one dark spot shaped like a pumpkin seed on the top of his forehead. I used to rub that spot like it was a good-luck penny. I figured his breed was part everything, with his big hound-dog eyes, those large feet he slapped in front of him like clown shoes, and that mismatched coloring pieced together like a crazy quilt.

By the time Papa was close enough for me to make out what he was saying, Buzz had scooted under the house. "Where's that goddam worthless mutt?" he yelled. "He ain't worth killing."

I couldn't say a word. I couldn't even move. My mouth was as dry as if I'd swallowed the cup of dirt. All I could think about was how Papa would slaughter the pigs in the smokehouse. I always got attached to one of them, so I made a point of being as far away from the smokehouse as possible when killing time came. I wanted no part of wash pots filled with boiling-hot water and the hanging, splitting, and dressing of the meat. But I did show up about the time sausage was frying in the deep black skillet.

"Goddammit, Lilly. You better mind me and get that dog." Papa's eyes were moist and almost closed, like they had Vaseline smeared on them. He turned around and around in a circle trying to find Buzz, almost falling. He was drunk, really drunk. He lurched toward me, and I jumped up. Buzz must have thought Papa was going to hurt me because he shot out from under the porch, growling and circling us. Papa lunged at him, slicing the hoe through the air. I tried to stay between Papa and Buzz, never even thinking that I might get hit.

As we continued to dance around each other, the screen door slapped shut at last, and Mama came out screaming at Papa. His face and large nose flushed red above his white collared shirt buttoned to the top under his overalls. But other than that he didn't pay Mama a bit of attention as he, Buzz, and I continued to waltz around each other, the hoe thudding hard whenever it hit the ground.

"I mean it, Tot," she said, using the name everyone (but me) called him. "Don't make no sense to be scaring Lilly like that. Put it down."

But he was having none of it. He seemed to get madder and madder, and the hoe seemed closer to Buzz with every swing.

Suddenly Mama flew down the front steps, a long butcher knife in her hand, the same knife she always sharpened on the pedaling wheel before Papa killed the hogs. But not even the knife seemed to sway him. Papa, three times as big as she was, towered above her.

"Go on, Lilly. Get in the house," Mama said. I could see the look in her eyes, the fear and hatred that made her seem as wild as a rabid dog. I ran up onto the porch and, thankfully, Buzz followed.

Papa's eyes flashed anger at me as I stared at him through the screen door, my breath coming in quick gasps.

"Go on home and leave that dog alone," Mama said. She kept that butcher knife raised and pointed at him the whole time, jabbing it a few times in his direction when his temper flared back up. He dropped the hoe at last, and Mama backed him all the way down the steep driveway to the dirt road. And he left, lumbering and swaying his way back home.

As I watched this scene, I felt like I was suffocating, as if someone had stuck a sack of cotton over my head. I'd heard Mama tell my father how Papa had beaten her as a child. When she was little and he got to drinking, one of his buddies would rush to the house to warn my grandmother that Papa was headed home. She'd hustle the four boys and my mother out of bed to make a run for the barn, hiding in the hay for the rest of the night. Other times, without warning, Papa barged into their bedrooms, hickory stick in hand, and the beatings began.

After that day, I still rode on top of Papa's wagon and helped him feed the cows and guinea hens, but I never trusted him again. I remember telling myself I'd better be careful about who I let myself love. It was likely they'd turn on you. I also realized it was a good idea to have a knife nearby whenever possible.

Not long after, Buzz disappeared. I figured he just wandered off. Thankfully, it never occurred to me then that Papa might have gotten his way after all.

MANY YEARS later, when I first started working at Goodyear, the union guys liked to tell the women that they were going to "pick" us. That is, they were going to catch us and pick each pubic hair from our bodies. Like so much that happened there, when you put it in words and see it on paper, it sounds too unreal to believe. But they were always up to some prank or another, often making work a dangerous sport.

One day, a woman worker, fed up with the constant haranguing, actually dropped her pants and dared the men to do it. With her pants bunched around her ankles, she stood there in her plain white underwear. The guys backed off her but kept up their nonsense with the rest of us. I knew I'd never do what she did, but I also knew they often made good on their word, one time pinning down one of the new young guys and picking him clean. I went home and found one of Charles's knives to carry in my pocket, the hard leather sheath resting against my thigh in case they ever decided to test me.

Countless times throughout the years at Goodyear when I needed courage, I remembered how Mama had finally tamed Papa that summer afternoon. I never doubted my mother would have used the butcher knife that day, and in my moments of fear and anger, I never doubted I'd use my own knife if necessary.

THE PLACE where I grew up during the 1940s is a small bend in the road along the foot of Choccolocco Mountain in northeast Alabama. Just like those pinch-faced gray possums that roamed the pine forests, the people in that small community in the foothills of the Appalachians knew a thing or two about survival. They worked in the cotton or steel mills or scratched a living from the dirt. Some worked in the foundries or the army depot in nearby Anniston or, if they were lucky, had a good-paying job at Goodyear in Gadsden. The folks I knew would walk over broken glass to help a neighbor and just as soon kill you if you did them wrong.

In 1946, I was in second grade when my father came home from the navy and my parents bought land from Papa to build a slightly bigger house across the road from him. Life started looking up for my family then. It took me a while to adjust to the gleam from the naked bulb hanging off the thin cord from the ceiling, since I'd been so used to the soft glow of gaslight. A couple of years later, we got indoor plumbing and things really changed for the better. Gone were the days of tiptoeing through the wet grass in the black of night, wondering if I'd step on a rattlesnake on the way to the outhouse.

Our new house wasn't much to look at, but we were lucky. We were the only ones in Possum Trot, besides the brick mason, who owned a television. Daddy worked the night shift at the Anniston Army Depot six days a week, where he reworked engines on the battered military tanks sent home from Korea and later from Vietnam and the Middle East. Before we bought the TV, in the evenings when Daddy was gone, Mama and I had nowhere to go and nothing to do—except for Saturday evening, when we turned on the radio, silent all week to save batteries, and listened to the

Grand Ole Opry. But once we got the TV, folks gathered in every corner and doorway of our small house many evenings to watch the nightly news.

During the day, I had to come up with my own entertainment, and I ran wild, disappearing for hours to climb trees and explore the woods. My cousin Louise and I spent entire days searching for caves or hunting for arrowheads in the Indian cemetery. We also loved to mimic the holy dancing we saw at the church campground down the road.

Despite these wistful memories, nearly all of my childhood was spent in endless work. In the misty summer mornings Mama and I picked beans and okra before the sun started blazing down on us. After we headed back to the house to bathe and change, we spent the rest of the day hulling peas, skinning tomatoes, and blanching vegetables to can for the winter. We only stopped canning to sleep. On the weekends we roamed the woods to fill our syrup buckets with huckleberries and blackberries for jam and cobbler, slapping the itchy bites from the invisible chiggers with Listerine to keep them from driving us crazy.

Growing up, I never lacked for essentials, and I certainly never went hungry. I knew we were better off than a good many folks. Of course, I was also painfully aware that we weren't as well off as some others—like my best friend, Sandra. I'd known her since first grade. While I wore homemade bloomers, Sandra could afford silk panties. Every day she came to school in a coordinated sweater and skirt, never without a perfect strand of pearls. Even the teachers called her "little princess."

Sandra's family lived in New Liberty, a neighborhood where no one whitewashed their trees or kept chickens running around the front yard. There, children didn't have to share a bedroom with their grandmother, like I did. Sitting in front of the large mirror at Sandra's elegant dressing table, I'd angle her hand mirror every which way to see my reflection, hoping to improve my profile. But there it always was, clear as day, the bump in the middle of my nose, the same mysterious Indian nose as Granny Mac's and Daddy's.

Every time I came home from Sandra's, I felt inferior. Just the sight of my dingy white house and dusty dirt yard made me ashamed even though I knew how far we'd come. I dared not say anything about my disappointment. I saw how hard my parents worked. But the older I got, the more transparent the differences in my life and Sandra's became, and my sense of embarrassment stayed with me, as indelible as a birthmark. I was keenly aware that all this privilege was due to Goodyear, where Sandra's father worked. New Liberty was where the Goodyear families lived. And it's where, more than anywhere, I wanted to be.

I used to stare at the Goodyear plant when I passed it on my annual summer Greyhound bus trip to Aunt Mattie Bell and Uncle Hoyt's small duplex house in Gadsden. Right before you got into town, there was the plant, next to the Coosa River. A giant red-brick building with slits for windows, it sprawled for blocks behind a tall steel fence like a fortress. The huge smokestacks billowed black smoke. Riding past the plant, I dreamed about what it would have been like to ride around in a brand-new Mercury every few years like Sandra. Or I imagined swimming in the Gulf Coast during spring break like she did. I even fantasized about how smooth my hands would be if my daddy worked at Goodyear. Maybe even best of all, if he did, I'd never have to pick cotton again.

ALL MY life I'd been surrounded by one continuous cotton field. I started picking cotton there before I entered first grade and had been picking ever since. It was the only job around, and I was in the field every weekend with my cousin Louise making extra money for the family. When I was older, during the summer Louise and I chopped cotton before it matured in order to earn some spending money of our own. We slung our hoes into the ground, attacking the johnsongrass that spread like gossip between the rows, sputtering complaints to each other that we dared not offer to any-one else. It wasn't just the cotton. When we picked corn, we bel-lyached the same way, row after row, as cornstalks slapped our bare necks and scratched our hands.

At the end of the day, two men shouldered a pole between them and hooked our sack of cotton onto the P ring as Papa—all six foot five of him—loomed above me and slid a heavy metal ball across the bar to determine how many pounds we'd plucked from the prickly stalks. It took days to fill our long, skinny sacks. Sometimes it felt like I was trying to fill the sack with clouds.

Each time Papa weighed my sack, I held my breath, willing the ball to move farther. I enjoyed the anticipation of weighing my day's work. Being paid meant not having to listen to Mama tell me no for the hundredth time. It meant I could save for the ready-made dress that was hanging in the window at Hudson's department store in town. I was by now darn right sick of the homemade dresses my mother sewed from feed sacks. Yes, clothes were a focus of mine in those days. I was a teenager, after all.

In the fall of my ninth-grade year, I fell in love with the outfit of all outfits. I pined away for one thing more than anything else: a cheerleading outfit. I'd tried out for the squad with Sandra, and I made the cut. I was so thrilled, I actually thought my whole life was going to change for the better, until I realized I had no way to get to the evening basketball games and the outfit would cost a whopping $25.

Mama didn't drive, but that didn't really matter because Daddy needed the car to get to work every night anyway. But even that wasn't the point. Neither of them had ever set foot in school, so there was no reason to think they'd do so now, just because I'd made the cheerleading squad. I finally convinced one of the bas-ketball coaches to pick me up and take me to the games. But when I told my parents at supper that I needed to buy the outfit, Mama about scared me and Daddy to death.

She stopped eating and slapped her hand against the wooden table. "Let me tell you one thing, young lady. My best dress coat didn't even cost twenty-five dollars! You're going have to pay for that outfit."

How could I have forgotten how Mama acted any time I wanted anything? She worried nonstop about whether we had enough money to pay the bills. All her talk made me think we were on the verge of having the lights cut off. If she wasn't calculating what we needed for next week's groceries, she was reminiscing about not having any sugar or any paper for the butter during the war rationing. And if it was anybody's fault, it was Roosevelt's: Mama blamed him for the Depression and the fact that when Daddy made a dollar a day working in the brickyard, two cents went to Social Security.

That night at supper as I felt the tears fill my eyes, I pictured how the salesman had shown the team the sweaters, how all of us girls fell so hard. We'd never seen anything so glamorous— the dark gold sweater with the purple capital letters RW for "Roy Webb" sewn in the middle, the gold silk skirt that flashed purple when you twirled, the delicate beanie to pin in your hair. Until that moment, I'd never wanted anything as much as that cheerleading outfit.

LATER, LYING in bed seething as Granny Mac snored away beside me, I reminded myself that Mama had been through a lot, and my life, cheerleading outfit or not, was roses compared with hers. Of course, being Mama, she rarely talked about her past. That would be a waste of time. I wondered so often what had made her so hard. But the only relic that she'd kept was a tattered Bible with a few funny-spelled names and ghostly dates scribbled in light pencil inside the cover.

It was only Granny Mac, Daddy's mother, who liked to tell stories about her past. But whenever she'd launch into one about my father's family, Mama hushed her. All I knew about Granny Mac herself was that she grew up an orphan in Georgia. I looked over at her sleeping peacefully and wished she were awake to distract me from my anger and my aching want.

She'd found another way to use her storytelling skills, and she loved to do so when it was pitch-dark outside. Her dark Indian eyes would glitter in the bedroom we shared, her long black hair flowing loosely, freed from the braided bun she wore during the day, as she told me ghost story after ghost story. She about kept me from ever going to sleep with all those stories. There was the one about the murdered man whose blood seeped down the walls of the house when it rained. But the worst story was her favorite one, about the pig who dragged a baby under our house and ate it. As I'd slide under my quilt, she'd tell me to be still and listen. Didn't I hear that baby screaming under our room? It never occurred to me to ask whose baby it was or whether or not anyone ever came looking for it.

I hated that story, maybe in part because it reminded me in some strange way of another family story that was rarely spoken of, this one involving me: how I almost tore Mama in two when I was born and almost died myself. I first heard the story as I lay waiting for sleep on a pallet with the other children on the farm in Alpine, Alabama, where Aunt Lucille had taken us to pick scuppernongs, a type of muscadine grape. Behind the thin bedsheet hanging between the kitchen and the main room, Aunt Lucille told the other women about Mama being in labor for three days, my daddy unable to do anything but smoke and cry in the barn. Even with the help of two doctors and a nurse, we almost didn't make it. Aunt Lucille said my face was bruised and my body crooked. Many years later, I asked Mama about it. She only said that during labor her bones wouldn't separate. According to Aunt Lucille, Mama's body was so torn up, she wasn't able to have more children. That would explain why I was an only child.

Sometimes when Mama looked at me with that look of sour disapproval—like she did that night at dinner—I thought that maybe she'd never forgiven me for denying her more babies. I'd also wonder if she ever got over the time I almost burned her up. Mama had grabbed a piece of black coal I'd gotten hold of as a baby, and her skirt brushed against the smoldering coals in the fireplace. Fire blazed up her back. Daddy tried to put it out, but her whole backside burned. They couldn't afford a doctor, so he just bandaged her up. Whenever I saw the scars, I wanted to peel the scablike skin off her back to reveal the unharmed flesh underneath, which I imagined would be as pure and smooth as the white trunk of a sycamore tree.

On the rare occasion when my mother did talk about her family, it was clear that she'd had to carry too big a burden as a young girl. Her mother, Lillie (my namesake), was part Cherokee, a petite woman with a powerful touch, known for her herbal remedies and giving ease to women in labor with the tea she mixed from the roots of cotton plants. But when she came down with cancer, my grandmother couldn't heal herself, and died young. This left Mama to care for her four brothers, and for this reason, she never made it past the sixth grade in school.

Although Mama didn't grumble about what happened to her, she did judge the world with a harsh eye. I can't tell you how many times I heard Daddy whisper, "Hush now, Edna, that's not our business," before he took a cigarette from the pack of Camels in his shirt pocket and lit it.

Mama had the right way to snap beans, the right way to bake a coconut cake, piece a quilt, milk a cow, and break a chicken's neck. Whenever Granny Mac cooked supper, Mama made a comment: The sweet potatoes were too sweet, the meat too salty. Every night after supper, Granny Mac cleaned up the kitchen. And every night my mother came right behind her and cleaned the kitchen again. No one else could keep the kitchen as spotless as it was supposed to be.

Sweet Granny Mac claimed she was hard of hearing and

pretended not to hear Mama's put-downs. She went about her business, smiling and accepting things as they were, and never stood up to Mama. Maybe Granny Mac just didn't want to be orphaned again. (And she never was; years later when Granny Mac was sick and dying, Mama took care of her like she had her own mother, changing her diapers and bathing her from head to toe.)

That night, as I went to sleep still seething with a sense of unfairness and aching for that darn cheerleader's outfit, I tried to remind myself that Mama had her reasons to be tough. And, hard as it was, I forced myself to remember the times she'd been kind. I thought about when I'd contracted yellow jaundice from the contaminated water at school and been laid up for months, how she'd tended to me. I would get the chills all the time, and Mama seemed to sense when the cold came over me and gently wrapped my feet with a warm blanket she'd heated by the stove each night. Sometimes when she finished, she sat silent for a minute at the foot of my bed, her hand resting on my bundled feet. But I knew I couldn't expect her to understand what I was feeling now—how badly I wanted to step beyond my life as it was and into a new club where cheers and champions and a beautiful outfit awaited me. Feelings were luxuries for rich people. And the words "I want" were just not in her vocabulary.

So THE next weekend I picked cotton with Louise, trying to earn some money toward the outfit. The strap from the cotton sack might as well have been a snake around my neck. I remember saying to Louise, out of nowhere, "When I grow up, I'll never pick another piece of cotton again." Louise laughed, her face red and sweaty in the bright sunlight. I guess I'd said it before, but that fall day, everything felt different. I stood for a minute, looking at the spot where a hawk had been moments before, yearning to fly out of that field with him.

From across the field Mama yelled at me to quit daydreaming. So I picked a boll and stuffed it into my sack, flecks of red from my bleeding hands trailing across it. Louise's stooped figure moved in the row ahead of me. Behind her, every once in a while a piece of forgotten cotton fluttered above the bare stalks. Bending over, the sun beating on my back, I felt my promise in my bones. I wasn't going to be like Mama, stuck in the same place I grew up. I wasn't going to live like this forever. I was going somewhere special. I knew it like you know the wind is blowing even though it's invisible.

I finally did find a way to finish paying for the cheerleader's outfit when the squad sponsored a bake sale at the Halloween carnival and we all split the money. Scrounging up a way to keep my dream alive, I realized that whatever I wanted I had to make happen. I also discovered that refusing to take no for an answer can help make the impossible possible.

CHAPTER 2

Marrying Charles

IIIIIIIIIIIIIIIIIIIIIIIIIIIIIIIIIIIIIIIIIIIIIIIIIIIIIIIIIIIIIIIIIIIIIIIIIIIIIIIIIIIIIIIIIIIIIIIIIIIIIIIIIIIIIIIIIIIIIIIIIIIIIIIIII

Once a woman has given you her heart, you can never get rid of the rest of her.

—SIR JOHN VANBRUGH

THE FIRST time I saw Charles I was in ninth grade. As I boarded the school bus that day, I was struck by the handsome driver with the sharp blue eyes and easy, wide smile. In fact, I was smitten. Now I had a whole new subject to study on the way to and from school. The regular driver, Charles's father, had found full-time carpentry work, and so Charles, a high school senior, replaced him, driving the bus for the rest of the year. Since my stop was the first on Charles's route, I was always the first on the bus. Once those doors closed behind me, I wouldn't even sit down. I'd drape myself over the metal bar next to Charles and start talking. As we bounced over the rocky dirt road in the early morning, I'd often interrupt our conversation with a playful "Watch out for the pothole!"

Charles always said that he'd noticed me several months beforehand when for the first time I walked into Asberry Baptist Church one day wearing my red sling-back shoes. My family didn't attend church, but I'd convinced my mother to let me go to the closest church in our community. I was eager to get out of the house on Sundays and thrilled to wear the fancy heels I begged her to buy for the occasion.

Of course, I was more interested in seeing my friends than in being saved. Squirming on the hard wooden pew, I studied the women's colorful hats in the pew in front of me instead of listening to the preacher. Charles was always more serious about church than I was. He took great pride in the fact that his grandfather, Reverend Holder, along with hill farmers from surrounding communities like Skull Mountain, Dry Bone Hollow, and Ant Hill, had built the one-room church made of stone.

It wasn't long before we started dating. Living in a town the size of a frog pond, we didn't have much to do. Most of the time, we went to the drive-in theater and stopped at Dairy Queen for a hamburger afterward. Sometimes we hung out at the cemetery, dodging through the graves, some dating back to the Civil War, to sit under the large oak tree smack-dab in the middle of all those headstones.

But as much as I adored Charles, there was another young man in my life. I grew up playing with my stepcousin Johnny, who was the son of Papa's third wife, Beulah. Johnny was quite a bit older than I was, already a pilot in the air force. When I turned fourteen, he sent me a letter telling me I'd grown into the prettiest girl he'd ever seen. His flattery fired up my imagination. I'd never felt very pretty. In fact, in first grade I cried so hard for curls that my mother finally took me to Ruth's Beauty Parlor, where she got her once-a-year perm. There the beautician wrapped my hair in steel curlers, their spikes digging into my scalp. She covered my head with a thick milky-green shampoo before she hooked me up to a silver octopus whose electric legs transformed my plain pageboy into perfect Shirley Temple curls.

Inspired by Johnny's letters, I dreamed of traveling the world with him, asking my mother every day after school, "Has the mail come?" I'd moon over the framed picture Beulah gave me that I kept on my dresser. As I admired his smooth face, his expression so serious, I imagined him flying fighter planes in Korea. In my reverie, I saw myself an officer's wife, entertaining other officers' wives.

When Charles would visit, I hid Johnny's picture in my top drawer even though he never went into my bedroom. The truth was that my daydreams about Johnny were a kind of comfort to me. I worried that Charles still pined for his first girlfriend. Her mother had gotten pregnant out of wedlock, and when her daddy hassled Charles so badly, afraid the same thing would happen to his daughter, Charles moved on. My fears proved to be true when he started dating her again during his first year at Jacksonville State University when he and I didn't see each other as much. Finally, he broke it off with her for good, and we started dating exclusively.

Meanwhile, I'd finally come to my senses about Johnny. He was halfway across the ocean most of the time, and when I saw his sisters around, they insisted that he was dating dozens of beautiful girls. I finally realized that I didn't know the first thing about love if I was moping around for someone I barely knew anymore. We'd simply played together as kids. What I loved had nothing to do with him: I loved the idea of him and my fantasy of living in exotic places.

Living out in the country, I didn't know the ways of the world. What I knew about sex I overheard my uncles teasing about at Aunt Lucille's dairy farm or learned from my friends in the locker room at school. When I discovered I was bleeding for the first time, I was terrified. Without a word, my mother handed me torn bedsheets.

But despite my lack of worldliness, I had my secret ambitions. Even though most girls, if they weren't already married, worked in the cotton mills or became secretaries after graduation—the really smart ones studying to become teachers or nurses—I wanted to be a lawyer when I was in high school. Where my aspirations came from I haven't the foggiest, since we didn't keep a single book in our home.

Later, encouraged by my math teacher Mrs. Self, I decided I wanted to be an engineer. In class I marveled at the fact that she could catch a mistake before a student finished solving an equation on the blackboard. I whizzed through my math tests, the purple ink always damp, emanating a strong, almost skunkish smell from the mimeograph machine. For me, calculating numbers felt like listening to my favorite music.

Mrs. Self also happened to play bridge with Mr. and Mrs. Gray, the most educated couple I knew. On Saturdays they drove from Jacksonville to our house to buy fresh butter. When I heard the sound of a car in the driveway I'd peer out the window to see Mr. Gray, a retired chemistry professor, behind the wheel of his red convertible, his bow tie somehow still neatly tied. I wondered if he slept in it. He was so different from my uncles, more like my history teacher, a slim, energetic man the boys made fun of for living with his two aunts and walking to school carrying an umbrella.

Sometimes I was invited to the Grays' house in town. Eating dinner in their formal dining room, I worried about which fork to use as I tasted unfamiliar dishes like asparagus casserole served on delicate, rose-patterned china. I recalled what Granny Mac said about how my father had the finest of everything and drank from crystal glasses at their mahogany dining room table. My father's father, who'd been a foreman for Southern Railroad, supervising the black crew fixing the railroad tracks, sounded downright rich. Returning a gun he borrowed for Granny Mac to keep for protection while he traveled all over Georgia with his crew, he accidentally shot himself in the groin as his wagon bounced over the tracks. Gangrene killed him. After his death, Granny Mac packed up all the fancy furniture and fine china—except for a tea set she now kept in the trunk under her bed—and moved with my father to Aunt Lucille's farm in Alabama, where she kept most everything stored away.

When it came to my education, it was Mrs. Self who had hopes for me, and she asked Mrs. Gray for help. She wanted Mrs. Gray to convince my mother to let me take college courses at Jacksonville State University, a teachers' college only a short walk up the hill from Jacksonville High School, half the day during my senior year. Mama said no, of course. It cost too much. Anyway, a high school education was all a girl needed. So my senior year, at my mother's insistence, I took home economics instead of earning college credits, almost failing my sewing assignments.

I'll never forget the sting I felt when the week before graduation, the principal stopped me in the hall and congratulated me for being near the top of my class of one hundred. On the way to class, I was sick to my stomach, as if I'd swallowed a bottle of castor oil.

I found my way around most of my mother's objections, but I didn't know how to work around that conundrum. I've often speculated about how different my life would have been if I'd gone the eight miles down the road to Jacksonville State University. Later, when I went to work, I took every seminar and training class I was offered. But it wasn't the same.

NOT LONG after I realized I couldn't go to college, I took the picture of Johnny and gave it back to Beulah. I wrote him my last letter. I didn't know Johnny the way I'd come to know Charles, a steady worker and a churchgoing man. Johnny was a figment of my imagination. I'd seen Charles, calm and competent, steer a school bus from slipping off an icy bridge. Charles was the one who taught me how to drive. We circled the school parking lot in his Chevrolet or blew down the white road made of chert gravel in front of my house, a trail of milky dust fading behind us. It didn't matter what we did or where I went with Charles. We always enjoyed each other's company. Being with Charles made me forget how lonely I was as an only child. And on some level I knew he was the one, the way you just know some things, deep in your soul.

During my senior year Charles dropped out of Jacksonville State University to take a full-time job at General Electric, located about twenty miles outside Possum Trot, so that he could earn a steady paycheck. The last thing he wanted to do was farm for a living like his father, Willis. When relatives provided Willis, an illegitimate child, a place to live on their farm, he was treated as an outcast. While the rest of the family ate supper, Willis fed the cows and pigs. Later, Willis treated Charles almost as harshly on their family farm. I knew Charles admired the fact that my father wasn't a farmer and respected his job as a diesel-tank mechanic.

Once Charles was employed with a decent salary and benefits, he bought from his aunt Sudy a piece of land, located several miles from my house. Then he immediately started building our home. By December of my senior year the walls were dried in. I don't remember Charles ever formally proposing. We just talked about it like we did everything else. At least part of the reason we decided to get married when we did was that we could afford it.

The day I told my mother I wanted to marry Charles, I was sure she'd pitch a fit. I wasn't used to her saying yes to anything I wanted. And in this case she needed to agree, as I was still a minor. In my heart, I wanted more than anything to marry Charles. There was hope: He was the only boy of the few I'd dated whom she'd liked, and she appreciated the fact that Charles was such a hard worker.

I stood in the kitchen doorway and tried to gather my courage. I waited until she was in the middle of cooking fried apple pies; that way I wouldn't have to look her in the eye. Then I told her, fast and to the point.

When she turned away from the black skillet and looked at me, she simply asked, "Are you sure?"

I nodded. I was seventeen. I was ready.

She finished frying her first batch of pies, then made me sit down at the wooden table. "You know, what you see is what you marry. What you see across the table won't change all those years you'll be married, so don't think you can change another person," she said.

I sat silently, sweating in the warm kitchen. Grease dripped down the side of the black skillet on the stove. Now I had nowhere to look but straight into her eyes.

"I suppose now you'll have someone else to count on besides me and your daddy," she said. Then she stood up. "If that's what you want, I'll sign the papers." She turned to start chopping more apples for her next batch.

It was that matter-of-fact. She didn't even have to discuss it with my father. I was more than a little stunned. I had been ready for a fight. Instead, I wanted to jump up and dance, but I sat at the table for a minute trying to contain myself and figure out how to say thank you. When Mama started frying the next batch, I stood beside her, chopping the rest of the apples in silent gratitude, picturing the whole time what my own kitchen would look like.

ONE COLD afternoon when school let out for the Christmas holiday, I got married. Charles picked me up at school and rushed me home to change. My mother had taken me shopping earlier in the week and helped me find my dress. It was perfect. In my bedroom, shivering a little, I pulled the glistening navy dress over my body. Pinning my hat on my head, I looked at myself in the mirror above my dresser, my face blurred behind the silver netting sprinkled in rhinestones. I touched my white collar, all stitched in pearls. I felt important and grown-up. I grabbed my pocketbook off the bed, ready to show Charles how wonderful I looked. Then I thought of my mother; I wanted her to see me, too, to recognize me as all grown up. I stood still, listening for her in the kitchen. It was silent.

Charles was waiting in the car, so I took one last look at myself, trying shake off my disappointment that my mother hadn't been there to see me off. I didn't expect my parents to come to the wedding. No one in my family had been married in a church, and my mother had made sure I understood that this occasion warranted the least amount of expense and attention. I guess Charles's parents felt the same way, because they didn't come either.

On the way to the preacher's house, we picked up my cousin Louise and my friend Carolyn, who giggled all the way there. On the surface it felt like just another outing with friends, except that I was so dressed up and excited. When the preacher opened the door, he was still wearing the dirty coveralls he wore driving his peddling truck to sell flour and seed. He told Charles and me to take a seat on his sofa in the living room. I thought he was going to make us wait while he changed, but he just stood in front of us and started preaching.

"Now look each other in the eye and hear what I have to say." Louise and Carolyn stood behind him smiling almost as much as I was. Our smiles disappeared pretty quickly, though, when it became clear that we were in for a sermon. I could see my friends' eyes turn gradually toward the window to the pastor's tree-lined yard as they braced themselves. My mind wandered back to the times when Louise and I were little, how we liked to go to the nearby Congregational Holiness Campground to watch the holy dancing in the wooden tabernacle, whitewashed a dull white like the concrete bunk buildings surrounding it. Later, when we played in the woods, she stood on top of uprooted pine trees, blown over by recent tornadoes, and acted like the preacher while I swayed my hands in the air singing "Jesus Loves Me."

The preacher snapped me out of my reverie when he asked, "Have you thought this through?" and paused for our response. A shock went through my body, a startling sensation as strange as hitting your funny bone. When we didn't answer right away, he said, "Marriage is a lifelong commitment. Once you're married, it's for eternity. You will have to look at the world differently. When you're married, you're no longer an individual, but part of a whole. The marriage, not yourself, comes first."

All of a sudden I didn't want to look Charles in the eye. I could get lost in those blue eyes, usually full of comfort and promise, but in that moment I felt I needed to separate myself. The preacher's forceful words unsettled me. I was glad the netting covered my face. The words he used, like *covenant* and *sacrament*, sounded ominous. Now I felt like a mischievous schoolchild being scolded by the principal rather than the dressed-up, grown-up woman I'd been looking at in my mirror.

As the preacher carried on, I pretended to adjust my netting, worried that Charles could see my concern, wondering if he really loved me as he'd said he did. I reminded myself that everyone in the family had whispered that I was pregnant; otherwise, why would I marry before I finished high school? One of my aunts had marked her calendar, waiting for me to start showing. The preacher's funereal tone of voice made me question what the rush had been anyway. I suddenly felt I might need some more time to think. Yes, he'd been my best friend for the past three years, and so I'd been convinced I knew Charles well. Until now. Did I know him well enough to bind myself to him forever? If Charles was thinking the same thing, he didn't flinch. That reassured me a little, but I continued fidgeting to avoid looking him in the eyes. My head itched like I had a swarm of mosquitoes under my hat. When the preacher made us stand up and started the official ceremony, I thought I was going to faint. I could barely repeat my vows. I couldn't help but think that if he had given us the same sermon the day before, I'd have backed out. As it was, I was dressed and we were already there. I decided we'd just have to follow through and hope it worked out.

In the car, it seemed that Charles had been stirred up by the preacher's words after all. All the way to Atlanta, where we planned to celebrate our honeymoon, we didn't say a word. Neither of us even spoke up to say we needed to stop for a restroom break. When we got to the motel, we both ran straight to the bathrooms before even glancing at the man behind the desk or bothering to check in. It wasn't until we stood in front of Rich's department store, listening to Christmas music, admiring the winter wonderland and watching Mr. and Mrs. Claus wave to the shoppers, that our mood finally lifted.

WHEN WE returned from our weekend honeymoon, Charles still hadn't finished building our new house, so we lived at my parents' house. In the mornings I had to blink twice when I saw Charles, not Granny Mac, sprawled in the twin bed across the room from me. Granny Mac had moved in with my aunt Lucille, where she'd lived before. She was still nearby, but I secretly missed the sound of her bustling around in the early-morning light as she wrapped her long dark braid in a bun around her head. I'd forgotten how irritated I used to get when she rummaged through my belongings. Instead, I remembered all the times I was upset with my mother and Granny Mac sat me down on the bed. She'd scoot out her wooden trunk, tucked under her bed. Handing me a gold bracelet or her opal ring to wear, remnants of the life she lived before my grandfather left her widowed so young, she smiled and hummed as she set her hand-painted teacups on the quilt for us to play tea.

Now when I opened my eyes, Charles shared the bedroom I'd slept in since I was seven, its walls plastered with pictures of Ginger Rogers and Fred Astaire. His large frame almost swallowed the small bed. On the weekends, Charles and I spent the night at his family's house in his childhood bedroom, his younger brother and sister following us around and staring at us like we were aliens from Mars who'd landed in the cornfield.

After we married, I went back to school. The only difference in my routine was that when I came home in the afternoons, I joined

Charles, my father, and his uncles to help finish the house Charles was building for us. I completed my homework later in the evening, when it was too dark to work.

That April, the day I turned eighteen, we moved into our unfinished house. My mother rocked in her chair on the front porch and cried. Her tears took me by surprise. It was one of the few times I'd seen her cry. After all that fussing over the years, my mother didn't want me to leave. And when I did, she'd expected me to move a stone's throw from her like she did with Papa. I looked around one last time. The path I cut through the woods to Louise's house would soon be overgrown with wisteria and sumac vines. I recalled how Louise and I used to make a game of throwing cotton bolls at each other when no one was looking. I thought about how much I'd miss my father, who loved to make a special treat of any occasion. Those trips to town on Saturday, he looked like a king dressed in his best suit and one of his dark felt hats. Before we left, he always slipped me a quarter to buy an Archie comic book and a Hershey bar at Watson's Drugstore. I wondered what happened to the miniature doll bed he made me from apple crates—the one I used to stuff Buzz into—that Christmas Mama said there wasn't any money for presents.

As I loaded my few belongings into Charles's car, my eyes rested on Papa's house across the road. He was one person I wouldn't miss.

Driving away, passing fields that would be ready for planting soon, Charles held the steering wheel, his arms taut from years of farmwork and the last months framing our house. As I clasped the box holding Granny Mac's fragile teacup set in my lap, I wanted to grab Charles's arm and stop the car.

THE MORNING Charles laid down the law, I sat on our bed in our bedroom, fully dressed and ready for school, my stomach clenched with anxiety. Charles was still in the kitchen finishing the ham and biscuits I'd made for us before he set out for work and dropped me off at school on his way. I hadn't eaten a bite.

Now I looked out the window at the dirt Charles had prepared for my flower garden. When I'd reminded him about the senior trip that morning at breakfast, he acted surprised. My trip was only two weeks away, and then there was graduation. I wanted to be with the friends I'd spent my childhood with before we went our separate ways.

"But you've known all along I wanted to go," I'd insisted. Mrs. Self's school trips were famous. I'd looked forward all year to seeing the White House and New York City.

"It's not a good idea," he'd said without emotion.

I could feel that familiar anger well up in me. It may have been his law, but it sure wasn't mine. I'd worked hard for that trip. For weeks my father had driven me up every back road in Calhoun County to sell the second-most magazine subscriptions in my high school so that I could afford to go. I'd told Charles months earlier that I was going. Over breakfast, as he tried his best to eat his food while it was still hot, we went back and forth until, exasperated, he finally said, "You're married now. Married people don't go on trips alone."

He meant married women. Surely, he wasn't worried about the rowdy boys in my class who drove across the state line to buy liquor in Georgia every weekend. I suspected they'd misbehave as usual on the trip, but that had nothing to do with me. I remembered that Charles had made sure that I was indifferent when he made me throw out a silly necklace one of them had given me a long time ago. I sighed as the morning light streamed through the window, a strange contrast to my dark mood. Charles clearly expected me to be a "good wife," and that meant I was to stay at home where I belonged.

But this wasn't one of our ordinary squabbles over blankets or thermostats. I hated the way, in the middle of the night, Charles, fast asleep, jerked the blankets to his side of the bed, leaving me with one thin sheet, shivering. It killed me when he changed the thermostat behind my back; he insisted on keeping it at 65 degrees, practically freezing me to death. Now I really felt left out in the cold. I so wanted to find a way through this. I thought and thought as I smoothed the bedspread over and over again, knowing I'd be late for school and Charles for work. And it hurt even more because I had to admit to myself that Mama was right this time. She'd told me when we were shopping for my wedding dress that Charles would never let me go on the trip. I didn't believe her—why did he have to *let* me, anyway? I'd read the *Good Housekeeping* advice at Mrs. Gray's house—that a good wife didn't question her husband's judgment because he is master of the house—but that wasn't supposed to apply to me. Daddy had never told my mother what to do. And I felt like I could almost always get my way with him. If Daddy had nothing but a dollar left in his pocket and I wanted a steak, he'd buy it.

I called to mind the time I was determined to have a coat my mother refused to buy. One late afternoon right before my father left for work, I'd found him in the living room flipping through one of my comic books. Dressed in his denim pants and the white work shirt Mama starched as stiff as barn wood, he smelled like diesel fuel, a smell I'd almost come to like.

I sidled up next to him and asked him if he'd get me that coat I'd been talking about. He kept his money folded neatly in his pocket. He didn't look up but turned the page, the palm of his hands calloused as hard as a butternut in places, the whites of his fingernails stained an indelible black from engine grease.

"Sugar, if you want that coat, I'll get you that coat."

It was August and hot as blue blazes outside, but I wore that coat every day. Mama was so mad that, for months, every time I turned around I found myself with more chores to do.

I got up from the bed at last and opened my closet door to look for that coat. Did I have any say-so in this relationship? Feeling the thick brown wool, I knew that even though I had my own money for the trip, I wasn't in control of my life. Our ideas about marriage, specifically what it meant to be a wife, were as diametrically opposed as two magnets facing each other the wrong way. Suddenly I felt like a fool. I should have known that our different backgrounds would come between us. Religion and the traditional values that accompanied it loomed large in Charles's family. He often reminisced about the Sunday picnics after church when the old folks gathered to gossip while the young folks played horseshoes the whole afternoon. His sister would tell how when they'd be sitting on the porch on Sundays and the preacher came by, Charles ran around slinging all the dirty dishes into the stove and stuffing the dirty clothes into the wringer washing machine.

Charles's best memories centered on the church, his second home. My main memory of church was Mama complaining the few times we went about the reverend dipping into the church offerings to pay for his gas. And she had absolutely no patience for those snake-handling preachers.

Still in my bedroom a half hour later, I just couldn't let go of that coat. I didn't want to see Charles, never mind ride with him all the way to school. I knew he was patiently waiting for me, probably hoping I'd accept his decision if only he gave me time. He'd been clear that it was his decision to make. As he sat at our brand-new kitchen table, Charles had flat-out insisted, "If you loved me, you'd stay home."

His eyes had widened in disbelief when I said, "If you loved *me*, you'd let me go."

As I took my treasured coat out of our closet, I knew I was going to Washington no matter what Charles said or how upset he was. It was way too hot to wear that coat on a sunny spring day, but it was my shield, as it had been with my mother many springs earlier. I put it on, ready to go to school, my blood still burning. In the car, Charles reminded me that a husband cleaves unto his wife; they become one flesh.

Now I understood the true meaning of my wedding sermon. When the preacher had said that the marriage would come first, he'd meant Charles would, and there'd be a price to pay if I didn't submit.

I had only been in Washington one day when I called Charles at GE on the pay phone to check in. A coworker answered and told me Charles was on his way to the hospital in an ambulance; no one knew what had happened. I thought that maybe he'd had a heart attack, so I took the next train home.

At the time, Charles was running tubes in the furnace room, where it's so hot you're supposed to take salt tablets to keep from becoming dehydrated. Charles hadn't taken them that day, nor had he drunk enough water. But he wouldn't admit he'd gotten dehydrated on purpose. I knew in my gut that he'd done so in order to get me to come home early.

It took a long time for me to get over his stunt, and I wished a thousand times I hadn't come home. I had always known that there's one thing I hated more than anything else: being told that I couldn't do something. Now I knew what was second on my list: being tricked and manipulated. In our first few months of marriage, Charles had crossed both lines.

Not long after that, we argued over the hospital bill that we had to spend what was left of my trip money to pay. Night after night, while he read his Bible, I pretended to sleep, not wanting to talk or kiss him good night. I was stiff with anger. I felt as if my heart had closed.

One night, after about a week of this, I pulled the covers over my head extra hard and asked roughly when he was going to turn the light out.

He sighed. That irritated me even more. Finally, I heard him put his Bible on his bedside table, where he always left it. The room became quiet. We lay in silence, the only sound the cicadas' crescendo outside our window. I thought about my uncle who'd told everyone we'd be separated in a year. I could feel sadness creeping in, softening me. I didn't know how this was ever going to be resolved, but I was tired of being mad.

Charles pulled the covers from my face and leaned into me. I didn't push him away. We found each other again in the dark.

"I don't want you to be upset anymore. I don't want to lose my best friend," he whispered later.

Before we fell asleep, we promised we'd always talk through our troubles whenever we disagreed. Throughout our marriage, this pact served us well. After that night, no matter how angry we got with each other, one of us would back down and end the argument by reminding the other that we were best friends.

I began to realize that no one's marriage is perfect; you just make the best marriage possible. My senior trip wasn't the first or last time Charles got into his religious mode, thinking he was lord and master and forgetting that I was a real person. But I knew Charles loved me like no one else.

TOWARD THE end of my senior year, I interviewed at General Electric, where Charles worked. The Monday after graduation Charles and I drove to his friend's house, where we carpooled with him and some other guys sixteen miles into the small town of Oxford. I clocked in at GE, thinking the sooner I started working, the sooner we'd be able to put a little more distance between us and the life I so wanted to leave behind. I was going to be like Aunt Robbie, who like many women during World War II had been hired in at Goodyear while the men were fighting the war.

As one of the younger women at GE, I tended to keep to myself. The older, more experienced women worked the upper end of the conveyor belt. Down at my end of the line, we put the finishing touches on the tubes made for televisions and radios. All the women dressed in white uniforms, so we could spot any debris that might corrupt the tubes.

Operating the foot pedal, I welded together two threadlike filaments. With hundreds of tubes coming down the line, no one had time to talk. You could only go to the restroom during a break. At first, I felt like that episode of *I Love Lucy* where she's working in the chocolate factory and the belt speeds up so fast she has to stuff her mouth and hat and brassiere with chocolate drops. We couldn't stuff our bras with scrap material, but before we left the plant, management would rifle through the aspirin and lipstick in our purses, looking for pieces of scrap.

At first, my foot hammered the pedal too hard and I generated too much scrap. Even after I got the hang of it, the machine would get too hot, scorching the filament. But I learned to block out my surroundings and focus on lightly tapping the pedal. There was nothing I could do about the machine's temperature.

We were paid by the piece and given a bonus after we made a certain number of tubes. When we exceeded the production numbers, we were quickly broken up, our synchronicity scattered, so that we wouldn't have to be paid extra. But when it came to the men there, often the women worked against themselves, acting as ridiculous as schoolgirls. I was glad I was married and not caught up in all that nonsense.

One supervisor had a bad habit of choosing one woman at a time to pick on. When he came around to picking at me, I got so frustrated that I actually started looking for another job, interviewing at Sears and the nearby hospital. When I realized I could make $40 a week somewhere else, or hang in there and keep making $150, I decided to tough it out. I refused to be run off. So I kept earning my paycheck, saving for a new dining room suite we'd put on layaway.

||||||||||||

AFTER ABOUT a year of working, Charles, who had joined the National Guard, was stationed at Fort Belvoir right outside Washington, D.C., for six months. I wanted to take a week off to go see him. At my age now, I know six months isn't so long in the grand scheme of things, but back then I missed Charles so much it felt like a part of me had been amputated. When I put in my request, the foreman said no. We usually got vacation time in July, when the plant shut down, or around Christmas, when production slowed, so my union representative said there wasn't much I could do about it.

I told the foreman I was going anyway and he'd see me the following week. I really expected to be fired, but I knew I could find a job somewhere else, with more responsibility and better treatment, just less pay. I was willing to take that risk.

The night my father drove Sandra and me to the Atlanta airport, I almost didn't make it onto the plane. I'd convinced Sandra to go with me, since her husband was stationed there as well. We scrimped and saved for our plane tickets and took the cheapest flight, the red-eye. Sandra balked at the sight of the plane. I didn't want to climb those steps into the plane's tiny door any more than she did, but she announced that she was staying home. I said, "Oh, no. You are going with me," and dragged her onto the plane.

Things only got worse when we arrived. It occurred to me as we zipped past Fort Belvoir on the Greyhound bus that something was wrong. Charles had told me to catch the bus to the base, but I'd never seen a city bus. In my mind, the word *bus* meant Trailways or Greyhound. I jumped out of my seat and told the driver we needed to turn around. He said, "Lady, you're on the wrong bus. We're not stopping, so you might as well sit down."

I stepped down closer to him and heard myself say in my best Edna imitation, "Listen, you have to stop this bus right now." By then, the base was miles behind us. The passengers became quiet, peering over the tops of the headrests. He stopped the bus.

Dressed in skirts and heels, with cars and trucks whizzing by us, Sandra and I lugged our suitcases across the six-lane highway. I found a pay phone at a gas station and called a cab. I'd never been so happy to see Charles in all my life. That week we never left the base. I'd spent all my sightseeing money on cab fare, which cost more than my plane ticket.

The next Monday morning when I showed up at work, my supervisor didn't say a word. Back on the line, as I singed the two tiny threads together and tapped my foot pedal ever so slightly, I replayed telling him I'd be back in a week, feeling the satisfaction of speaking up, of having choices. After I returned from visiting Charles, my supervisor never picked on me again.

Two YEARS later, since I'd been the last one to be hired, I was the first one to go when GE went into layoff mode. Shortly afterward, I found out I was pregnant. Even though I wanted to look for a new job, Charles and I had always planned on having two kids, so it also felt natural to focus on building our family. I settled in at home, cooking, gardening, and tending to our new daughter, Vickie. It turned out that my mother was right. Home economics came in handy after all.

She may not have come to my wedding, but every day my mother, dressed in a man's jumpsuit, appeared on my doorstep. Charles begged me to ask her if she could please stay home a couple of days a week so we could have the house to ourselves. I was grateful for the fact that she slung that soiled pile of cloth diapers through the wringer washer on the porch daily. Nursing Vickie, I'd watch her through the window as she unpinned the frozen diapers off the clothesline, her hands stiff and red with cold.

I was also grateful for how she doted on her granddaughter. It reminded me of how she took to Uncle Howard's two boys, Billy and Buddy. When I was young, the boys, still toddlers, lived with us for several months. She rocked and loved those boys like I'd never seen. After their mother moved away with them, my mother grieved. Watching her care for Vickie, I knew she and Vickie would have the close relationship she and I never could.

Three years after Vickie was born, Phillip came along. His birth was the first time I made headlines, when the *Anniston Star* read, JACKSONVILLE WOMAN BEATS THE STORK. As we sped to the hospital in the middle of the night, escorted by the policeman who'd stopped us for speeding, we had no idea that the strange screeching sound we heard was Vickie's poor cat, who'd been asleep on the engine—after that, he didn't stick around much longer. Seconds after Charles dropped me off at the emergency room—he hadn't even parked the car—I delivered Phillip.

Nothing I'd known had prepared me for motherhood, and as Vickie and Phillip grew I was scared not to go to the doctor at the slightest hint of sickness. Uncle Howard used to say that Papa killed my grandmother Lillie when she had cancer. Spending all his money on liquor, Papa neglected to take her to the doctor. He also crippled his son Leonard when he refused to get Leonard's broken leg set. Like the cat sleeping on our warm engine, one day Leonard just took a notion and disappeared. So any time of day or night, if the children showed a sign of a fever or ear infection, I hauled them to the doctor, Edna sitting in the backseat of my car soothing the sick child in her lap.

EVEN THOUGH I read Dr. Spock religiously, as a young mother I was overwhelmed by the fatigue and rawness of my emotions, spinning from tears to frustration in a second. And Phillip, allergic to everything he ate and even his baby blanket and sheets, cried through each night of his first two years. He never slept, despite the soy formula I had shipped on a Trailways bus and delivered to Crow Drugs each week.

Throughout the night, I'd sit in the wooden rocking chair in his room, holding him in my arms. Otherwise, he screamed. Mute with exhaustion, I felt especially vulnerable, as tender as the soft spot on his newborn head. When Charles left for work in the morning, I listened to his car crank up and envisioned eighteen-wheeler trucks smashing into him on the way to work. Then I'd follow my imagined tragic scenario to a vision of me, alone, trying to raise Vickie and Phillip.

Many mornings I brought myself back to reality by admiring the beautiful straw flowers and zinnias outside my bedroom window. One of the first things I'd done when Charles and I settled in that spring of my senior year was plant a flower garden. Mama never did grow anything you couldn't pick and eat. Planting my annual seeds was comfort I'd chosen a different path. One particular morning after rocking Phillip all night, gazing beyond my blooming flowers, I was struck by the familiar sight of fields I'd known as a child. I closed my eyes and continued to rock Phillip. The truth of the matter was that I was living the same life as my mother.

CHAPTER 3

Going to Work

||||||||||||||||||||||||||||||||||||||||||||||||||||||||||||||||||||||||||||||||||||||||||||||||||||||||||||||||||||

A strong woman is a woman determined to do something others are determined not be done.

—MARGE PIERCY

EACH TIME I took Vickie and Phillip to the doctor or went to see my own doctor, Dr. Stout, Charles said, "You're just hunting for somewhere to go." I didn't look forward to doctor visits, but I was glad to get out of the house. During the last visit to Dr. Stout's office, when he couldn't find anything wrong with my shoulder and knee, both of which had been hurting, he'd commented, "You're perfectly fine. You just seem a little tired." I shrugged. He pressed, asking if everything at home was okay. I smiled. Of course it was.

Dr. Stout patted my hand, concerned. "Well, I know it's not the children. They look fine." Holding my hand, he continued. "What about Charles? How's his job?"

I told him that Charles worked as a license inspector for the county. I pulled my hand from his clasp and grabbed Phillip, now about to start school, to stop him from spinning the stool next to the examining table. Dr. Stout started to write something on a piece of white paper, then stopped and took off his round spectacles. Deep grooves cut across the sides of his face from the tight glasses. He wiped the lens with a white handkerchief he took from in his pocket. Placing his glasses back on his face, he commented as he finished writing, "In my experience, if it's not job troubles, then it's one of two things." Finally, I was going to get an answer. "You're dealing with either an alcoholic or a religious fanatic."

I shook my head. I'd never thought of Charles as a fanatic about anything, except maybe his coin collection. "No, Charles doesn't drink. He's a deacon in our church." I didn't say anything else. Neither did Dr. Stout; he simply handed me the piece of paper. I could barely read his scribble. It was a prescription for an antidepressant.

When the door closed behind Dr. Stout, I crumpled up the paper and threw it into the trash can. I couldn't afford the prescription, and Charles wouldn't hear of me taking it anyway.

DR. STOUT was right; everything wasn't fine. I thought about the real answers to his questions on the way home. The only place I went besides the grocery store was the Baptist church. If Charles had his way, we'd have gone to church every day; as it was, we were there at least four times a week. I didn't know how or when it had happened, but my world had become too small. I still spoke to Sandra some over the phone, and we had dinner with Charles's family or mine every Sunday, but during these dinners I felt like I was repeating the same conversation. I sometimes worried I'd never experience that sense of wonder you feel meeting a new friend or traveling to a new place for the first time. I was afraid the major milestones of my life, marriage and childbirth, were past. Was it foolish to hope I still had something exciting ahead of me, something even important, that I could have a life of my own?

I had told Dr. Stout that Charles was a license inspector; what I hadn't explained was the fact that Charles and I had struggled for years to make ends meet. After the GE plant closed, Charles worked part-time at Railway Express Agency. He took the weekend shift that no one else wanted until his supervisor realized how reliable he was and offered him a full-time job. Ten years later the company was sold to Greyhound, so he'd found work as a license inspector, traveling to businesses throughout Calhoun County to verify that the owners were up-to-date with their annual fees. He also checked the status of people's mobile-home licenses. I worried about his safety—especially after his windshield was shot out. Now the sheriff accompanied him when he issued citations.

What I also hadn't told Dr. Stout was that Charles's job was only part-time, and the income, even with his supplement from the National Guard and selling encyclopedias, just wasn't enough. We had tried to make everything count: eating pinto beans when we were saving for furniture, picking berries in the woods to sell. I even learned to sew the children's clothes, and I'd go to town and browse the stores to copy the patterns I saw hanging on the racks, just like my mother did. We paid cash for everything we bought, as Charles didn't believe in credit. The money from the pies I baked and sold to the neighbors and Charles's unsuccessful peanut- and sweet-potato-growing ventures wasn't enough—especially when everywhere he worked shut down.

Not long after that appointment with Dr. Stout, I took Phillip to see the pediatrician, Dr. Luther, a tall, boisterous woman who piloted her own plane. I never knew what to expect when we visited her office, decorated with pictures from South African safaris. The summer Vickie caught the measles, she thundered, "Whoever heard of sending a five-year-old to vacation Bible school?" Not once did she let me pay for the children's medicine, sending me home with boxes of samples when they needed them.

At this visit, Dr. Luther asked Phillip what he'd gotten for Christmas, and he barely answered. She shot her eyes at me, surprised. "Is this the best he can speak?" She signed him up that same day for testing at a rehabilitation center in Birmingham. During the weeks leading up to the appointment, I'd wake up in the middle of the night to find myself standing at the kitchen counter eating the cakes Edna baked for us every week. I must have gained twenty pounds by the time we took Phillip for his evaluation.

On the day Phillip was tested the doctors immediately checked to see if he was tongue-tied. I'd thought that was just an expression; to consider it a real possibility was horrifying. Then the doctors put that poor child through every test imaginable. I'm sure they thought that we were straight from *The Beverly Hillbillies* and didn't own a refrigerator when Phillip identified the picture of a safe as an icebox. He was right. It looked exactly like the old rusty icebox in Edna's kitchen, where she stored her sewing material.

The doctors concluded from Phillip's tests and my interview that he was behind on his speech development because I was so worn out from his chronic allergies and asthma that I didn't sing and talk to him the way I did Vickie. I'd also taken it for granted that Vickie did all his talking for him, like a little mother hen. He needed speech therapy twice a week to catch up to other children his age.

It tore my heart in two that although I'd given Phillip all I had, still it wasn't enough. I knew what the doctors had no way of diagnosing: Each day at home, I'd find myself plagued by a discontent I didn't understand. I was constantly, needlessly restless. I'd hear the dying echo of a delivery truck traveling to its unknown destination, and I'd feel an aching loneliness. I'd been left behind.

THE MARITAL arguments started not too long after Phillip's diagnosis. I'd taken Phillip to one of his first appointments with the speech therapist. An unusually cold spell had struck that day, and my car broke down on the way home from town. There I was on an empty country road, without one penny to my name and no way to get help. I stared at the flat tire on the dented green Plymouth we'd drained our savings to buy. In pitch darkness, I looked up at the stars and told myself, *No more.*

Somehow I changed that flat tire by myself, while Vickie comforted Phillip, tired and crying in the backseat. With each twist of the lug wrench, I felt a piece of myself come unhinged. No matter how hard we tried, something always set us back.

With the last lug tightened, I sat back on my heels, my arms aching. I couldn't do it anymore. I couldn't live without any savings; I wouldn't raise Vickie and Phillip without a real future.

On the way home, as the headlights illuminated the endless row of tall, sturdy cedars lining the country road, I silently recited the one psalm I knew by heart: the Twenty-third. I glanced in the rearview mirror; Phillip's head rested in Vickie's lap. Her head drooped at an awkward angle against the backseat. From the time I'd brought Phillip home from the hospital as a newborn Vickie had been by my side, my assistant mother. Sometimes I thought she had far more patience than I did. I leaned my right arm across the back of my seat, brushing the cold vinyl, to prop up her head as best I could. I wanted to scoop the children up and hold on to them as tightly as possible, never letting them experience pain or frustration again. Turning into the driveway, the gravel crunching underneath the wobbly tire, I'd made up my mind. I was going back to work.

CHARLES AND I argued about it well past midnight. He couldn't understand why I wouldn't let him be the sole provider—the way things were supposed to be, and had been since biblical times, he said. I couldn't justify my position in a way that Charles accepted. Countless times in the months afterward we rehashed the same argument: circling each other, the tension in our marriage escalating while my desire for a job grew inside me as relentlessly as kudzu.

When Charles had given Vickie, now in elementary school, only a dollar for spending money for her most recent Sunday-school trip to Rock City in Chattanooga, Tennessee, I was beside myself. Standing in the kitchen trying to follow the recipe off the

Campbell's soup can for the green bean casserole I was fixing for dinner, I shook my head to myself, thinking about Vickie's embarrassment the day before when she hadn't been able to buy anything at the gift shop like the rest of the group. I hadn't had a chance to discuss this with Charles yet, and I was anxious to do so, unable to get anything right all day when sewing or cleaning.

I heard Charles come in the front door, and my agitation increased. I knew he'd take off his blue windbreaker and hang it on the coatrack in the hall before he went to wash his hands. I waited for him to come into the kitchen and sit at the table to talk while I finished cooking supper. When he finally walked in, he started a pot of coffee, a gesture that usually gave me a sense of comfort but that now irritated me. I didn't ask him about his day like I always did. I barely let him sit down before I said, "Next time Vickie goes on a retreat, she needs more than a dollar."

He put a spoonful of sugar into his empty coffee cup before he answered. "I don't know why she needs more than that. That's plenty to cover her lunch."

"That's only enough for a hot dog and Coke. It doesn't leave anything for the gift shop."

"She doesn't need anything from the gift shop."

"She just wanted a little something to take home. That's all." The coffeepot started percolating loudly, the brown liquid splashing furiously against the small glass knob on the metal top.

Charles stared at the coffeepot. "She'll have to learn she can't always have what everyone else does."

For the life of me, I couldn't understand why Charles thought it was okay for our kids not to have the same opportunities as everybody else. If anyone knew how *that* felt, it was Charles. He had been the child who carried eggs and butter to school to pay for his lunches, wearing the same three outfits throughout the week. When we were growing up, my family was downright rich compared with his.

"But, Charles, she should have the same as everyone else, or she'll feel left out. You don't want that, do you?"

He got up and stood by the coffeepot to wait for it to finish percolating before he said what I knew he would. "I managed without and she can too."

How many times had Charles told me that he'd survived as a child with less than the other kids and so could Vickie and Phillip? "You know, just because I walked a mile to the bus stop doesn't mean I think Vickie and Phillip should have to do the same." I took the green beans I'd snapped and rinsed them one more time before placing them in a mixing bowl. "That makes about as much sense as your mother baking her cakes on Saturday and locking them up until Sunday," I continued in disbelief. I never did understand why Sunday was the only day sweets and fried chicken were allowed in Charles's family.

Charles didn't answer me. He poured his coffee and retreated to the living room with his cup.

"You need to do something about this pile of magazines in the den. I'm tired of the mess," he yelled from the hallway.

I opened the drawer to find a mixing spoon and slammed it shut.

When we argued we were both on automatic, our frustrations becoming so intense, a thick invisible wall stood between us. We were trying so hard to be heard that we couldn't hear each other. I didn't understand some of Charles's stubborn, crazy notions. We were so different at times. Charles found satisfaction scavenging up and down alleys and roads to find what he thought were perfectly good items someone had thrown away. He'd walk into the house lugging home his latest prize—a broken glass cabinet or lopsided bookshelves that he actually planned to use as furniture in our house. One day he brought home a gigantic barrel of every color of ribbon imaginable. For years the neighborhood women came to the house, staying as long as it took to roll up the endless yards of ribbon they needed.

I loved nothing better than finding a good deal at a discount store, but I wasn't interested in furnishing my house with castoffs. More than anything, I wanted Vickie and Phillip to have a different childhood than we'd had; I wanted to do more than just get by. Charles had all he'd ever wanted: a wife and family. He liked the predictable routine I'd created—one that meant the car was washed, lawn mowed, cakes baked, and, yes, even the doorknobs polished every week. When I challenged him, I turned his dream upside down. He thought I was saying he was a failure.

I wasn't. Deep down, *I* felt like the failure.

SOON AFTER the night I had the flat tire, I started experiencing searing headaches. Sometimes my head hurt so badly, I couldn't see. I'd had the same "sick" headaches as a young girl. My mother would take me into Piedmont, guiding me up the long flight of wooden stairs to the doctor's office, where he always gave me a small red pill that made me sleep for what seemed like days. Now, as an adult, I'd lie in my dark bedroom with the curtains closed and a wet washcloth over my eyes, keeping an ear out for the children.

As Charles and I scrambled weekly to pay for gas and speech therapy, he finally considered letting me work part-time. Frustrated with his own part-time job, Charles continued to search for a better, full-time opportunity. One afternoon he came home and told me about an opening at H&R Block in Anniston, the county seat, only a twenty-minute drive from our house. We went to Anniston whenever we needed something from Sears or J. C. Penney. The job sounded like a good possibility for Charles; but when he mentioned that it was part-time during tax season and that there was a math test to pass, I said, "Let me take it."

In the fall of 1968, I signed up for the H&R Block tax-preparation course, and I passed the test a month later. The manager who hired me the following January agreed to let me skip lunch and leave at four-thirty to pick up Vickie and Phillip from Mrs. Harris's after-school care.

I immediately fell in love with the job. I no longer felt so out of sorts, like some pollywog adrift in the water; instead, I had a goal to fulfill. I was paid minimum wage, $2.90 hour, against a draw, which was based on the number of tax returns I completed. The more returns I finished, the more I earned. We were paid $5 for each return, and I quickly devised a system to maximize my effort.

Each day I eagerly awaited customers, sitting behind my desk in my pink dress, navy hose, and white shoes, ready to operate my electronic calculator, the size of a shoe box, whose whirring muted the sound of the receptionist snapping her Juicy Fruit gum. It wasn't long before the boss's wife took me aside and suggested that I wear a different color combination. I stuck to polyester pant suits after that. At lunch I sat at my small metal desk, the gray carpet around me stained from coffee spills, and stirred my beef bouillon cubes in my cup of hot water until they dissolved. I kept my bottom desk drawer stocked with boxes of Lipton's instant chicken noodle soup and Nestlé's hot chocolate mix. Throughout the afternoon I sipped hot chocolate, my tongue trying to nudge loose the tiny pieces of rubbery marshmallow wedged in my teeth.

I never knew who would come walking through the door from one day to the next. It could be a restaurant owner with years of greasy, jumbled receipts I'd have to sort into order. The time the door swung open and a man appeared in the office carrying a large dry-cleaning box used to store a woman's winter coat, the other agents averted their eyes and tried to look busy. I offered to help the man. Once he sat down, I handed him several books of matches we always gave our customers from a well-stocked bowl on my desk. He pulled a small ledger from the cardboard box, standing almost as tall as he was. Inside the black leather ledger were pages of perfectly kept records in a tight, neat script. I didn't ask about his odd record-keeping system, and he didn't offer an explanation.

Although I'd started working motivated solely by financial pressures, I soon found a greater reward as I exercised skills I didn't know I possessed. I enjoyed aspects of the job most people hated. I was the only one in the office who actually liked it when we had to piece together the copy machine the supervisor dismantled on purpose, to test whether we could fix it on our own. Tinkering with the copier parts, I thought about the hours my father spent in the garage repairing his cars for an extra buck. That wasn't work for him. He enjoyed it. Now I knew why.

At the end of the day when I clocked out, I rushed to pick up Vickie and Phillip. After I put the kids to bed, I left Charles, who, of course, was beside himself that I was leaving, at home watching *All in the Family* and returned to H&R Block to finish filling out the forms stacked up by my desk. During the three and a half months of my first tax season, I somehow managed to prepare five thousand returns.

Charles resented my long hours; they were hard on everyone. He'd immediately regretted agreeing to my working. In his eyes, my job took me away from our family and church, and he complained about everything to do with it—especially the fact that I was sometimes alone in the office late at night with only my manager.

The following summer I was offered a full-time position. I didn't even consult with Charles. I knew he'd say no if I asked him about working the entire year. He'd only agreed to my working in the first place because it was something I could do during the short tax season, from January to April. I felt as though I was finally coming into my own, and I wasn't about to let him take that away from me.

I accepted the offer on the spot.

||||||||||||

WHEN I did tell Charles I'd taken a full-time position as the office manager, he acted as betrayed as if I'd had an affair. To show him I was no longer willing to be told how to live my life, at the end of my first week as office manager I marched, paycheck in hand, to the First National Bank in Anniston and opened my own checking account. When I'd completed all the forms, the banker pushed the papers back across the desk at me. I asked him what I'd missed.

He looked at my wedding ring. "Are you married?"

"Yes." I looked at his left hand, trying to see where this conversation was headed.

"You forgot to fill in your husband's name."

I tasted the bitter residue from the packet of saccharin I'd poured into the cup of coffee he'd offered me when I sat down. I handed the forms back to him. "I'm opening a separate account."

He was quiet for a minute. "It's happening more and more these days," he said.

"What's that?" I glanced at the *Anniston Star* sitting on his desk. I thought he was referring to the headlines about the Vietnam War protests. My father, who worked at the Anniston Army Depot, viewed any antiwar sentiment as un-American; the demonstrations made Charles, a member of the National Guard, furious. I secretly sympathized with the protestors.

"You must be getting a divorce."

"No, sir. As a matter of fact, I'm not."

He shook his head. I wondered if he was going to give the paperwork back to me.

He rifled through it, signing below my name before he pulled an account booklet from his drawer.

"There must be some reason you're opening a separate account," he said, more to himself than to me, as he wrote my name at the top with my new account number and the amount I was depositing underneath.

I didn't elaborate. I didn't say that with my own bank account, I could prove to Charles how much of a difference my paycheck would make; and if I wanted to spend more on myself or the children, who was to stop me?

He handed the blank account booklet to me. "You'll receive your new checks in the mail in about two weeks."

A few days later, when I opened a charge card at Wakefield's department store and applied for a Standard Oil gas card, I received the same response the banker had given me. This time I wasn't surprised. When I told Charles about the account, he blew a gasket, raising his voice and then retreating to the garage for hours to wash and polish his car. The first time we split the household bills at the end of the month, he calmed down a bit.

Charles settled down even more when we were able to buy our dream house in Jacksonville several months later. For years, we'd drive into town on Sunday afternoons to admire houses and see what was on the market; now Vickie, tired of being so far from school, was begging us to move. We made a budget and started our search in earnest. Charles and I soon found a redbrick ranch house that we all loved on a small hill, tucked near the end of a long street at the foot of a wooded ridge. The yard was big enough for Charles to build a work shed in one day. The best part was that it was only blocks from school and the Jacksonville Baptist Church. In spite of its proximity to public places, our new home was located on a quiet street, and it wasn't uncommon for us to see deer grazing in our yard or wake up to the ghostly mist of a morning fog.

Meanwhile, significant social movements were sweeping the country. Historic civil rights struggles were taking root in Alabama. No one in my family was sympathetic to the African Americans and northern agitators advocating change. I lived in a community where change came slowly, if at all; and when it did, it was often violent—as in the case of the firebombing of the Greyhound bus carrying Freedom Riders outside Anniston in 1961.

Both my parents had voted for George Wallace for governor in 1962. They applauded him when he stood in the schoolhouse door at the University of Alabama and so famously declared, "Segregation now, segregation tomorrow, segregation forever." His ranting and raving reminded me too much of Papa for him to get my vote. When politics came up for discussion at the Sunday dinner table, I kept my thoughts to myself to keep the peace. My parents' voice was not my voice, as segregation seemed like a grave injustice to me.

When I opened a bank account to prove to Charles that he was being unfair, I made no conscious connection with the bra-burning feminists. At the same time, I felt a yearning so many women like me at all levels of society were feeling. I was determined to find a new path. I'd learned early on not to take no for an answer, and in the end I got my way by working. My daily path was no longer confined to trips to the grocery store and church. Charles and I also no longer worried about how to pay for speech therapy. Charles had initially dismissed Dr. Luther's concern over Phillip, saying he'd come around in his own time, but when he saw Phillip's progress, he seemed relieved. As Phillip improved by leaps and bounds each week at therapy, I was overwhelmed with joy. Now I could even treat him to ice cream afterward.

As GRATEFUL as I was for the new challenges and the freedom more money gave me, many days I came close to giving up. I was unprepared for how tired I was working full-time—a feeling more debilitating than that leaden fatigue I'd experienced in the first trimester of pregnancy. I often wondered if I had the stamina to keep the pace up.

I'll never forget the late afternoon I found Vickie and Phillip sitting on the curb outside Mrs. Harris's house waiting for me in the descending darkness. Driving up to the house, I saw them huddled together, alone, in the dusk. Mrs. Harris had somewhere to go and had left them when I was running late. I was saturated with guilt. I hated that feeling of giving up my most important job—caring for my children—to someone else. I even felt jealous when Edna or Charles's sister took care of the children.

One cool fall evening when I was making Hamburger Helper, Vickie asked me if she could help me cook. (Mixing a meal from a box and opening two cans of sweet peas wasn't Edna's definition of preparing a meal, but it was quick.) I let her pop open the soft can of Pillsbury crescent rolls by pressing it with the back of a spoon. As she folded the sticky dough on the pan she asked, "Can we make doughnuts after dinner?" At least once a week before I'd started at H&R Block, we made doughnuts together as a family, creating our own assembly line.

I opened a cabinet to see if we had the ingredients (even though I knew we didn't) before I said, "We're out of yeast and powdered sugar."

Vickie sighed. "But we haven't cooked them in such a long time."

"I haven't had time to go to the grocery store," I replied too harshly. Noticing the dust balls by Vickie's feet, I thought, *I haven't had time to vacuum, scrub the toilets, or wash a month's worth of laundry, either.* Vickie's simple request irritated me because it highlighted my inability to get everything done; still, I was ashamed of my own irritation.

Hearing Vickie's frustrated tone, I felt like the worst mother in the world. In the frenetic mornings getting ready for school and work, I yelled at the children when they didn't deserve it. Watching Phillip scramble into my car, his shoes untied, I wanted to rewind and start the morning over, attending to everyone's last little need. Instead, I was frazzled. Every morning as Vickie rushed out the door I frantically tried to brush her knotted hair. I watched her traipse into school wearing a mismatched outfit she'd proudly chosen herself, her blond hair still tangled in the back from her tossing in her sleep. The other little girls in her class walked by with perfect ponytails their mothers had lovingly fixed. No matter how much planning and organizing I did, I had to live with the fact someone or something was not always tended to properly. I had to face the self-loathing this created. Vickie's question made me realize that I didn't want to quit making doughnuts or carving pumpkins or baking Christmas cookies because I was too tired to get it all done.

I told Charles before bed that night that I'd quit work. At first he looked surprised, despite the fact that he'd staged his own protest by ambushing me almost daily with arguments on why I should quit. Then he hugged me as if the University of Alabama had just scored a touchdown. I was glad when he let me go and went to brush his teeth. I didn't feel victorious; I felt deflated. I remembered all the times before I started working when I went to the A&P. I'd hold my breath during checkout as the cashier punched in the prices on the cash register. I was always within cents of my $20 limit, having kept a running tally of the groceries in my head, calculating the math before I placed each new item in my cart. To my relief, not once did I have to return anything to the shelves.

The next evening, before I started cooking dinner, I gathered the family in the living room. Charles told Vickie and Phillip that I was quitting.

Phillip asked, "Can we still go to Jack's for a hamburger?"

A hamburger cost fifteen cents. That expense would have to go. I recalled all the times I unsuccessfully begged my mother for a bicycle or piano lessons. I couldn't believe it, but here I was telling Phillip *no*.

"We'll have to eat at home from now on. Hamburgers are too expensive."

Phillip jumped up and started mimicking Cousin Cliff, singing the jingle for the Jack's ad on TV. "You'll go back, back, back . . . to Jack's, Jack's, Jack's . . . for more, more, more!"

Vickie hushed Phillip and asked why I didn't want to work any-more. When I explained that I couldn't get all the housework done, she was silent at first, then she, too, became animated. "We can pitch in. I'll clean my room every night before bed, and Phillip can clean his." Vickie jumped up and ran into her bedroom, returning with a pencil and the lined writing paper she practiced her cursive writing on. "I'll make a list for me and one for Phillip, and we can hang it on the refrigerator so we don't forget."

Right then, I knew that whether I chose to stay at home or continue working, I'd have to live with the guilt inherent in each decision.

I asked Phillip to find my car keys. We were going to Jack's for dinner.

Once we made our decision, we created new family rituals. On Saturdays we divided the chores and cleaned the house. I made Charles do his own laundry after he ruined almost all of my clothes with the blue ink pens he forgot to empty out of his shirt pocket. Between morning church and evening services on Sundays I'd fix a big pot of spaghetti or soak some pinto beans with ham hock that Vickie would warm up during the week. As she got older, she learned to make corn bread and slaw to go with supper. Phillip liked to tease her about burning everything she cooked, but she looked after him, and they were always close. During Christmas vacation, the whole family gathered around the card table fold-ing reminders to fifteen thousand H&R Block clients to complete their tax returns early. Then we stuffed the envelopes and sepa-rated them by zip code. Charles and I gave the kids the $400 H&R paid me.

Charles began shouldering a good portion of the responsibili-ties that had once fallen solely to me, such as picking up the kids from Mrs. Harris's. As Vickie and Phillip became more involved in school activities, Charles was the one who participated in the PTA meetings, attended Phillip's football and baseball games, and worked the concessions when Vickie was a cheerleader and in the marching band—I was grateful that not once did she have to worry about buying a uniform. Over time, he became accustomed to my working, and the day my paycheck became greater than his he finally accepted the fact that I had a knack for what I did. Eventually, he found a good job he liked as the housing administrator at Fort McClellan and stayed there until he retired, working his way up to the rank of command sergeant major and finishing his college degree.

CONTENT AT H&R Block, I thought once I started there, I'd stay and manage the office, prepare returns during tax season, and teach the fall tax-preparation class at night for the rest of my career. Working the line at GE, I might as well have been one anonymous figure in a string of cutout paper dolls. Now I had a chance to define myself through hard work. The seventies were a rocky time as far as the economy was concerned, beginning with the oil embargo in 1973, a result of the Arab-Israeli conflict. Exorbitant oil prices were soon followed by debilitating inflation, widespread layoffs, and the energy crisis defining the decade. What this meant for me was a layoff from H&R Block four years after I started working full-time.

When the state auditor who visited our office regularly recommended me for a position at an accounting firm in Gadsden, I took it. After a short stint there—I got tired of my paycheck bouncing—I became the officer manager at a small gynecologists' office. My most challenging task, besides typing on a broken typewriter, was stocking up on boxes of Zest crackers and gigantic jars of pickles each month.

Hoping to go back full-time when the economy picked up, I also moonlighted at H&R Block. The doctors' office just wasn't for me, in more ways than one: I knew I was in the wrong place when they offered to perform a hysterectomy on me. Like the other women in the office, the doctors told me, I could keep the insurance check when it arrived, pocketing the much-needed few hundred dollars, in exchange for letting them sharpen their surgery skills. I was hard up for cash but not desperate enough to give away a perfectly good uterus.

Before long, I was talking to a friend at church and found out about an opening at Jacksonville State University in the financial aid office. I wasted no time pursuing the job. At the end of the interview, the financial aid director, Larry, a lanky guy with a mustache, told me, "You've got my vote. Now my wife and secretary just have to approve." An easygoing, kind woman, his wife warned me that working with Larry would be like walking on eggshells, since he had low blood sugar. As his assistant, I got along with him just fine. Whenever he'd get really cranky, he'd pull a boiled egg from his coat pocket, or as if he were a magician, a sausage biscuit would appear out of nowhere. Most of the time he just paced the office eating spoonfuls of peanut butter from the largest jar I'd ever seen.

The day I started work, I walked onto campus thinking about what my life would have been like had I gone there, if only my mother had let me earn college credit my senior year. I didn't dwell on it too much. In my own way, I'd gotten to college after all. Working on campus and helping eager, grateful students in need go to college was something I looked forward to daily.

Unfortunately, without my own college degree, I could only achieve so much financial success at the university. After I'd been working with Larry for three years, H&R Block contacted me, as I'd hoped, to become the district manager for the Anniston office when my old manager left. By then H&R Block had around seven thousand offices and opened a new office seemingly every minute. The pay was double my university salary, and as much as I enjoyed helping students and appreciated the academic setting, I had to move on.

I returned to H&R Block in 1976 and stayed there until 1979, in the end managing fourteen offices. One busy morning as I was reading *Business Week*, I was struck by an article about Goodyear. Just as the technology behind making tires was changing with the newly constructed radial-tire plant built in 1976, so, too, was management philosophy; it was now emphasizing a team approach.

I thought about the stories I heard growing up, the bloody tales of violence between union men and management. They were legendary, like the well-known local ghost stories. I remembered Aunt Robbie talking about her own uncle, who went into hiding during a strike to keep from being killed. My uncles had often referred to "the reign of terror," the time before World War II when workers tried to unionize and labor organizers were beaten viciously on the main street in the middle of the day. According to the article, times had changed.

I finished the article and held the magazine in my lap, considering, for the first time, the real possibility of working at Goodyear—the article had also said that women were becoming part of this new management team. I had no idea what went on behind those red-brick walls sprawling for acres next to the Coosa River. How a tire was actually made was beyond my comprehension. I thought about my friend Sandra wearing a different sweater set every day and the beach vacations and shiny Mercurys Goodyear provided her and her family. Maybe working at Goodyear could give me that stability I needed for the rest of my working life. I'd started late, entering the workforce when I was thirty-one, and I'd gone as far as I could at H&R Block without moving to another state.

One of my most pressing concerns was college tuition now that Vickie was almost halfway through college at Jacksonville State University. Seeing both Vickie and Phillip successfully attend college was one of my greatest dreams, and I'd cashed out my retirement each time I'd made a job change to create a college savings plan.

For a while, I'd been worried that Vickie was headed down the wrong path and wouldn't even make it as the first person in our family to go to college. She'd been such a well-behaved young girl, but she'd started hanging with a rough crowd about the time she learned how to drive. Her teen years had certainly put a strain on Charles and me. She and her friends would do things like get one friend's little dog drunk. Thank goodness, by the time she graduated from high school, she'd finally settled down. I couldn't help but feel that my work-induced absence partly caused her rebellion. Maybe she'd been too responsible too young and wanted freedom from the burden of being such a good and helpful child. Now in her second year of college, she was serious about her studies, and too busy working part-time at the Dairy Dip (and as a receptionist at my office during tax season) to get into too much trouble. I wanted to make sure she would have whatever she needed to keep her life on track.

As I approached forty-one, I was also beginning to realize that life was moving faster than I'd planned. There was only so much time left to accomplish what needed to get done—to establish a greater sense of security for my family. Phillip would be in college soon, and I still needed to build a good retirement. I felt I wouldn't have many more chances left to achieve a certain degree of professional success. The youthful luxury of imagining I had all the time in the world to get it right was long gone. Facing the last half of my life, I understood how important the choices I made were.

I'd also been taken off guard by Edna's recent diagnosis of mouth cancer during the summer. Considering that my grandmother Lillie had died young from cancer, Edna was convinced she was also going to die. After the woman behind the Merle Norman counter told her they didn't have any makeup to cover her sallow complexion, Edna liked to say, "Don't worry about buying me anything—I won't be living by the time Christmas comes."

In light of the fact that she'd had colon cancer ten years earlier, the diagnosis wasn't surprising. She'd also dipped snuff and smoked all her life. She never understood why when we'd moved into our new house in town, I made her stand on the front step to smoke; one reason was that I'd had enough of customers blowing smoke in my face all day at the office, but I also hated the stale smell of cigarette smoke clinging to my upholstered furniture.

What didn't make sense was the idea of burying my mother. In her late fifties, she was too young, and I wasn't ready to stand at her graveside. As difficult as she could be to deal with, the idea of life without Edna gave me a strange sense of vertigo. Now, as I saw what Edna called "liver spots" beginning to appear on the back of my hands, I felt the inevitable limitations of time constricting me as surely as the small wrinkles punctuating my knuckles like parentheses. My aging alarmed me.

I PLACED the magazine on my desk, planning to take it home and show Charles. Just thinking about the fact that Goodyear was hiring female managers for the first time in the history of the company gave me goose bumps. I rubbed my arms and relished what felt like a door opening when I'd thought for sure, at this point in my life, the doors were only closing.

Charles seemed surprised when I informed him of my decision to apply for a position at Goodyear. I took a personal day and put in my application anyway. As I sat in the human resources office filling out the endless forms, I read the plaque that hung on the wall in front of me. I mouthed the Vince Lombardi quotation engraved in gold to myself: FOOTBALL IS A LOT LIKE LIFE; IT REQUIRES PERSEVERANCE, SELF-DENIAL, HARD WORK, SACRIFICE, DEDICATION, AND RESPECT FOR AUTHORITY. It made sense to me. If that was what was required to work there, I was ready. A signed picture of coach Bear Bryant hung next to the plaque. I couldn't wait to tell Charles—when Phillip was born on the same day as "the Bear," he couldn't have been more tickled.

After the long interview, I wondered how many other women

had applied. The only women I'd seen so far were secretaries in the front offices where I'd submitted my application, but I knew Aunt Robbie had worked there. One time when I was a little girl, I'd asked her what she did. She laughed at first. Then she said she'd started in shipping, where she "cut the tits off tires," meaning, she finally explained, that she sliced the thin rubber protrusions off. I thought about her wielding a razor with the same hands she used for knitting and tatting. Aunt Robbie had been hired during World War II, when women manned the plant, making jeep tires, rubber soles for shoes, raincoats, and anything else the military needed. Even after the men returned from war, she managed to stay— refusing, she told me, to accept Goodyear's offer in 1960 to buy her a brand-new house if she'd take early retirement. By then, she and Uncle Howard had built their own nice house with a swimming pool. She worked at Goodyear for twenty-seven years, until heart problems and a back injury forced her to retire.

Leaving the plant after my interview, I passed photographs of the men from "Mahogany Row" in Akron, Ohio, lining the paneled hallway—the same men whose biographies I had no idea I'd be memorizing soon. I stopped for a minute and took a deep breath, staring at the black-and-white portraits of these men who exuded such a sense of power. I tried to imagine their lives: how it felt to run a corporation, travel the world, and dine at the country club. It was a life about which I could only fantasize. At least I had this chance to make my life better—a chance I'd never believed possible as a child.

On the way home I stopped to check on my mother. Blocking the doorway, she was dressed in her housecoat, her dentures still sitting in their usual spot on her bathroom sink now that her mouth was too sore for her to wear them. I announced that I'd applied to work as a manager at Goodyear. She didn't offer to let me in but cut her sharp eyes at me and asked, "Shouldn't you be doing what a woman's supposed to do?"

My shoulders tightened. A familiar feeling of frustration flooded my stomach. No matter how old I was, it always snuck up on me when something Edna said hurt my feelings. Throughout my life there had remained something stuck between us, something as elemental as two charged electrons repelling each other. It wasn't one particular thing she did or said but the accumulation of all of the small things: the hard look that could stare a hole right through you, the critical tone of voice, the wall she erected between herself and the rest of the world even though she was always doing for others—myself and the children included.

Vickie was the one who got the best of Edna those early years of her childhood when she and Phillip stayed with her on the farm in the summer while I worked at H&R Block. She was so good to Vickie, I'd have to remind her that she had two grandchildren. When the children became more independent, I'd go through phases of distancing myself from Edna, being too busy with work, even when she and my father moved a stone's throw away after Papa died. I'd often fooled myself into thinking that I no longer cared whether or not I measured up in her eyes, yet here I was again, returning to her doorstep, seeking her recognition.

When Edna finally decided to invite me in, I didn't stay. I searched for my car keys in my purse and told her to get some rest. She looked tired. It was clear she didn't feel well. Besides, I was too old for such childish nonsense, and I knew enough to recognize and accept that Edna was doing the best she could, as she always had. Really, how could I fault her if she didn't know how to love me the way I wanted, if she never once said the words "I love you"? How could I blame her for only knowing how to survive by freezing her feelings, playing dead like a possum? It was the one thing I'd learned to do best, and it's what would keep me alive during the hard times waiting for me just around the corner at Goodyear.

CHAPTER 4

Becoming a Rubber Worker

||||||||||||||||||||||||||||||||||||||||||||||||||||||||||||||||||||||||||||||||||||||||||||||||||||||||||||

*Life should not be estimated exclusively by the standards
of dollars and cents. I am not disposed to complain that I
have planted and others have gathered fruit. A man has
cause for regret only when he sows and no one reaps.*

—CHARLES GOODYEAR

WHEN I started training at Goodyear, I joined the stream
of workers driving to Gadsden before each shift. A small
city on the Coosa River, Gadsden is circled by hills brimming with
iron ore, coal, and limestone—the three ingredients necessary for
making steel. Generation after generation of families had migrated
from the surrounding foothills to find a better way of life at Re-
public Steel (the heart of this industrial city) and smaller factories,
producing everything from wire to stovepipes. When Goodyear
opened its doors in 1929, men from small bluffs and hollows named
Gnatville and Turkeytown had a new opportunity to earn what
seemed like a fortune, compared with their fathers, who had made
only pennies a day farming. At that time, President Hoover had
actually pushed a button at the White House to raise the American
flag at the plant.

In 1979, I, too, faced a new opportunity at Goodyear, but my first time inside the plant, I felt like I'd stuck my head in a barrel of hot roofing tar. No exaggeration. It smelled that bad, and I wondered, "Do I really want to work here?" The deafening machinery made my ears buzz, fumes from the curing pits almost choked me, tire-building equipment reared back like gigantic spiders on their hind legs, and machines called banburies, which looked like three-story cake mixers, spit out four-hundred-pound batches of black rubber marshmallows. Several times a day, from that day forward, I asked myself if I really knew what I'd gotten myself into.

For six months I trained in the plant's various departments in the five main divisions: the tube plant, the mill, the truck side, the passenger side, and the radial plant. I marveled at the fact that I was working in a fifty-acre maze, with miles and miles of conveyor belts and daily reports about "near misses." It would take only a second to lose your fingers in the tire machine if you placed your hands on a "pinch point"—the spot where the cutter, as sharp as a guillotine, did its slicing.

Lying in bed at night, I'd mull over the stories people told about the accidents that happened. One such story, in which a factory worker in the nearby Union City plant in Tennessee had suffocated to death when he was rolled up in a machine for two hundred yards, haunted me. I kept mentally replaying that moment when his father, who had been working the same shift, had to pull his body out.

After listening to stories like this, I thought I understood how quickly a machine could become a death trap, but the idea never really hit home until the day I had my physical at the doctor's office, located at the back of the plant. As I sat waiting for my examination, two distraught men carried in their coworker who'd been caught in the mill, a machine that operates two gigantic rollers moving in opposite directions. The mill is so hot that it softens rubber into liquid to be extruded. I found out later that they'd heard him screaming but thought he was yelling that he was taking

a break. Instead, he'd been pinned between the moving rollers. I
grew nauseous smelling his burned flesh. His clothes had melted
into his skin, and his arm was hanging by a single thread of muscle.
After that, I began each shift with a prayer that I'd leave like I came
in: alive, and with all my body parts attached.

Despite the hazardous machines, I looked forward to each day,
which was always different from the last. My squadron of five attended seminars and toured fabric mills and retread plants in Alabama and Tennessee. I learned how to prep the stock, build tires,
cut hot rubber in the mill room, and withstand a sandstorm of
white chalk in the tube room. I'd lug home thick training man-
uals explaining the process of making tires or managing a team
of workers. I took test after test on every topic imaginable, learning the biographies of men such as the founding father, Frank A.
Seiberling, who started the company in 1928, and P. W. Litchfield,
president when the Gadsden plant opened in 1929—the same year
that Goodyear became the largest tire manufacturer in the world.
I was even held accountable for memorizing the educational background, religious denomination, and children's names of the top
brass in Akron.

As I studied the history of the company, I was especially moved
by the strange story of Charles Goodyear, who discovered the vul-
canization process for rubber but died penniless. What I admired
about Goodyear was his determination and sense of purpose in
developing a way to make a viable form of rubber. Until his addition of sulfur to the mix, rubber softened into a gooey blob in hot
weather and hardened into brittle pieces in cold weather. He never
gave up his search despite the odds against him and the fact that he
was destitute, continually in and out of debtors' prison. I admired
his resilience but wondered how his family, who lived on the brink
of disaster, endured the sacrifices they had to make. He never prof-
ited from his invention and died ignorant of how dramatically his
efforts would change the future.

After several months of classroom time, I began working as a supervisor trainee in stock prep on the night shift with my mentor, Andrew, a bear of a man who encouraged me in every possible way. He gave me management books to read outside of work, and pushed me to become a member of an Anniston business club (where I would work my way up to becoming the first female president). His confidence in me helped quell my fears about the machinery and bolstered my nascent belief in my ability to be a good manager.

I was lucky I had Andrew to lean on. He warned me to choose my words and actions carefully. Anything could be twisted, and I didn't dare joke with the guys. He'd remind me that half the people in the plant were related to one another somehow, and I'd better be careful whose feathers I ruffled or I'd pass those people on the way down.

Even Andrew, who'd seen quite a bit as a supervisor, couldn't begin to predict the crazy snafus I'd run into just because I was a woman. One night when we were short two people on the schedule after the race weekend at NASCAR, Andrew asked me to run the overtime clock. No big deal. I went upstairs and starting calling workers to see who could come in at 1:00 A.M. On my next shift, the men I'd called cussed me like a yard dog. They wanted to be taken off the calling list. Their wives had pitched a fit when they heard a strange woman's voice in the middle of the night. From then on, I handed the phone to the janitor, who'd give me a quick wink before he asked someone's wife if he could speak to her husband in the dead of night.

When I completed my training, I felt like I was on top of the world. The day I received my department assignment as a new manager, I sat in the conference room next to the other four trainees in my squadron. One training manager, a real hoot, warned us, "When you become a manager, it'll be tough running your departments. I'm the only one who'll tell you the truth. Being a manager is just like falling off a cliff." Since training had felt as unnatural as jumping out of an airplane, his remark didn't surprise me. I appreciated his honesty and was ready to prove I had the mettle to be a good manager—to show that I could motivate my team and withstand the daily dissonance of deadly machinery.

I genuinely believed I could be an important part of Goodyear's future, fostering a better relationship between management and the union, or "bargaining men." Even more important, women in management were relatively new, and I was one of two women on my squadron—the other woman, Cindy, had been promoted from the union. The squadron represented a range of backgrounds. One of the men had come from shipping, another had worked at IBM, and the third worked as an assistant store manager at J. C. Penney.

I felt like a trailblazer. Both Andrew and the human resources manager had told me many times through those weeks that I had a bright future at Goodyear, and that meant a lot to me. I wanted to matter, and I was ready to fulfill these high expectations. If I could make it, then the door would open for more women to follow. I already knew all too well about the woman who'd gone through training the year before me and had quit soon after being assigned the night shift, a typical assignment for new managers. I wasn't quite sure why she quit, but for whatever reason, I felt compelled to prove something on her behalf. As the roomful of rookies left following our last meeting together, I looked forward to the day when there would be more women joining me.

MY FIRST job as supervisor was in stock prep on the third shift, from 11:00 P.M. to 7:00 A.M., in the radial division. I knew from the beginning that being a female supervisor wouldn't be easy, but nothing had prepared me for the daily hassle from both the union guys and upper management. One old-timer who'd been there for forty years was so enraged when I was made supervisor that he immediately requested to be transferred to another department. Another old man flat-out announced, "I take orders from a bitch at home, and I'm not taking orders from a bitch at work."

It wasn't surprising that these men resented me; they'd never answered to a woman before. I tried to stay calm. I didn't want the men to have something more to complain about by becoming too emotional. It would take a while for them to accept me, and I tried to rise to each challenge—even ridiculous ones, such as the time one guy insisted, "I bet you can't find me a recipe my wife would like or doesn't already have." Maybe he was trying to prove I didn't have the right stuff even at home, where I was "supposed" to be. I brought him a chicken and corn bread recipe, wishing he'd focus on what really mattered. He seemed satisfied.

While the men I supervised resented a woman being in a position of authority, some of my supervisors feared that I wouldn't pull my weight. I had only been on the floor in stock prep a few days before one shift foreman took me out onto the back dock, where he thought no one would hear him. In a low voice, he grumbled, "I've got this other loser [referring to an African American worker], and now I have you, and you're a damn woman." He actually scratched his crotch, so I just focused on the Y-shaped vein popping out smack-dab in the middle of his forehead. "I don't want either one of you. You'll ruin my record, and I'm gonna get rid of both of you." As far he and some of the others were concerned, I might as well have been a missionary in a strange land, trying to convert them to a new religion.

I DIDN'T say anything to Andrew or anybody else, imagining that these situations would fade away as naturally as fog burning off the foothills in the morning sun. I couldn't turn to Cindy for support— she decided to go back into the union not long after becoming a manager. She'd been assigned to the mill room, where raw rubber is mixed. During the mixing process, lampblack (also known as black carbon) is released. As fine as talcum powder, the lampblack seeps into every pore of your skin, making lungs bleed and sweat blacken. Cindy had such an adverse reaction to the chemicals that she requested to be transferred back to where she'd started.

I hoped I could talk to Barbara, a tough old bird who'd become supervisor of the tire room. In the bathroom one evening, I asked her how she handled the stress of being the only other female manager. She let a string of cuss words fly before she told me, "You can't trust a soul," and cautioned me that if I planned to stay, I'd better watch my back. Eventually she left, too; I assumed she'd had all she could take from the men.

As a supervisor, I immediately learned to tune out all of the cussing. It didn't take too long, either, for me to understand that I could never let my guard down. Whenever we were in the office together, one of my shift foremen—a tall, blue-eyed man named Donald—would grin and make the most inappropriate comments, without warning. Donald always dressed neatly and had a good-natured manner of speaking, so it sometimes took me a minute to register what he'd said. We'd be talking about work, and out of the blue he'd interject, "That must be one of them French bras you're wearing, because it's got those things up high and your nipples are showing." Or he'd catch me retrieving a file from the file cabinet, and he'd observe, "If you kept bending over at the file cabinet, you might get something rammed in your ass that you don't want. I know I could take care of that." As his words sank in, I kept my head averted, shame spreading its red flush across my face, shock and embarrassment flooding my body.

After a few of these awkward moments, I learned to steel myself for his comments. When Donald inspected my department, despite the fact that it was spotless and in order, he'd say things like, "Goddammit, Lilly, this looks like a whorehouse."

I wouldn't flinch. "Really?" I'd reply. "I wouldn't know. I've never been to a whorehouse."

I CONTINUED to give upper management the benefit of the doubt until the night in stock prep when I was overseeing the mills. When we ran out of stock on one of the machines, my supervisor barked at me, "Lilly, load her with that scrap rubber over there. The worst thing you can do is let her go down."

The scruffy union fellow running the mill, who looked like he might as well have been on one of the FBI's Most Wanted posters at the post office, shook his head. "If you put the scrap in this machine, both the caps on each end will bust, and it will be a real hard fix," he said.

I didn't believe him, and told my supervisor what he'd said. "Aw, hell, that guy don't want to work. He just wants to sit on his ass," was his response. So I did what my supervisor instructed me to do and made the operator load up the scrap rubber. I heard a loud explosion and was sick to my stomach. Sure enough, the mill was down all night. I knew I'd been taken by my supervisor. Throughout the night, as we struggled to get the mill up and running again, Barbara's and Andrew's words echoed in my mind.

ONE OF the other shift foremen, Stan, a bowlegged man who talked too quickly, didn't try to trick me. He announced his suspicions of me loudly and clearly the minute I became part of his department. He warned everyone that I was keeping information about people in a little black book because I was "a member of the ERA." (I carried a steno pad around with me to take notes and record information to keep from making mistakes.) By then I had been moved from stock prep, where I'd been for about a year, to final finish, where the tires go after they're cured in the pits and have traveled on overhead conveyors to cool, passing into the trimmer where the rubber tips are cut off. Once they reach final finish, if a tire is a blackwall, it goes immediately on the hook lines for two people to inspect by spinning and feeling for defects. If the tire is a whitewall, it travels to the blue paint machines to be sprayed so that the finish is protected during shipping. All of the tires are ground down by the force grinders to balance them out before being stamped and packed onto a truck for shipping.

In final finish, Stan never bothered to give me instructions on how to operate the machinery. There were several panels with some fiddly old wiring, so it took me a while to understand the mechanics; but the union electricians who saw me sticking with it helped me. One night when we had one mechanical problem after another, I called Stan onto the floor for help. He immediately blamed my rib dressers, threatening to send them home.

"My guys aren't the problem. My crew is running more tires than ever," I pointed out to him.

He turned red in the face and said, "What did you just say? Are you calling me a liar, when you have no idea what you're talking about?"

"No, sir, I was just telling you the rib dressers have done their jobs. That's my responsibility—that I do know."

He started yelling and waving his arms at me, and went on like this for at least thirty minutes—in front of my team. There was nowhere for me to go and nothing for me to do but stand there and take it, until he suggested that we go to the computer room and settle our differences.

There he went on and on about what I was doing wrong. I finally said, "You're right. You're the boss. We'll run everything your way. Just tell me what you want." He moved his chair so close to me that I couldn't move and leaned forward with his beet-red face in mine. I stared at his ears, puzzled by the stray patches of hair.

"Where did you come from? You think you're so smart. You're

not a manager and don't know a damn thing about anything. You're Goodyear's mistake."

"Look, all I want to do is my job, but I can't do anything if you won't let me." I asked him to let me go back to work, but he wasn't through with me. My nerves were shot and my stomach was in knots, but something about the intensity of his anger cautioned me to roll up inside myself and play dead like someone being attacked by a bear is supposed to do, hoping the bear becomes discouraged by the lack of response. I was finally able to leave when the engineer manager arrived.

When I talked to Andrew about the situation, he explained that Stan couldn't be all bad. He couldn't be a complete jerk if he'd taken in his brother-in-law when both the boy's parents died unexpectedly. I tried to let our differences go, and when I did, Stan realized that I didn't hold grudges or spy on people. Finally, he started to give me a chance. With Stan I learned I had to meet people in the middle and try to understand their personalities, even changing my attitude when necessary to make a relationship work. Before I knew it, we were able to work together without acrimony.

I didn't mention this incident, or any of the others, to Charles. During those first couple of years, Charles never knew the extent of what I was dealing with at Goodyear. We communicated mostly through notes on the stove; when I was home, he was at work, and vice versa. Our shifts just worked out that way. He was traveling a fair amount for his job at Fort McClellan, while also finishing the college degree he'd never completed when moving up in rank in the National Guard. The real reason I didn't confide in him, though, is that I tried to leave work at work. I refused to let my troubles at work consume my family life, and when we talked, we were solving other problems at home—now Phillip was in high school and Vickie off at college. He never even set foot inside the Goodyear plant. I thought I could handle my own problems, so I adjusted to the

situation, like a contorted tree twisting its way around another tree
that's too close, eager to find just enough space in which to grow.

THERE WERE enough dependable people at Goodyear to keep me
going. The first time I cut a batch of rubber running the tuber in
stock prep, my supervisor gave me a dull knife—even though I'd
asked for a sharper one. When the blade got stuck in the rubber,
another man came over and jerked it out for me. He pointed the
knife in the direction of the man across the room, who'd lost his
thumb cutting rubber. "Let me show the right way so you don't
end up like him," he said, slicing the thick white sheet that made
me think of whale blubber. There were other simple acts of kindness, too, like when the guys helped me with faulty wiring on the
old machines, or let me in on the best type of shoes to wear on the
concrete floor.

Once the guys got to know me, they usually came around—
even the most stubborn. The day I was introduced to one of the
millwrights, he leaned close to me and said, "Well, you think you
should be here, don't you?" He was a big ole boy with scraggly long
hair. His breath was foul.

"Yeah, I think I should be here," I said. I wanted to ask him
when was the last time he took a bath.

He hitched up the waist of his stained khakis over his belly and
said, "Well, you know, it gets hot out here and sometimes I wear
cutoffs without anything underneath, and I might have to drop my
shorts to cool off." He spit a stream of tobacco juice onto the floor
beside me. "Or fart."

I didn't move away from the brown spittle.

"I'm responsible for your production and making sure you're
paid properly, so don't go changing your habits on my account. Just
because I'm female doesn't mean I require anything different."

That day he remained unconvinced, but he soon changed his
tune once we'd spent some time together. It didn't matter whether

I was male or female—the union guys would have had to test me. That was the nature of the relationship between management and the union men. Respect was never a given for anybody. Just as a coach has to earn the respect of the players, managers, who had a history of stepping on men's necks, had to gain the confidence of their crew. Once they saw I was willing to drag one-hundred-pound rolls of material off the conveyor by myself if someone wasn't around to help, and work overtime on the weekends when they were sick of doing it, most of them started calling me Miss Lilly with a real sense of regard.

THE SUPPORT of a few good men carried me a long way, and I could never have survived without the help of guys like the night engineer supervisor, who stood up for me when I was blamed for something I didn't do. Everyone knew the machines were supposed to be running when you walked on the floor and when you walked off. Once a machine goes down, it might not start up again. It's like a wreck on the interstate—especially down the line in the pits, where tires are cured. Those presses never stop running, and the tires keep coming, so you have to take them off the conveyor belt and stack them. Before you know it, you could have three thousand tires you've got to work back in at some point.

In stock prep, the objective is to make sure a tuber never shuts down. The department is about as large as a town block, with trucks, skids of rubber to load, and a six-eight and a twelve-six tuber, both of which produce tire components. Heated rubber goes from the mills down into the huge tuber, which, like a sausage grinder, heats and mixes the different types of rubber before the operator puts in the die with a tread design. Then the rubber's excreted out in the shape of tread that is weighed and cooled, sometimes traveling through water. A huge saw cuts the tread before two people offload the tread from the conveyor onto the flat leaves of a truck.

I hadn't been in the department long when the eight-inch tuber went down two hours into my shift. A ball of rubber caught up under the machine, causing the belt to break. The shift foreman blamed me, but one of the night supervisors, whose face, after he'd been caught in a press, looked like it had been slashed with a knife, stood up for me during a meeting the next day. He explained to the group of disgruntled men that the ball of rubber had built up from a piece of loose rubber scrap over time, and I didn't have anything to do with it.

I was grateful for his willingness to go against the gang. This was an exception to what usually went on, which was that any time the production was down, it was my fault. Ultimately I learned I had to take care of myself; I had to work harder and smarter than the rest. I started coming in two hours earlier than my shift to check the schedule, make sure stock was ready, and get any updates. That's when Edna began saying, as she did through the rest of my Goodyear career, that she never knew anybody who took twelve hours to work an eight-hour shift.

If my experience had been all bad in the beginning, I couldn't have made it; but I was like the lab rat that keeps coming back for more because it never knows when it pushes the lever if food will come out or not. I was constantly seeking approval, unable to predict when Goodyear would reward or punish me.

I HAD my first formal evaluation in 1981, after I'd been supervisor in final finish for a year. During the meeting in the cramped office of the department foreman, Jeff, it was made abundantly clear that I didn't understand the unwritten expectations of me, didn't know what a woman was supposed to deliver, so to speak. As Jeff asked me a few questions about the machinery in final finish, he chain-smoked, surprised when I gave him the right answers.

The next thing I knew, he started talking about how well *he'd* done at Goodyear, and explained in detail his wife's personal connections with the top dogs at corporate headquarters in Akron. After he finally quit talking about himself, I thought we were about to get down to the business of my performance and future. Instead, he said, "Well, I rank you an eleven out of twelve. If you want a better score, you can meet me at the Ramada Inn."

I stared at him blankly for a moment. Surely, he was just joking. I was used to crude remarks, but Jeff stared right back at me, expecting an answer—just as if he'd asked me another question about the machinery.

I glanced at the clock. We'd been in his office for over an hour.

I replied, "I'm not sure I understand."

He exhaled cigarette smoke in my direction before he repeated himself. My temples throbbed. I felt a jolt of anger. I told myself to breathe and think, and not to do anything I'd regret. Despite all his big talk, Jeff was a small guy, always tan from playing golf. Where did he find time for that? I'd heard from coworkers that he was untouchable because he had a relative high up in management. It wasn't as if he wasn't liked, either. I remembered seeing him plenty of times after work, hanging out in the parking lot with a group of guys, drinking beer out of a cooler in one of their cars.

I asked, "How can you do that based on my performance?"

"In a place like this, Lilly, it's more important that your bosses like you than that you do a good job." A wisp of smoke trailed out of one of his nostrils.

I calculated Vickie's college tuition. Phillip would be in college before I knew it. I still had a few years ahead of me before Vickie and Phillip were independent. Then there were the household bills and expenses that Charles's paycheck didn't cover.

I didn't know what to say that wouldn't make the situation worse, so I stood up and walked toward the door. Out of the corner of my eye, I saw Jeff smash his cigarette with a rough jab into the overflowing aluminum ashtray on his desk.

That night I couldn't sleep. The following day I tried to ask Jeff about my evaluation. When I approached him, he said, "Nothing you say matters. You're at the bottom, where you'll stay." I pressed him to tell me why, but he only replied, "That's where I want you. You've made the wrong people mad these past few months and caused me a lot of trouble." Several days later I tried to talk to another manager about the problem. He replied in an unconcerned tone, "What are you so worried about? If there's a layoff, you'll go anyway, so don't worry about it. You're okay."

It wasn't much longer after this that Goodyear said it was cutting back on supervisors and demoted me, moving me from final finish to special tire trials in July 1981.

I WAS more than upset about being moved to special tire trials, where I was excluded from manager meetings and training seminars. Soon after this demotion, I slipped on a grease spot in the parking lot, breaking my nose on a speed bump. The Goodyear nurse gave me some Darvocet to take when I got home, but I was in so much pain that the usual one-hour drive took me two hours. Finally at home, I slept upright to keep from choking on my own blood. The next day, Charles took me to the hospital for emergency surgery. While I was in the hospital, the only person from the plant who contacted me was one of my supervisors, who only called to see if I had extra tickets for the football game on Saturday. When I returned to work, my nose was swollen and the guys started calling me "squaw." I'd always hated the crook in my nose, and now I felt even more self-conscious and vulnerable. I wanted to hide my injury, to become invisible.

In special tire trials I was anything but invisible. I worked with only one other employee, Dennis, who'd been at the plant for thirty years. He informed me right off the bat that he'd gotten his business degree at Jacksonville State University and had been part of the management at Goodyear. Realizing that he didn't like the long hours and hard work, he'd convinced Goodyear that he had a nervous condition. He was demoted, as he'd wanted, but was still paid the same—a fact of which he never quit reminding me.

Our working relationship started out pretty good until he started telling me about his personal problems, especially with a woman he called "the redhead." They'd worked together in the tube plant, had an affair, and now she lived with him. You'd think Goodyear was Peyton Place, the way gossip ran rampant at the plant. Everyone referred to Dennis as "Goodyear's number one pimp." I figured I could handle him as the weeks passed and he continued to tell me in more and more detail about his sex life, his fights with the redhead, and his money problems. That's just the way he was, and I hoped that if I brushed his words aside and did my best in the new position, he would quit talking that way.

Every time we prepared to run trials on the floor, we met in the office to discuss our schedule, and before too long, like clockwork, Dennis would start in about his sex life. "That redhead is sure good in bed when she wants to be, but you know I'd rather go to bed with you."

I got the impression Dennis actually thought I should appreciate his remarks. When I tried to ignore him and review our schedule, he'd continue, "All the women say I'm good in bed."

Funny, I thought, *how this short little fellow who isn't much to look at thinks he's God's gift to women.* "We'd better get started," I'd insist, wishing he'd keep his mind on work.

One day Dennis pulled a nail clipper from his pocket and started clipping his nails. "You're gonna be my next woman. You'll see what I mean," he commented as dirty yellow slivers fell onto the desk.

It didn't matter that I didn't respond. He didn't skip a beat in his harangue.

"I bet the first thing you do when you go to the hotel on the company trips is get in bed with somebody and stay there all weekend. Next trip, I'll go, and you can take me to bed with you."

I wanted to say what was really on my mind, but instead I said, "That's probably not a good idea."

His eyes narrowed. He swept the clippings into his hand and dropped them into the plastic trash bin. "We'd have a good time together on the trip to New Orleans. I'd be the best thing that ever happened to you."

Finally, my patience worn thin, I said, "I'll be busy working with the presentations and speakers."

"That's not a problem," he said, examining his hand with the precision of a woman checking her nail polish.

"Well, you can do whatever you want, but you can't go with me." I took my clipboard with our schedule and headed to the floor, despite the fact that we hadn't discussed what we were doing first. He started snipping the fingernails on his left hand with angry snaps of the clipper.

DENNIS SOON became obsessive about trying to get me into bed with him: rubbing up against me, hugging me around the waist, or running his hand up and down my back whenever we ran tire trials together. Frustrated that he was getting nowhere with me, he took on a sharper tone. After he went through his usual litany of sexual escapades, he'd say, "You know, if you don't start doing more in this department, I'm not sure how much longer you'll have a job. You think you're so smart, but you don't have any credibility, and that's one thing I can give you if you know what's good for you. It's a shame, but a lot of people around here just have to be moved when they can't perform. And it looks like, to me, you're not real good at this."

I didn't want to make him any angrier, so I tried to keep my voice even, like the automated tone of a seasoned secretary. "You know I'm married, and even if I wasn't, I don't get involved with the people at work."

"That's not what I've heard."

"We've got work to do," I said, starting to feel light-headed. A chocolate milk shake from McDonald's was all I'd eaten for dinner.

"That's a shame. I think I'll get you started and you can run four tire trials today. You haven't been running as many as the other guys. You haven't been doing your job right lately, and I'd hate to have to talk to my supervisor about you. You know, he owes me a big favor. That's why I can get people moved from their jobs when I want."

Even though I'd already checked the records and knew I was averaging more trials than Dennis each day without any help from him, how did I know he didn't have something on the supervisor? They'd worked together a long time, and he'd talk about how they hung out together at a strip club called the Fuzzy Duck. He'd already spread the rumor throughout the plant that we were going together. I had no idea what else Dennis was capable of. He reminded me of an assassin bug—an insect that sneaks up behind a boll weevil when it's eating cotton and stabs it with his stinger, sucking its insides out like soup. Then the assassin bug actually gets inside the boll weevil's body and waits to ambush another one.

After several months of Dennis's incessant threats to have me moved, I grew so anxious I could barely eat or drink. I became de-hydrated to the point of being hospitalized for several days. That's when I had to let on to Charles, at least to some extent, the trouble I was having with Dennis. As I suspected, he wanted me to talk to a supervisor if Dennis didn't stop. I felt that I couldn't talk to anyone. Andrew was my training manager, and had no say in the operations where I was. Jeff was already furious at me for rebuffing him, and I was still trying to overcome being demoted in the first place. I couldn't cause trouble when I was already seen as a trouble-maker. Since Charles couldn't fix the situation, he grew more frustrated and unreasonable each time we discussed it. I downplayed the truth of the matter in order to keep him calm.

||||||||||||

I FORGED ahead, doing my best to be irreproachable, but even though I wore a plain denim shirt, Dennis still commanded me to "turn around and hold up your shoulders so I can see what you've got." While we were catching tires, he'd comment, "You don't have a bra on, do you? You know I'm partial to women with large breasts. That's another reason I don't know why I took up with the redhead, because she never did have much to begin with, before the operation."

He meant her recent mastectomy.

I withheld even the most innocuous personal information; something as simple as mentioning that I was on a diet turned into a constant refrain not to lose too much weight or "I'd lose my greatest asset." Listening to him, I was reminded of the shame that snuck up on me sometimes as a teenager when I struggled to adjust to the startling fullness of my changing body. I withered, tucking inward like a leaf after a hard freeze, wishing for the freedom I felt as a child unaware of my sexual identity. I started keeping my hair cut short.

At times, my dread of going to work almost paralyzed me. I couldn't fix my problem in a logical way, like you could a defective tire. When there's a tire hold and the machines stop running, you have to figure out where in the process something went wrong. Was there too much rubber, too much of a certain chemical, or the wrong temperature setting? You trace each step in the process, searching for clues until you find the mistake. Then you fix it and start over with the right formula.

I couldn't fix Dennis.

I'd think about my father, who worked like a dog for thirty-two years, and wonder what he'd endured that he never discussed with my mother or me. I could feel in my bones that fear both my parents had of sudden hardship that can turn your life upside down in a minute. My mother had lost her own mother so young, and my daddy had lost his father, a foreman for Southern Railroad, when he was fifteen. Not long after that, he and Granny Mac moved to Alabama to live with Aunt Lucille.

Uprooted at such a young age, my father craved stability. His entire life he'd missed only one shift of work that I knew of. That was to get a tooth pulled, and he used a vacation day, afraid that if he didn't go to work he'd have a blemish on his record and jeopardize his job security. I lived with the same kind of fear of an unexpected disaster, and I took great comfort in the fact that I could take care of myself and the children if something ever happened to Charles. That year running tire trials, I had no choice but to put up with Dennis. I did just that, until the situation became critical—when the redhead moved out of Dennis's house.

It was early May 1982 when I walked by the office and Dennis hollered at me, "If I'm not here, you just sit at your desk all day and do nothing when you need to be running three tire trials instead of two." He was the one who stayed in his office all day on the phone, talking to women and doing God knows what.

After making a public spectacle, he went onto the floor and started taping loads of tires I'd already run to be run again. When I asked him what presses and tire machines he wanted me to start checking, he grabbed my hand and pulled me close.

"You stick tight by me today and help me because I don't feel like working. I'm a little down." He squeezed my hand. "I need you to cheer me up." He reached over and ran his hand around the top of my blue shirt like he was about to button it up. The second time he did that, I said, "I'll be happy to button the top button if you want me to," and I stepped away from him.

Back at the force machine, he kept his hand on my back,

rubbing it in circles. Twice he intentionally touched my breast before he said, "You're shaking me up. Now what are you going to do about it?"

It was like trying to clean up broken glass; every time you think you've gotten up every last shard, you catch another glint waiting for your bare feet. I turned my back to him, my stomach burning with what felt like hot lava churning inside it, and walked to the other side of the machine. He was so angry that I wouldn't go with him to his empty house that night that nothing I did for the next couple of days was good enough.

Finally one morning, even though I'd checked all the tires, he wanted me to do more. When I balked, he said, "You just don't want to work. When my boss gets back, he needs to know this, and I'll have your job."

I was exhausted from worrying about when he was going to make good on his threats. It was time to get help. The only person I could talk to was Bruce, the union division chairman, who in his position was accustomed to resolving problems. He agreed to go with me to human resources. That very afternoon we met with Eddie, the personnel specialist for the radial division.

In the meeting, the last place I wanted to be, I explained the situation, the last thing on earth I wanted to do. "All I want is for him to keep his hands off me and quit telling me about his sex life," I said. "Please just make him keep his hands to himself and quit overloading me."

After a few minutes of listening, Eddie, whose face had flushed to the same deep auburn as his hair, stood up and walked to the door. He changed his mind, sat back down, and looked past me. Seeing his agitation, I was beginning to feel like I was the one who'd done something wrong. He finally picked up the phone, held the receiver as if he'd forgotten the phone number, and called his secretary to page Bo, the division superintendent, and ask him to come into our meeting. When Bo heard what I had to say, he looked at me skeptically. "With our new company policy, we'll have to do an internal investigation, which might take a few days," he said matter-of-factly. That was exactly what I was trying to prevent. I just wanted the situation to be handled and Dennis, who everyone knew had a problem with women, straightened out.

Then Eddie said, "You can go on home now, and we'll let you know when we've finished and what've we've found." His face was still flushed.

Overpowered by the bitter, vomitlike smell embedded in my clothes from the plant's persistent fumes, I felt like I might faint. "But what about Dennis? Is he staying?"

"Yes, there's no reason for him to go home. He has a good career here and a proven track record, and we're going to keep him," Eddie said, looking at Bo, who nodded.

My hands were shaking. I might as well have had six cups of coffee. "I'll stay."

"You go on home now. Don't worry, we'll pay you," Bo assured me.

Something stubborn rose up inside me. These guys weren't going to get away with this. I had as much a right to my job as Dennis had to his. As a little girl sitting in the dark movie theater while my parents shopped at Blackwelder's grocery store, I'd seen hundreds of westerns starring Gene Autry. A simple lesson had been ingrained in me on those countless Saturday afternoons: The man in the white hat always wins. No matter how many times he might get knocked down and have to dust off his pants, in the end, the good guy prevails.

I slid my hands under my thighs and sat up straighter. "If Dennis stays, I stay."

AFTER THAT meeting, I immediately went to a pay phone and called the Equal Employment Opportunity Commission (EEOC) in Birmingham. The man I spoke to informed me that I had to file the charge in person. I explained to him that by the time I made it to Birmingham the following week I'd probably be out of a job. He went ahead and took my information over the phone but made sure I understood that they were backlogged, with too many cases and too few caseworkers. My file was at the bottom of a large stack. Hanging up the phone, I dropped another quarter into the slot and called my doctor.

When he took my blood pressure late that afternoon, it had shot up sky high.

I WAS unsure about the EEOC process, and though I knew from working at H&R Block that sex discrimination in the workplace was illegal under Title VII of the Civil Rights Act of 1964, I had no real understanding of the law. I had no idea that it had only been two years since the EEOC had issued guidelines defining sex discrimination, establishing the term *sexual harassment*. I also didn't know that in 1976 the court had recognized that a male supervisor's advances toward a female employee were viewed as harassment, or that in 1977 the court had also ruled that retaliation against a woman in the workplace for rejecting the sexual advances of her boss is a violation of Title VII. Like so many women then and now, I'd experienced both of these situations.

When I talked to Charles about contacting an attorney, we agreed that we'd put off making the car payment if necessary. I called Jack, an attorney whom I'd met through the Anniston business club I'd joined at Andrew's urging. He'd recently opened a private practice. In the meantime the internal investigation was conducted, and Goodyear circled their wagons. Word of the investigation had gotten around the plant, and I heard that people were told that if they were interested in a career at Goodyear, they'd stay out of it.

One woman, Kristie, who'd witnessed the harassment and had

sympathized with me in the break room, had a sudden change of heart. She had previously confided in me that management had skipped over her for a promotion because she was recently married and would probably have kids. She'd even asked me how to deal with that situation. Now she changed her allegiance. She went so far as to grab my arm when I walked by her and berate me for ruining people's careers by causing such a mess. I was floored—particularly because I knew that Dennis had treated her the same way. After that, she refused to speak to me. Many years later, she admitted to me that she came to regret her actions when she was later harassed in another department.

AT THE beginning of the EEOC's investigation, I met with Eddie and Bo. They indicated that Dennis had admitted to all my statements, except to having touched my breasts. Then, as if washing his hands of the subject, Bo remarked that Dennis was staying put in his department and I'd be transferred.

I was flabbergasted. Bo came around his desk and sat on the edge of it, leaning toward me in an almost fatherly way. "So far it looks like you have a terrible record. There are a lot of things you need to do differently. You could start by learning how to ride a motorcycle or water-ski on the weekends. If you want to succeed here, that's my suggestion."

Did people really say things like this? Did he really expect me to hang out with the guys on the weekends, fishing and drinking, as if downing a few beers with the boys would make everything all right? And what was all this about my "poor" performance? This meeting was supposed to be about Dennis's behavior, not my evaluation.

"Then why hasn't anyone told me this before?" I managed to say.

"You know, it's hard to tell a person when they're doing a bad job. Your supervisors actually have been telling you things, but you just haven't picked up on their right meaning." He returned to his chair.

"When I came to Goodyear, I had an excellent track record in management with good recommendations," I reminded him.

"Well, you might not belong in manufacturing, then," he concluded, opening his drawer to look for something. "And you've been moved already, in a very short time here."

My ears were starting to buzz. "But I've always been told I was being cross-trained, and only the people who were going to be promoted were cross-trained. Isn't that right?"

He closed the drawer, toothpick in hand. "I think you've missed something along the way here, but right now, since you're having a hard time getting ahead, we feel it's in your best interest to work in quality control. It's a temporary assignment and you'll still be a supervisor, but maybe you can earn some credibility there." He started picking his teeth. There was nothing else for me to say.

As the EEOC conducted its investigation, I worked alone on the floor in quality control, checking the quality of the tires against the specs by running tread and testing the weight and width of the tires. Throughout the plant, people avoided me. Some people quit talking to me outright, while others continued to criticize me for causing trouble. I couldn't fault people for wanting to keep their jobs, but those who knew the truth turned a blind eye, and I don't know how they slept at night.

Laura was the only one willing to speak the truth. A petite woman with an engineering degree from Auburn, Laura worked the computers in final finish. When we'd talked about our jobs in the past, she'd complained that the men worried her to death with all their propositions. She agreed to talk to Jack and tell him her story. It was a huge relief to know that at least one person was willing to stand up with me.

About six months later I won the right to sue, which meant I had permission to file a lawsuit within ninety days. Now I had to choose the next step. Proving Dennis did and said the things he did was a "he said, she said" scenario with no guarantees, Jack explained. He asked me what I really wanted to accomplish. That I knew: I wanted my rightful job back. With this in mind, Jack negotiated an agreement with Goodyear to reinstate me as a supervisor.

The day I met with Eddie and George, one of the department foremen, about my reinstatement, I was a nervous wreck. We were in an office about the size of a cubbyhole when they gave me my job back. Relieved that the madness was finally over, I said, "That's all I wanted. I don't mind working hard or even being cussed out. I can put up with a lot, but just don't let anyone harass me like Dennis did. And don't lie about my performance," I added.

Eddie started pacing and cussing and said, "Well, all I know is no goddam government is going to tell me how to run my department." George quieted him quickly, and they hustled me out of there.

Despite the tone of that conference, I faced my future at Goodyear believing that justice had prevailed, just as it always did in those westerns I loved as a child. I truly thought I'd successfully refused to be bullied out of my job. I believed the strength of the recent federal laws and the support of the decent people I worked with would sustain me. After two hellish years, I was ready to let the memory of my experience fade, just as I'd forgotten the pain of my first childbirth in order to endure a second labor. Refusing to let my doubts outweigh my hopes, I was determined to continue my career and to be treated fairly. I really thought things would change at Goodyear, but as with any twisted romance, I should have known better.

CHAPTER 5

Lighthearted, Light-Footed Lilly

||||||||||||||||||||||||||||||||||||||||||||||||||||||||||||||||||||||||||||||||||||||||||||||||||||||

Remember, Ginger Rogers did everything [Fred Astaire]
did . . . backwards and in high heels.

—BOB THAVES, *Frank and Ernest*

I CARRIED THE red velvet cake Edna had baked into the break room. The rule was that whenever you bought something new—a house, a truck, or even a washing machine—you had to bring something homemade to work. I didn't have time to bake anything, so Edna, who stocked her pantry with a gallon of Watkins vanilla for her weekly baking, whipped up hummingbird or Italian cream cakes for me when I needed something. This evening I wasn't celebrating a specific occasion, only that I was glad to be back as a supervisor on the late-night shift in final finish after the past year I'd spent isolated in quality control, waiting for the outcome of the EEOC investigation. The cake was heavy. Edna had doubled her recipe as usual, and still it would be gone in an hour. Setting the Tupperware cake carrier on the break-room table, I snapped the cover off and placed a plastic cake cutter next to the cake. I thought I might even cut myself a piece—hands down, no one made a better cake than Edna, and her cakes were the only ones I ate at work. I didn't trust the guys who, in an attempt to pay back other pranksters, had managed a time or two to slip pubic hairs into the batter behind their wives' backs. At least that's what they said, smirking, after we'd all eaten a piece.

I arranged a stack of colorful paper plates and plastic forks next to the cake, optimistic that I had another opportunity to make things work. I didn't want to hold a grudge like my mother did. So many times she took any perceived slight from friends or family, held on, and wouldn't let it go. All the things that had transpired the previous couple of years had been filed away in what Charles liked to call "File 13," a phrase he'd picked up from the military to refer to the trash. Now I'd officially filed away those events; it was time to move on, time to return to normal.

While I was licking icing off my finger, Pete, who worked the curing presses, walked in. Every week he went around the different departments taking orders for the steaks and baked potatoes he cooked on the scalding-hot twenty-foot-high machine in the middle of the Saturday-night shift. I hadn't seen him in a long time.

"No licking all the icing off the cake." He laughed and dropped some change into the Coke machine to grab a Mountain Dew. "I'm sure glad to see the cake maker's been at it again." All the guys referred to Edna that way.

I started cutting large slices of cake. "Would you like a piece?" I offered.

I handed him the biggest slice. Two tire builders I didn't recognize came into the room.

"Hey, save a piece for me," one said.

I gave him a piece. The other guy shook his head, his mouth set tight, when I offered him one. "Tell me, Lilly, why'd you have to go and sue Goodyear?" he asked.

The mood in the room changed from lighthearted to somber as suddenly as if the power had gone out. The heaviness returned to my chest and reached down to the depths of my bowels. Sometimes it felt as real as someone pushing me against a wall with two hands pressed hard on my sternum. "I didn't," I said, wiping up crumbs from the cake's soft open gash.

"Then how come that's what everybody says?" he continued, crossing his arms, his legs planted in a wide stance.

No matter how many times I'd already answered this question, I'd never be "true blue and gold," as the union guys liked to say in reference to their loyalty to Goodyear. "I didn't sue. I filed a complaint. If I'd sued, I wouldn't be here."

"Whatever you did, it's not right. You're always causing a whole heap of hurt when we got enough on our hands already." He looked at me as though I'd turned into a witch about to cast a spell on him. I wondered if he'd had anything to do with the recent rigging of my locker with firecrackers. "In fact, now I think about it, I don't want to be anywhere near you." He nodded at his buddy, looking at his plate so he'd hurry up and finish.

"Come on. I can't stand being in the same room with her." He turned to leave. Pete and the other guy followed.

I hoped that things wouldn't turn ugly. When it came to practical jokes or retaliation, you never knew what the guys could come up with. You were lucky if you got away with something harmless like the wet pickle I found in my purse once. Sometimes things could take a dark turn, like the time the guy slipped a syringe full of liquid laxative into his daily honey bun, which kept disappearing from his locker. The unsuspecting prankster landed in the hospital for days. It was hard to find anything funny about that, but it didn't stop their nonsense.

I couldn't let them dampen my spirits. I had to make the best of this second chance that I'd fought so hard to gain. The next phase of my career at Goodyear would be different; it had to be better than my rocky start.

I cut myself a piece of Edna's cake and left the rest for the others.

||||||||||||

TIME HAS a strange way of slipping up on you when you work in a manufacturing plant on the night shift; you feel like you've entered the Twilight Zone, and it takes a while, when you walk outside in the morning, to adjust to the rhythm of the regular world. One morning I'd stopped at Hardee's for my biscuit and was reading the *Anniston Star* as I enjoyed my breakfast. My eyes focused on the year at the top of the newspaper: 1986. I looked again. Was it really 1986? Disoriented, as if swimming up from the depths of sleep, I felt like I'd been lost inside a dream. I grappled with the date the way you do sometimes with a simple word you know how to spell but that one day, all of a sudden, looks wrong. Where had the last several years gone? When was I going to do something else in life besides work?

Then I noticed an advertisement for ballroom dance lessons at the bottom of the page, four for $10, at a small dance studio in Anniston. I closed my eyes and saw the page that as a little girl I'd torn from *Life* magazine and posted above my bed—a picture of Ginger Rogers, in a glamorous pink gown, waltzing with Fred Astaire. Ever since cheerleading had given me a taste of performing, I'd fantasized about learning how to dance. The reality was, I'd never done more than square-dance in high school gym class. The thought of dancing lessons sparked a sense of excitement I hadn't felt in a long time. I blew on my coffee, waiting for it to cool. I couldn't keep letting time slip away from me. I saved the page to show Charles. I wanted him to join me.

"I don't have time for that nonsense" was his immediate response.

I pestered him, but he held firm: "I don't know how to dance."

"Neither do I. That's the whole point."

"Men don't take ballroom dancing."

"Sure they do. It takes two people, remember?"

We went back and forth like this a few times because I truly wanted Charles as my partner in my new adventure, but I didn't want to fight with him about it if he didn't approve.

I finally told him, "Fine. If you change your mind, you know where to find me," and signed up by myself.

I immediately fell in love with dancing. A couple of days a week, before my shift, Hector, a slim, flamboyant Texan with a head of slicked-back black hair who had more energy than anyone I'd ever met, taught me how to dance. I lived for my lessons despite Charles's constant questions about Hector and the other people taking lessons. I'd tell Charles there was nothing to worry about. He tried his best to dislike Hector, but Hector's charm disarmed even Charles.

During dance lessons, I glided across the floor with Hector learning the tango, while Sabrina, Hector's wife, sat on a bench watching us. "Smile, Lilly, smile," Sabrina repeated as she tapped her foot to the beat of the music. We spun across the shellacked floor, and I caught my somber expression in the mirror. I wanted to smile, but I couldn't. For the first few months of dancing, I'd stand in front of my bathroom mirror, feeling ridiculous, practicing how to smile. Until I met Hector, whenever I smiled, I unconsciously covered my mouth with my hand, ashamed of the unfamiliar feeling of joy.

After a while, when it came to dancing, I didn't need Sabrina's encouragement. I dreamed of becoming an accomplished dancer, of challenging myself and experiencing something new. I started competing on the weekends at showcases in Atlanta held at places like the Holiday Inn, places large enough to accommodate a ballroom and the hundreds of people who expected to be entertained. Before I participated in my first showcase, I asked Hector what we should wear, thinking jeans might be okay. "Honey, wear the best you've got. Better than even your Sunday best." Polyester pant suits aside, that meant the dress I wore to Vickie's wedding.

I'd shopped for that dress at my favorite family-owned discount store. I thought I'd found a fabulous dress until the woman helping me asked, "Now, how many daughters do you have?" Just one, I told her. "Well, then, dear, don't you think you better go to the department store and find a special dress for yourself?" Somewhat embarrassed but grateful for her advice, I went to the regular department store and chose a burgundy dress etched with cranberry-colored satin. The dress, now carefully stored in my closet, would be perfect for the showcase.

The moment the music started, that first showcase transformed me from the drab, capable manager that had become my chosen identity into someone "footloose and fancy-free." I couldn't quit smiling. I felt a joyous release I'd never known, inspiring my performance and encouraging the audience's enthusiasm for Hector and me. We continued to compete in showcases, and once I got so carried away that I flung my arm in a dramatic sweep, hitting Hector in the face and almost knocking him to the floor. We still placed first that day.

AROUND THE time I started taking dance lessons, Eddie became one of my department foremen in final finish; it seemed the air around us was charged with static electricity when we interacted. He made me jittery, the vein under my left eye twitching slightly when we talked. Rumors of layoffs were circulating throughout the plant as well, and even of management positions possibly being cut, a first for the Gadsden operation. The uncontrollable fluctuations in the economy loomed like some infectious disease gone awry. Maybe someone would find a cure before it caught up with me and my family. Now that Vickie had found her footing in the world and Phillip, who'd also graduated from Jacksonville State University, was starting his real estate career, they, too, were susceptible to the unpredictable economic highs and lows.

Unfortunately, the talk was true, and I was let go with a good number of other managers. The week I was laid off from Goodyear I walked into the dance studio greeted by a bouquet of balloons, one saying YOU WILL BE SUCCESSFUL. I wasn't so sure.

In the past, layoffs had often been temporary, and most workers were eventually called back. In light of the increasing inflation, Goodyear organized a job-skills session at the company clubhouse, since such a large layoff was predicted. Sitting across the cardboard table from a woman dressed in a blue suit, I filled out a questionnaire about myself.

While she read it, I stared through the large bay of windows overlooking the golf course where Eddie and Jeff often played on the weekends, unsure how I was going to manage to find another job and unclear if I wanted to stay in manufacturing.

She asked me how my job at Goodyear was.

"Great," I said.

"How well do you run your department?"

"Great."

"Okay, can you tell me more about yourself and your family?"

"My family's great."

"I see," she said, fiddling with the floppy tie around her neck, some strange version of a man's necktie I supposed.

"How long has it been since your last job interview?"

"Pretty long," I said trying to calculate the years.

"I see. Well, I think the place we need to start is how to answer a question when you're being interviewed. The first thing is you need to say something else besides 'great.' The interviewer can't get a sense of who you are with just a one-word response."

I'd survived the last ten years by building a wall around my emotions and creating a mask to hide how I really felt. I hadn't always been this way, so mistrustful and closed-off. Now I needed to open up for a prospective employer?

"Great," I said.

||||||||||||

BEING LAID off meant I was forced to slow down, and once I did, I slept more than I had in years. I'd had no idea how tired I really was from the long hours and all of the overtime. I'd also had no idea what disarray the house was in. Rumbling around in the back of my mind all those years I'd been working were the teetering piles of photo albums and scrapbooks I'd planned to start filling. I had bags of special stickers and colored paper. They sat next to the stacks of accumulated family photos and the children's elementary school artwork and schoolwork. The clutter drove Charles crazy, but I wouldn't let him throw anything away. He went behind me anyway, organizing the disorder. Sometimes he demanded that I get rid of the outdated catalogs and magazines. I'd follow behind him, snatching a few magazines from him.

"There are some good recipes in that magazine. You can't throw that one out."

"You can't keep everything." He'd grab the magazines back.

"What about your coin collection?" I'd fuss.

"That's different. It's worth something."

"And you could fill the walls of every Cracker Barrel in America with all those rusty tools in your workshop."

"That's not the same either. Anyway, they're in my toolshed. You don't have to look at them."

"I have to look at all the stuff you bring home and put in the garage. It doesn't make sense. You get rid of my stuff just so you can have more room to bring home someone else's trash."

One time when Charles was still working at Railway Express Agency he actually brought home someone else's wedding dress, which had been damaged in shipping. I often teased him about that, but he was proud of the fact. He'd point out that Vickie had played dress-up in it until she'd worn it out.

Instead of facing the layers of emotional debris collecting around my heart or the detritus scattered throughout my house, I threw myself into my job search. I updated my résumé and bought a copy of *What Color Is Your Parachute?* I also bought the book *Color Me Beautiful*, about how to dress according to whether you're a fall, winter, summer, or spring—I was a spring. Reading in my job-hunting book that, for every $10,000 you earned, it took a month to find a job with a comparable salary kicked me into high gear, armed with the right color palette for my wardrobe, of course.

With my background in accounting, I gravitated to an opening for an Allstate agent to run the Jacksonville office. The Goodyear headhunter also informed me of another promising position for a manager at the Tyson chicken plant, so I called someone who'd worked at Goodyear with me but had also previously worked at both a chicken plant and an insurance agency. When I asked him about being an agent, he said that before he'd even deposited a commission check, he'd start worrying about how he was going to make another sale, to the point that he couldn't sleep most nights. When you're in sales, he explained, "You eat what you kill." If I could help it, I didn't want a job that created chronic worry about my income reliability and that sounded as unpredictable as walking barefoot on a sidewalk scattered with spiky brown gumballs from a sweet-gum tree.

With my resources limited, I knew I needed a steady paycheck. As part of the application process for Tyson, I'd even taken an industrial psychology test to see if I was suited for working as a manager in a poultry-processing plant. According to my profile, I was. I had also found out that the training for the Tyson job started several weeks earlier than Allstate's training, and it seemed clear what I needed to do.

LIKE AT Goodyear, at Tyson I had to learn every job on the production line. The plant, which produced all of the chicken for every

McDonald's east of the Mississippi, also packaged and shipped every part, except the feathers and the cackle, all over the world. The feet were a delicacy in China; the guts went into the process of making dog food; the flap over their bottom was supposedly used as a Japanese hors d'oeuvre; and the carcass was boiled for the tiny pieces of meat you find in your chicken noodle soup. My only problem was that the plant was located two hours south of Jacksonville in the small town of Ashland.

At first I made the long commute on the narrow, two-lane highway—until I skidded off the slick road in the fog. Shaken, I rented a small apartment in Ashland, a town with only one restaurant, the Dairy Queen. As someone remarked when I first moved there, "There are two things to do here: go fishing or watch the leaves fall."

I'd drive down Monday morning, the backseat full of food Edna had fixed. Charles usually came down one night a week, and I'd drive home on the weekends. I was so tired at night during the week that it didn't matter that I was alone because I went straight to bed after warming up leftovers and soaking in a long, hot bath.

Learning every job on the line meant learning how to hang chickens. In the hanging room, always darkened to trick the chickens into settling down for roosting, I stood, nauseous, next to an overcrowded bin of live chickens. I had to grab three at a time, flip them upside down, and hook their sharp feet onto the chains attached to a conveyor belt at about eye level. The stunned chickens often fought me, twisting and turning and agitating the rest of the group and scratching the devil out of my arms.

Another day, when I worked the killing room for the first time, I stood in my place in line on the far side of the sharp steel killing wheel. The entire time, my stomach was upset. To keep from being splattered in blood, I had my hair pulled tight in a hairnet under the plastic hat, and I sweated underneath the thick plastic raincoat I had to wear, drops of perspiration pooling under the folds of my breasts. Hundreds of chickens hanging upside down, a cease-less stream, moved toward me at an unnerving speed, their throats level with the rotating blade.

If the machine missed slitting a chicken's throat, I gave the chicken hanging upside down a hard rake across its naked throat with my butcher knife. The very first time I did this, I looked across the room through the large plate-glass window. My eyes met those of the group of men who, having hedged their bets against me, had lined up outside the window to watch. Women comprised most of the workforce there, six hundred to a shift, but a woman in management was still an anomaly.

Covered in blood that clung like blobs of red jelly to my hat and raincoat, I put myself on automatic to finish the business the kill-ing wheel missed. The men eventually bored of their sport and left. At the end of the shift, I stopped outside the window where the men had stood. I looked at the bloody floor where I'd been stand-ing. I doubted the men here had any tricks worse than the men at Goodyear and thought to myself that they hadn't bargained on the fact that I'd grown up on a farm and seen worse.

While at Tyson, I was in the studio dancing even more often. I competed in my first regional competition, in New Orleans, in early December, only several months after the layoff. During my first dance, as I sashayed across the floor, I got a thrill from the multilayered skirt that I would peel off after that dance to reveal a new outfit underneath. At the end of the judging, when the panel-ists announced that Hector and I had won first place, I held the heavy trophy I'd been awarded, an excitement and satisfaction I'd never felt before coursing through me.

IF I thought I had discovered joy through dancing, the excitement I felt when I saw Will, my first of three grandsons, born in March 1987, was unparalleled. That promising spring day was dampened only by the fact that he was born a month premature. Holding his sweet little body for the first time and touching those tiny fingers tickling my hand, I made a promise to myself that I'd do a better job being present for my grandchildren than I had with my own children, and I would also do everything I could to help Vickie.

By the time Will was almost two, no matter what the doctors tried, they couldn't knock out an infection that had cropped up in his lungs. They predicted he'd lose one of his lungs. Somehow Will had swallowed a peanut the wrong way and it had lodged itself in the soft membrane of his lungs, causing a bacterial infection. Vickie discovered it when he fell off the deck and broke his collarbone; the X-ray had shown a gooey mass as thick as peanut butter oozing across his lungs.

For weeks at the hospital, Vickie and her husband, Bill, never left Will's side, supported by their company's generous attitude toward family illness. Almost every hour, a nurse took Will's blood, his arms as torn up as if a desperate chicken had raked its claws across them. It got so that the minute Will saw a white coat walking through the door, he'd start screaming, and we'd have to restrain him. The doctor sent each blood sample to the Centers for Disease Control in Atlanta so they could recommend which antibiotic to try next.

To our relief, Will finally beat the infection. To my disappointment, I did not live up to the promise I'd made when he was born. My work schedule wouldn't let me. I'd started working at Goodyear again, and I was willing to let down my family because I was more concerned with satisfying Goodyear.

AFTER TRAINING at Tyson for nine months, the day I was supposed to start as a manager there, Goodyear called. They wanted me back. The economy was picking up, and with increased production they were in hiring mode. The pay was twice what I was making at Tyson; and because I hadn't been laid off longer than fifteen months, I was able to keep my seniority, accumulated sick and personal days, and benefits.

I couldn't say no to the better pay, and I rationalized that I had no other choice but to go back to earn more than double what I made at Tyson. In hindsight, I see that it's never that simple. You always have choices. I returned, driven to be recognized for my hard work and commitment, and I had given Goodyear the power to define me and my self-worth. But even more, Goodyear felt like home, and like the child of an alcoholic who marries an alcoholic, I gravitated to what felt familiar, an environment defined by fear and conflict, much like other parts of my life had been.

I knew what I was returning to, but my ability to tolerate what most people would find intolerable was pretty high, and I believed, a victim of my own highly efficient coping skills, that I could handle anything thrown my way. I minimized the negative experiences, gave significant play in my mind to any gesture or word of kindness, and normalized much of the Goodyear politics and policies. Often, however, I'd feel strangely detached from my reality, as if I were an outsider watching myself. My body, always poised in a heightened state of defense, finally started falling apart. Only then did I start to see the truth of the situation. My stubbornness kept me from realizing that you don't have to live a robotic, white-knuckle existence; you don't just have to survive. You can live a life full of grace.

How different my path would have been had I taken the All-state job—especially when they were more than willing to hire me without an MBA, since I'd scored so well on their test. To this day the woman who started running the Jacksonville office at that time still works there. She couldn't have had that many sleepless nights worrying about where her next commission check was coming from.

||||||||||||

BACK AT Goodyear, I was assigned to the glass house in the mill room, where the banburies mix rubber. I worked with one other person and was in charge of overseeing the setup operation for the banburies. Around four hundred pounds of rubber, carbon, sulfur, and a secret mix of additives are dumped into each banbury mixer, which creates a thick, black ooze. Steel rollers squeeze the ooze to continue the mixing process and eliminate any trapped air within the rubber—a process that sounds like fireworks going off. The rubber is then folded back and forth in a zigzag manner. Where I was working, there were guys on the floor, but I had no support staff and dealt mainly with the ongoing and offgoing shifts of truckers.

The union guys liked to say that working in the mill room would turn me into an old lady overnight. There were the endless skin problems, and every day was a bad-hair day. At the end of my shift I looked like I had greased my body with cooking oil and sprinkled myself with black baby powder. I wore a military cap with earflaps, but my blond hair turned a light shade of green anyway. No matter what creams I used, my neck stayed blistered. One guy's throat would get so irritated by the rubber poisoning that the inside looked like raw hamburger. Another guy couldn't get rid of the runny sores covering his arms, and someone else had the poisoning so badly that the chemicals turned the whites of his eyes gray. The doctor who gave me cortisone shots on a regular basis for my burned skin told me, "I don't know what that job pays you, but it's not worth this."

Of course, none of us went to the company hospital or requested being moved, because we feared losing our jobs. I took to wearing a turtleneck with my gray coveralls to cover my blistered skin. To keep the smell from suffocating me, I sprayed myself with much too much Eternity perfume before I started my shift, focusing a stream on the edge of my turtleneck so I could bury my nose in it every once in a while and inhale deeply.

I ENDURED the challenges at work by looking forward to the thrill I experienced dancing and competing in one showcase or competition after another. I spent as much time planning what to wear as I did practicing my moves. At each showcase, I scouted the costumes the other women wore. Sabrina would design elaborate costumes for me, and she and I would shop for all types of material—sequined, satin, chiffon, fringed—to bring to a seamstress in Hoke's Bluff who sewed them.

Charles eventually realized the fun he was missing and joined me at the dance studio. It struck me that taking lessons and stepping out of his role as a deacon and a sergeant took everything Charles could muster. One rainy afternoon right when he was supposed to start his first lesson, I was running late for my own lesson, and I came across him sitting alone in his car in the parking lot. He must have forgotten his umbrella. I knocked on his window. He rolled it down.

"You can share my umbrella."

He shook his head. "I'm not going in yet."

I pointed at my watch. "What in the world are you doing, then?"

"Finding my courage," he said.

To learn the moves, Charles took notes in a brown spiral notebook so he could study them later. He soon discovered what I'd always known: He had a great sense of rhythm. At home, for entertainment, we'd play Frank Sinatra on the stereo or pop a cassette tape into the boom box and fox-trot across the living room floor. Typical Charles: He started dragging home mirrors people discarded in the alley near our house, planning one day to line the garage with them so we would have our own private dance studio.

||||||||||||

WHILE I worked in the mill room, my father was dying. When he'd finally decided to retire almost ten years earlier, I'd just started at Goodyear. He'd wanted to retire earlier than he did, but Edna wouldn't let him. She wouldn't even let my father rest on the weekend—she'd have him mowing the widowed women's grass while she baked her cakes to take to them after he finished. It always amazed me when she'd sit in her rocker on the porch during her treatment for mouth cancer and talk about everything she needed to do. The minute she overcame the cancer, she got right back to her long list of chores.

The day my father went to the doctor shortly after his retirement, I drove with him. On the way to his car when the appointment was over, he didn't say a word.

I got into the passenger seat, and he started the engine. I couldn't stand it anymore. "What did the doctor say?"

He took the pack of Camels from his shirt pocket. I expected him to light his cigarette.

He placed the pack that I'd never seen him without since I was a child on the seat between us. "I have emphysema." He didn't say another word on the drive to his house. My mind swirled back to the times he drove me, snuggled against him, into Piedmont on Christmas Eve to pick out a present before the stores closed. Sometimes on the way home, he let me hold one side of the steering wheel. I was never afraid as long as he was there to lean on.

He left the cigarettes on the seat when he got out of the car. I waited a minute to go in and talk to Edna, watching a flock of cedar waxwings, drunk on the red berries, dive in and out of a stand of hollies in the neighbor's yard. I crushed the pack in my fist, the cellophane crinkling, and followed my father into the house.

He'd been smoking a pack a day since he was fifteen. In his remaining years, he never touched another cigarette.

||||||||||||

EDNA MIGHT have forced my father to work longer than necessary, but she also prolonged his life by feeding and caring for him. His last two years, attached to an oxygen tank, he could barely breathe, much less walk. I had to force myself to visit him because it undid me so to see him sick.

The day he died I'd gone to check on him and found him sitting in his favorite easy chair. He motioned for me to sit down on the sofa; it looked as if the skin on his arms was made of parchment, about to peel away as easily as the outside of an onion. His coloring was ashen, his breathing labored. A tray table with some untouched tomato soup and crackers sat next to him. On the nearby card table, he'd laid out his game of solitaire. Seeing the unfinished card game, I remembered how he used to play Rook with Louise and me; he was the only adult we knew who took time to play with us.

I called the doctor. He said I could call an ambulance or keep my father at home; he'd just been in the hospital over a week. I didn't want him to die at home, leaving the memory of his death lingering with Edna as her only company. I called an ambulance and jumped into his unwieldy brand-new 1988 Oldsmobile—what I liked to call his "two-bedroom car." I followed as fast as I could, my hands slipping on the steering wheel from the baby oil Edna rubbed on his arms to soothe his slack skin.

As fast as I drove, I didn't make it in time. He died as they transferred him from the gurney to the hospital bed. I was devastated that I didn't have a chance to let him know one last time that I loved him.

I couldn't cry at my father's funeral. I had to stay strong for my mother as we tended to the expected and unexpected matters of death. I spent countless hours dealing with the fact that he'd been buried on the wrong side of my parents' two plots. He was buried on the left, not the right. As is the custom standing at the marriage altar, the man is on the right and the woman on the left. To make matters worse, the headstone was placed on the empty grave where he should have been—and the company that made it had gone bankrupt, ruining any chance we had of correcting the problem.

For six months after my father died, I drove by the cemetery every morning after work. I'd park the car on the edge of the grass. Sometimes I'd sit by his grave, which faced east, aligning my father with the face of God on Judgment Day. The area where he was buried was still bare of grass, but the morning air was free of traffic fumes. I thought about how mild-mannered he was. I'd always been a picky eater as a child, and it sent one of my uncles over the top when I left food on my plate. He'd cuss me at table for not eating, saying, "You're just as finicky as your crazy father." I didn't know what he was talking about. Now I understood that it was the simple fact that my father was so unfamiliar to men like Papa and my uncles—he didn't talk ugly about women, and he never used the *n*-word like they did.

To keep my grief at bay, I parked myself on the sofa, ate too many potato chips, and spent hours watching QVC, mesmerized by each colorful purse or miraculous beauty product. I loved watching the live makeovers and listening to the callers; their voices eased my sense of loneliness, if only for a moment. Once something I ordered appeared on my doorstep, I sent it back or left it unopened on a stack in Vickie's old room. It was the process of falling in love with the item, pursuing it through my purchase, and anticipating its arrival that gave me a sense of fulfillment, not the actual item. By the time that special piece that was supposed to make me feel good again arrived, I'd have lost interest. I'd have found something else I wanted.

At this time, I became debilitated by mysterious aches and

pains, even getting tested for lupus. Choked by my sadness, I didn't know how to navigate through my grief or help my mother deal with hers. All I could do with any clarity was drive her—Edna didn't drive unless it was a tractor—to the three grocery stores she liked. We certainly didn't talk about our loss—then or ever.

The day I helped Edna sort through my father's clothes broke me. Gathering his old work shirts, still tainted with the licorice smell of diesel fuel, made me miss him more than I ever had. I sat on my parents' bed, a stack of his shirts in my lap, and buried my head in them, crying. Sitting on the same chenille bedspread my parents had used for as long as I could remember, my eyes swollen, my nose red, and gulping for air, I learned that the body sometimes tells us things the mind is afraid to face. Once I cried for the first time, I cried for weeks afterward, the phantom pains dissipating with my tears.

I LASTED a year in the glass house in the mill room. The male managers supervising the floor complained they'd been treated unfairly because I hadn't worked on the floor like everyone else who went to the glass house, so I was transferred to the tube plant, an older part of the operation. Before I left, some of the union guys pooled their money and bought me a fourteen-karat-gold bracelet. I wore that bracelet every day, grateful for their kindness and consideration, until I somehow lost it.

In no time I was laid off for a week, able to return only as a worker, not as a supervisor, to run tire trials. I later experienced another layoff, this one for ten weeks, and was called back to fill in for a supervisor who'd had a lung removed. I was beginning to think I was in a pinball machine being played by a lousy player, ricocheting without any rhyme or reason.

In 1990, I was fifty-two years old and I'd been married thirty-five years, more than half my life. I had been at Goodyear ten years, not including the time I worked at Tyson. That year, I was finally offered a permanent position replacing a supervisor in final finish on the second shift, from 3:00 P.M. to 11:00 P.M. Once again, unemployment and inflation were on the rise, and the conflict in the Middle East was heating up. Workers were afraid, and the mood at the plant was tense. A night after I disciplined a worker for not meeting production, some guys in a Trans Am with tinted windows followed me out of the plant. On the desolate two-lane highway, they rode my bumper, flashing their lights, and pulled up beside me.

I pressed the pedal of my six-cylinder Cutlass to the floorboard. Without any pickup, I went as fast as I could until I saw a house and pulled in to the driveway. The Trans Am eased in behind me, its lights shining in my rearview mirror before being switched off. I pressed the heel of my hand on the horn until they backed out. On the road again, I came across another section without any houses. The Trans Am's headlights appeared from nowhere, shining in my mirror. If I'd been a rabbit, my heart would have exploded. I promised myself that if I survived, I'd buy a gun. A knife in my pocket was no longer enough.

They followed me all the way to my driveway. The next day I went to Lewis Carroll Jeweler's, the only place in Anniston where you could leave your film to be developed, buy diamonds, and purchase a gun. I bought a gun.

I NEVER knew when someone would turn out to be an enemy or a friend. I first met Mitch, a training manager, during the EEOC investigation in 1982. One day while I was working alone in quality control, he approached me to say, "I don't know how you work alone like this." Throughout the years, Mitch did his best to support me, pushing the other managers to make me the female representative for management at the union hall even though they always chose one of the secretaries. It was men with attitudes like Mitch's who helped me stay.

A couple of years later, in 1992, I was told to go see one of the plant managers. I thought I was getting laid off again. Instead, the plant manager, Sid, a pleasant, quiet man I admired for his good nature and fairness, informed me that I'd been chosen as one of four managers to start the radial light-truck division, where SUV and passenger tires would be made. I figured that Mitch had nominated me.

In the new division we ran a skeleton crew on brand-new machinery, a nice change from so much of the old machinery that looked like it was held together with duct tape. Not long after the announcement about my promotion was made, the top brass from Akron, Ohio, came to Gadsden to meet with the chosen four in the company clubhouse, where upper management entertained the big dogs from other plants and held exclusive receptions in the small cafeteria. That day my new supervisor insisted that I go home.

"If they go to the meeting, shouldn't I?" I asked, referring to the three other managers, all male.

"No, you need to go on home," I was advised.

I knew not to push and went home, but I wrestled with why I couldn't go. I tried not to let it bother me too much, and I didn't dare protest. I just chalked it up to the way things were done. I was getting used to the idea that no matter what good things happened for me at Goodyear, I was never going to be accepted into the boys' club, and I couldn't let my disappointment depress me when I'd received the honor of being chosen to run the newest division of the plant, the one that represented the latest in tire technology.

I experienced another glorious moment when Hector and I competed at the National Ballroom Championship in Miami and won. Right before I went onto the floor, I called home and Phillip happened to answer the phone. He was checking on Oscar, our fourteen-year-old miniature dachshund, whom Phillip had bought with his own money as a young boy. Sometimes I thought Phillip loved Oscar more than he did the rest of us. Now Phillip sounded horrible. Oscar had died.

On the dance floor, for a moment before the music started, I wondered if I could shake my sadness over the unexpected news. But once I heard the upbeat rhythm of the music, I felt soothed. As I danced, I saw reflected all around me in the mirrors a different Lilly from the one who'd started her lessons so long ago. I saw a woman swirling in her black-and-white chiffon skirt, one whose swept-up hair was no longer a bleached-out blond but dyed a golden yellow, who looked like she owned the world. This woman relished the way her body moved. I felt that same sense of expansiveness I had as a child swimming in Nancy's Creek, flipping under the water, my body spinning, exploding with a powerful rush to float in peace until I crashed to the surface for air.

We placed first in all three categories: the tango, the waltz, and the East Coast swing.

IN THE radial division I worked with one supervisor I admired. He set an example I wanted to emulate, beginning our meetings by asking us to state three positive things about our previous shift. No matter what department I was in, though, the first thing I did when I went to my car was look around to make sure everything was okay—plenty of times managers had found their tires slashed. I'd never experienced vandalism to my car until I had to discipline several workers in a short period of time. The guy I wrote up who talked too much told me, "Lilly, I hate this job," and eventually quit. When I caught another guy sleeping on the job and wrote him up, he looked at me, exasperated, and asked, "Damn, Lilly, management doesn't want you around, so why are you hassling me?" He received a three-day suspension and threatened to make me pay for it. I bought a gas cap that locked. I didn't want sugar poured into my tank.

That wasn't enough. Soon a screw as big as a thumb was stuck into the side of my tire. Shortly afterward, when I walked to my car at the end of my shift, it was covered in about a gallon of tobacco juice. Once I had that cleaned off, my windshield was cut out with a glass cutter, leaving one side intact to ensure that when I drove over a bump, it would collapse on me.

I didn't let these tactics keep me from disciplining someone if necessary, but I entered a whole new territory the day I drove to Birmingham after work to a doctor's appointment to check on my chronic stomach ulcers. My car was driving funny on the way there. After my appointment, I couldn't get it started. A mechanic towed the car to the shop, inspected it, and asked me, "Have you made somebody mad?"

"Well, that's hard to say."

"In all my thirty-two years I've never seen anything like this."

"What's that?"

"Someone's tampered with your gear cable. Without it, you have no power steering or brakes. If you'd driven on the highway much longer, you could have been killed."

I told my boss, the business center manager, Eric, a slender, neat man who'd once played college football, but he merely commented, "You're getting paranoid."

But the vandalism didn't stop. My fenders were slashed and my car keyed. I went to Eddie, Eric's boss and next in seniority in upper management in my area. He said he'd look into it. I refused to leave his office until he promised that I could park my car next to the security guard's office at the gate. Only then did the vandalism stop.

AT THE end of this stressful year, in December 1995, Eric, who sometimes confided in me about how hard it was for his wife, a pharmaceutical rep, to work in an office full of men, handed me a piece of paper while we were down on the floor working. "This is going to be a great Christmas," he said with a smile. Written on the note was the biggest pay raise I'd ever received: I'd earned the Top Performance Award, an award I'd had no idea existed.

In the sixteen years I'd been at Goodyear, I'd received only a few raises after the change from cost-of-living increases to merit-based raises in the early eighties—one year earning all of $61 more per month. The highest raises I'd received throughout my career were those I received before I complained to the EEOC in 1982.

I thanked Eric and placed the torn paper in my pocket. A few months earlier I'd asked him how my pay ranked among my peers. Eric drew a circle representing minimum to maximum pay and put a line through the middle of it. "You're right below that middle line," he said. The reason I was so near the middle rather than lower was my attitude and enthusiasm. My lack of tire knowledge compared with that of the builders who'd been pro-moted into management held me back, but if I continued the way I was going, he told me, that would soon change. I would find out much later that I wasn't even being paid the minimum salary for the area managers.

I wasn't surprised I hadn't known about the Top Performance Award. Everything at Goodyear was top secret. Politicians and school groups touring the plant weren't allowed in the tire room, as if some student or schoolteacher might actually figure out how the tire machines operated and tell another company. So it was nothing unusual in offices with glass walls for a manager to slide someone a piece of paper with the amount written on it whenever anybody got a raise.

I was thrilled to receive the Top Performance Award but per-plexed that not a word was printed in the company newsletter about this honor. That was okay with me—I wanted to keep a low profile. The last thing I needed to do was provoke envy among my cowork-ers during tough economic times.

The one time I had made the company newsletter was in a story entitled "Lighthearted, Lightfooted Lilly," highlighting my winning competitions in ballroom dancing. I became something of a star in many people's eyes, and remained so for as long as I worked at Goodyear. Some folks at Goodyear even started taking a dance lesson or two themselves. For many, my greatest performance at Goodyear had nothing to do with tires.

CHAPTER 6

Up to My Knees in Alligators

|||||||||||||||||||||||||||||||||||||||||||||||||||||||||||||||||||||||||||||||||||||||||||||||||||||||||||||||||||||||||||||||||

A woman is like a tea bag—you can't tell how strong she is until you put her in hot water.

—ELEANOR ROOSEVELT

AFTER FOUR years as a supervisor in the radial light-truck division, in early spring of 1996, I was moved to the section of the tire room in the radial plant where the automatic radial full-stage (ARF) machines build tires. I continued to supervise the building of the smaller radial passenger tires on the older, more challenging machinery. The tire builders, according to the specifications logged into each machine's computer, assembled the components—the liner, ply, bead, chafer, belt, and, finally, tread—onto a steel drum. Then an elevator carried the uncured, or "green," tires on an overhead conveyor belt winding along the walls under the ceiling to the curing presses, where they were cured before they moved on to final finish.

As part of my job, I had to ensure that the department maintained sufficient inventory, that the correct specifications were set on the machines, that the tire builders met their production quota, and that the men always wore their safety gear. While I was supervising the tire builders, Jeff, who had tried to get me to go to the Ramada Inn with him so long ago, started auditing my area. One day he sauntered in and stood behind one of the tire builders, watching him work. Across the room alert signs flashed. Next to those signs hung the erasable board that listed the daily tally of injuries throughout the plant. Today: five reported injuries.

The last time Jeff had visited my department he'd neglected to fill out his safety audit as he usually did, marking the sheet while he was there. Instead, he sat at the break table shooting the breeze with a couple of guys, talking about his golf game and what kind of bait he'd used when he went fishing over the weekend. At our next managers' meeting in what we called the war room, I was shocked when he handed me my audit; he'd marked that the men in my department weren't dressed in their safety gear. I scanned the report; I was the only area manager on the summary report who'd been evaluated poorly.

Now I watched Jeff survey my builder, who, like all the other guys, was dressed in his giant goggles resembling insect eyes and the standard steel-toed boots. The loud machinery and industrial fans were deafening, so the guys also wore earplugs. The builder had no idea that Jeff stood behind him observing him and the entire department for his safety audit. The weekly audits were based on eight areas: safety, quality, production, waste, attendance, housekeeping, team meetings, and cost containment. This time I was right there with Jeff looking at my builder dressed in all of his safety gear. He couldn't pull that stunt on me again.

I walked past Jeff, the hot wind from one of the gigantic fans knocking against me, and nodded a quick hello. Over the years, despite his claims that he had a relative high up the food chain, he hadn't made it to top-level management as I know he'd expected to. In fact, he'd been demoted, his esteem throughout the plant dwindling over time, so that now he didn't carry the same clout he once did. Several times I'd seen the bigger guys, a few ex–Alabama football players, wrestle him down for entertainment as they drank beer in the parking lot after work.

Watching Jeff finally leave, I took a deep breath, trying to let go of my anxiety as I wondered what he'd written on the report this time.

JEFF CONTINUED to rate me poorly on my audits, and each week reading the audit summaries, I tried to let my anger move through me. When he downgraded me in the other areas as well as safety, maintaining that the tire-building machines weren't always running at full capacity, I tried to keep my composure. I tried to stand tall and throw back my shoulders just as I'd learned to do dancing. Once I'd overheard a woman talking at a dance showcase. We were in the bathroom primping. She was standing next to her friend and applying her red lipstick. She leaned toward her reflection, quiet for a minute as she concentrated on keeping the lipstick within the lines of her full lips. Satisfied, she straightened herself up, pointed the lipstick case at herself in the mirror. "You can win a competition with a smile, but it's how you hold yourself that counts," she said, and snapped that gold lipstick case shut. She dabbed her lips with Kleenex. "You have to look like you own the place. You have to hold your shoulders as if you have a shoe box between them. You might make a mistake with your feet, but the judges can't watch your steps the whole time. They're more impressed by how you handle yourself."

There wasn't much I could do to prove that Jeff was marking the audit sheet incorrectly. The only thing I could do was handle myself with grace.

As if things couldn't get worse, Eddie, who'd had his mind set against me since I had filed the sexual-harassment complaint against Goodyear years before, became one of my supervisors again, replacing Eric, who'd given me two annual raises and recognized my

work with the Top Performance Award only several months before. Managers were usually moved for one of three reasons: to replace someone who'd been promoted, to get more production from
a crew than the previous manager had, or as punishment. Eddie
was moved to my area as the business center manager because Eric
had been moved. I had to wonder what that would mean for me.

I'd worked for Eddie after the incident with the EEOC once
before, in final finish. He'd been my department foreman in 1986
for a short time before he informed me about my layoff, after which
I went to Tyson, so I was thrilled when he'd taken the time to write
me a congratulatory note about being chosen as one of four to start
up the radial light-truck division in 1992. His words—"You have
worked hard and improved a lot the past few years and you deserve
the opportunity"—had stayed with me. With his short, simple
note, I'd achieved recognition from someone who'd viewed me as
a troublemaker before. It was an important gesture, like the gold
bracelet the union guys had given me.

I reminded myself of these things when I became discouraged.
From his note, it sounded like Eddie's attitude had softened, but I
was worried; I'd recently heard from another supervisor that Eddie
had been told by the plant manager, who'd returned from Akron
to turn around the Gadsden plant, to get rid of the drunk and the
damn woman in his new department. I had been in a managers'
meeting with that plant manager, known for his hard, unforgiving ways, when he informed the group that Goodyear didn't need
women at the plant because they only created trouble. As his words
sank in at that meeting, I suspected I was right back where I'd
started so long ago.

I COULDN'T worry too much about Eddie and Jeff. My most immediate concern was my stomach, which had been acting up for a
long time but had suddenly gotten worse. My diet wasn't so great.
I went from eating too little to eating everything in sight. For a

couple of months when I went to the restroom, I waited a minute before I turned to flush, disheartened to see the red water in the toilet. I ignored the blood until, doubled over in pain one day, I couldn't deny the obvious anymore.

My physical problem ultimately resulted in colon surgery. The doctor said my problem was stress-related—my rectal muscles had tightened to the point that they ripped when food tried to pass through my body.

The charming joke at the plant was that I was having the two-way radio removed from my rear end. All the supervisors carried the radios, but the guys spent so much time swearing across the airwaves that I usually kept mine turned off. It drove them nuts when I wouldn't answer.

In the hospital room, lying in bed recovering, I said a prayer to myself and thanked God for letting me live. I was relieved that the surgery was over—I imagined the doctor stitching me back together like he was sewing a piece quilt—and the doctor didn't discover any cancer. I had been worried that I had colon cancer, which had killed my grandmother Lillie.

Like Edna might do, in a melodramatic daydream before my surgery, I tried to envision my funeral. Who would come? What would they say? I'm not sure what my family could say since I'd missed out on so many important moments in their lives, moments I couldn't relive. I still felt bad about not having helped Vickie with her wedding, the way a bride's mother should, and that had been ages ago. She and Bill had had a simple but beautiful ceremony on the first day of fall. I was working so much overtime that I couldn't be as involved with their wedding plans as I wanted to be. They handled everything, while Edna sewed the bridesmaids' dresses.

I'd barely shown up.

Just as I had not flown to Texas to see Charles receive his ranking as sergeant or been able to attend his college graduation ceremony.

And I hadn't spent enough time with my father before he died.

And what would the folks from Goodyear say after all was said and done? Would anybody say that I was a good manager, that I met my production goals, that I served the company well? Some would say I was a troublemaker, of course, but did it really matter what anybody said? What nagged me now was the larger question of what I'd really done with my life.

THE TREES outside my window, now bare, reminded me that Thanksgiving was fast approaching. It was my favorite holiday, and the idea of cooking the turkey with Charles and baking my grandsons' favorite pies relaxed me. In the most recent years, holidays had seemed more like a chore than a pleasure. This Thanksgiving, I was thankful for my health and felt a deep sense of gratitude for my family. I planned to enjoy our time together without letting my stress ruin our holiday, as it had done now for the past several years.

I thought I was handling the stress, keeping my work life and home life separate, but I wasn't. I'm ashamed to say that I'd been flaring up at home for entirely too long, and even in public, like the afternoon I was at the mall with Vickie picking up a pair of dance shoes. When I realized that the shoes hadn't been dyed the right color, I was so nasty to the man behind the counter that he called security. Now, during family vacations with Vickie and the grandkids, my body fell apart and I'd be sick in bed. I couldn't even enjoy my two grandsons—Will was already ten, and Ross, born five years after Will, was growing up fast. I'd tried to keep my promise to myself to be involved with the grandkids, but on our annual beach trips I'd collapse. And I was tough on Charles. Nothing he said or did made me happy.

BUT SOMETHING greater was going on. I understand now how the mistreatment of women can ruin their health and affect their fam-

ily life, but instead of directing my anger at Goodyear, I lashed out
at people who didn't deserve it or turned my frustrations inward.
Literally. My body had been telling me what I didn't want to face.
The job wasn't worth the suffering, but I wasn't ready to admit de-
feat. I told myself that the good outweighed the bad.

I convinced myself that I'd had many productive years at
Goodyear. It just depended on who my supervisor was and what
department I was in, but the doctor's words when he'd given me a
checkup rumbled around in my mind, refusing to leave. He'd insisted that I scale back at work or I'd find myself right back in his
office with possibly something worse to deal with. That concerned
me. I'd always seen myself as a lifer at Goodyear, working thirty
years, knowing when I retired that Charles and I would have the
security of full medical coverage. I also had to build up as much
retirement as possible to live on and reduce the debt we'd accumulated owning a home, buying cars, and paying for college.

Confined to the hospital bed with the TV turned to silent, I
watched Charles sleep in the chair beside me, comforted by his
presence. I still admired his broad shoulders and strong body.
When we were in the waiting room right before I was called back
for surgery, I caught the silhouette of a tall man talking to my doctor down the hall. My heart jumped at the sight of this handsome
man. It was Charles. After all these years, I could still feel the same
giddiness I felt as a schoolgirl.

We'd been through a lot together, and I was distressed about
how much time we'd spent apart. He'd been more than patient with
me. Too patient, probably. I felt like I'd abandoned him at times,
leaving him to raise the kids alone. The truth was, I'd neglected
those who cared about me most. Sometimes, going to work had
been easier than dealing with the messiness of family life. If Charles
hadn't been a Baptist, he and I would have probably divorced during those impossible years when the kids were teenagers.

Shifting my body trying to find a comfortable position, I hoped the pain medicine would kick in soon. I watched the silent image of Murphy Brown flitting on the screen across the room and reached for the control to set the bed higher. The searing sensations the pain pill hadn't dulled washed over me.

My body was telling me something, and I needed to listen. I needed my life to be different now, but what if it was too late? I prayed it wasn't.

AFTER THE surgery, I returned to work the last week before the plant closed on Christmas Eve, as it always did for the one-week holiday. Often when workers returned from a medical leave they were given a lighter load, and Eddie assigned me to work in one of the offices with Sharon, a secretary. Before this, I'd spoken to Sharon only in the mornings when I was coming off the night shift and she was starting her morning routine. I didn't know her well, but I knew she'd been at Goodyear much longer than I had.

Working with Sharon all day, I learned that she'd been a supervisor for eight years before she had to quit the night shift and take on less responsibility. She had been a single mother with a small child, and when her daughter's caregiver died of cancer, Sharon had to change her work routine. She told me she'd been approached several years earlier to return to being a supervisor.

"Why didn't you take the offer?" I asked, surprised that she was still a secretary.

"I did. I couldn't say no to thirty-two hundred dollars a month. And I was told I'd be given raises in the future to get me even with the men's salary."

"What happened?"

"I started working in the tire room, but I should have known something was up when I got my first paycheck and it was exactly the same as what I'd been making as a secretary."

"What did you do? Go talk to somebody about it?"

"At first, no. You know how things are. I hoped for the best and kept on working." She looked past me through the office window. I turned to see what she was looking at, a group of night supervisors huddled together, talking. I half expected them to put their hands together and do a group hurrah before running out onto some imaginary field. I turned back to Sharon.

"You were in same area I was when I was in the tire room. How many associates did you supervise?"

"Fifty-two men."

"That's a lot of builders to deal with."

"I know. I also had the truckers to deal with and had to oversee inspection, but some of the old-timers are really good, and then there are some who will fall asleep right there at the machine. I had this one guy who'd wander off on break every five minutes."

"Tell me about it. It's like herding cats at times. I had this one nest of people, and I had to time them when they went to the rest-room and when they went to eat. Sometimes I'd follow them with my stopwatch to make sure they didn't disappear forever.

"The guys were the least of my problems. My paycheck never changed. And the worst part was the guys on the floor probably made more than I did, and I was their supervisor."

"So what did you do?"

"After a couple of months, I asked about it and was told, 'We're working on it.' So I kept thinking my next paycheck would be right. About a month later, when it wasn't, I asked again when my salary increase was going to take effect. I was told the same thing. A couple of weeks later, I went back. You wouldn't believe what I was told then. I was informed, 'You're crazy as hell. We can't give you that kind of money.' "

I'd heard some bizarre things come out of people's mouths, and I knew how Sharon must have felt when she heard those words. "What did you say?"

"I said, 'That's right.' I *was* crazy as hell. Crazy as hell to keep doing what I was doing for the same pay. That's when I came back to this office."

"That was the best thing you could have done under the circumstances. You couldn't have kept working in the tire room the way things were."

"I know. I was offered a twenty percent raise, but that still meant I was nowhere near the base pay for a manager. And just last month they said, with the ticket being down, I'm on the list to be laid off."

There wasn't anything comforting to say about that.

Sharon opened her desk drawer and pulled out a pack of gum. "I really need a cigarette." She unwrapped a piece of gum and put it into her mouth. "If I'm laid off, I don't know what I'll do."

I could see the toll working at Goodyear had taken on her. Sharon was naturally tall and thin, but it looked like she'd lost a lot of weight recently; her khaki pants hung loose around her hips when she stood up.

The door opened and one of the morning supervisors walked in, eating a doughnut. "Morning, girls. What you got for me today?" Flecks of white icing fell on Sharon's desk as he peered over her shoulder at the list of shift workers.

Sharon rolled her eyes at me and handed him his report offs, a list of absent workers.

"Rick's laid out again?" he said with his mouth full while he scanned the sheet.

"Yeah. I don't know how long he's going to be out, but I got Dave to come in for him. And we have a floater to cover any gaps."

"Appreciate it. You girls be good now and don't get into any trouble today." He winked, closing the door and joining the other supervisors still huddled in conversation.

|||||||||||

IN SUCH a short period, I didn't have a chance to get to know Sharon very well, but I sympathized with her. Just the nature of the manufacturing work is hard enough on both men and women, and most people retired with a slew of ailments—back problems, pulmonary issues, heart disease. As one of my young tire build-ers told me before he quit, "This place is a death trap, and I don't plan to die here." Which was worse, a fatal mistake with the curing press or a slow disease from the toxic chemicals? I don't know. I do know what he couldn't understand, being so young: Goodyear gave families the ability to make more money than anywhere else. For most people that meant being able to send their children to college, breaking the cycle of disadvantage for the family, and that was worth the risks.

For others, like Sharon, the toll was becoming too great.

ON JANUARY 1, 1997, back in my regular department, I worked the start-up shift, from 5:00 P.M. to 7:00 A.M. I was glad when my shift was over. It's always a scary proposition to coax a cold machine up and running, especially when the guys are just as reluctant to start producing after a long holiday of lazing around. I wasn't in great shape myself. I still had a hitch in my giddy-up, as they say, from the recent surgery. I'd come in early to make sure the depart-ment was in order, and I could feel my lower back protesting that it wasn't used to my standing on the concrete floor for so long.

After our morning managers' meeting, Eddie asked me to step into his office. "I need to see you," he said.

When I saw the HR manager already seated, I thought, *Oh, my word, this will be some evaluation.* Eddie had sent me a self-evaluation form in the mail while I was at home after my colon surgery. Charles had driven me to the plant to return it, and I hadn't heard another word about it. I'd seen the other manag-ers being evaluated while I was working in the office and figured Eddie was waiting until the first of the year for mine. Different managers evaluated us at different times of the year, and these evaluations were sporadic at best. I'd probably had no more than ten in almost twenty years. The few raises I'd gotten were communicated to me on torn slips of paper with the percentage written on them. I hadn't been evaluated or given a raise since my performance award, an 8 percent raise, in December 1995.

The HR manager got right to the point. I was being terminated.

"We're experiencing severe cutbacks, and plans are in the works at corporate to phase out the entire Gadsden operation," he explained in the solemn voice of a well-rehearsed funeral director.

Before I could digest his words, Eddie chimed in, "Your performance has been poor this year. One of the lowest of everybody's."

My shock was replaced by a sense of guarded alarm. "How can you say that when I've never been evaluated?"

"We have your other evaluation that another manager did," Eddie replied.

"You mean the year I was given an award? That was my best year."

"No, I'm talking about Jeff's audits."

Great. The audits Jeff had lied about when he evaluated me. "You know my record's not that bad. You've seen my guys wear their gear, and you know my machines are always running."

"I don't know. I only know what I see written on these audits."

I could feel my adrenaline rising, and I wanted to argue and fight back. I had been out of the loop for a while now, being excluded from managers' meetings and not receiving some important memos. I clenched my toes inside my hard boots and repeated, "My record's not that bad and never has been." I tried to tell Eddie that not only were the audits wrong but that Jeff had started his nonsense again, and wanted me to go get a drink with him after work. Though I couldn't help but wonder if something was pathologically wrong with Jeff, I didn't dwell on his inappropriate remarks, knowing how precarious my position was at the moment.

"I trust Jeff is doing his job the way he's supposed to. As far as your job, we would have told you in November when we notified everyone else, but you were on sick leave," Eddie said, ready, it seemed, with an immediate response to any objection I might pose.

"Why not tell me in December when I was back for a week?"

"I didn't want to ruin your holidays."

I started to ask another question, but Eddie waved his hand across his throat in a gesture to cut me off, so I stopped.

"We'll talk in a minute," he said.

When the HR manager left, Eddie said, "Don't worry, Lilly, I don't have anyone to replace you. You're not going anywhere."

That's just the way it was. You were told one thing, and another happened.

Eddie sent me to meet with the "outplacement counselor" right after that meeting anyway. During our conversation I was exhausted, and not much the counselor said sank in. I was hoping I could take Eddie's word that I wasn't being let go, so I wasn't very open to dusting off my résumé and meeting her again at her office in Anniston to start another job search. Exasperated by my lack of interest in her help, she blurted out, "Why in heaven's name do you want to work for a company that treats you like this?"

It seemed pretty clear to me. Regardless of what the audits said, I *was* good at my job; I enjoyed it. Times were challenging, and it wouldn't be easy to find another well-paying job. Did she really think that at this juncture in my life there was something else out there besides being a greeter at Wal-Mart that would be an option? In the end, no matter where you go, you're shoveling the same scattlepoop from the barn, so after all the good and the bad I'd experienced, I certainly wasn't going to give up now. That would have been insane. I wasn't a quitter.

"You be here on the first and fifteenth of each month, and you'll see why I stay. I need to keep building my retirement." I was sixty years old. Goodyear was my career.

The following months I was on a constant roller-coaster ride, wondering if Goodyear would deliver on its plan to lay me off, but I stayed where I was. Another supervisor had a heart attack, and I split his shift, in addition to my own shift, with another manager. No more mention was made to me of my being terminated, and when I brought it up, I was told the same thing: There wasn't anybody to replace me, and there was no more mention of the plant closing. I worked more overtime that year, 1997, than in all my years there.

That meant, of course, that I didn't have time to enjoy Charles's retirement. He'd dreaded retiring, and when Fort McClellan offered to extend his position for two years as they prepared to close the base, he jumped at it. When he did retire, he threw himself into helping Phillip, who'd experienced his own ups and downs in the real estate industry, with some good years and some bad enough that I'd save the ketchup and mustard packets from fast-food restaurants for him. Now he was managing several apartment buildings, houses, and a historic bed-and-breakfast in Anniston.

Charles and Phillip hadn't been very close over the years, and Charles looked at the opportunity to help Phillip manage his properties and run a small company he bought that manufactured taxicab lights as a way to build a better relationship. But as financial pressures bore down on Phillip, he became difficult to work with, his mood swings growing more unpredictable. Charles stuck it out, though, in spite of the fact that I wasn't thrilled when he had to go knocking on apartment doors to collect rent or evict someone. That's not what I'd envisioned for his retirement, but I was still so consumed with hanging on at Goodyear, despite the doctor's concerns, that I wasn't focused on Charles.

By THE time the temperature had soared into a typical pattern of high nineties with little rain in sight that summer, my patience had begun to wear thin. Sometimes it was the small things that got under my skin most. In the tire room, everyone on my crew had been awarded a silver NASCAR racing jacket emblazoned with Goodyear's winged-foot logo for keeping the waste in the department to a minimum. Goodyear provided special tires for many of the race cars—the plant in Akron had its own speedway for testing them. With NASCAR so close by and all the guys such big race-car fans, the jackets were a big deal. Turns out the jacket ordered for me happened to be an extra-large. It might as well have been an overcoat. The guys couldn't quit laughing when I tried it on. I wore it once or twice and didn't say a word, but the slights added up, each as surprising as the unexpected shock from a paper cut. I gave the jacket to Charles. It was even too big for him.

I wouldn't say anything about something like the lovely jacket, but I did ask Eddie about his e-mails addressed to "Boys."

"Don't you realize you have something besides a boy on your team?"

"Lilly, we have work to do, and discussing this is a waste of my time, your time, and the company's time."

"Well, that's not how I see it. Did you ever think it's unfair that you're singling me out like this because I'm the only woman?"

The next time he sent a memo, he wrote, "Boys and lady."

Only a few days after that he cornered me alone in a small conference room and said, "Lilly, your production numbers are down again. You're not getting the job done."

I didn't see a shred of paperwork or one printout with figures to prove what he was saying. "Show me the production numbers and give me two weeks; I'll correct the problem," I said. He held a folder and a clipboard in his hand but didn't look at either.

"The problem is, two other area mangers are telling me they're pulling your weight."

"That's simply not true. Show me the production report and give me time to fix it, and you know I will."

"I can't do that."

I was tempted to grab his folder and see what he had in there. "Well, I can't fix a problem if I don't know what the problem is."

He sat down, his voice lowering as he placed the folder on the table. "You're just like me. You just keep coming back for more. You can't help it, can you?"

"I'm not sure what you're talking about."

"I just had a similar meeting with the plant manager. He was telling me the same thing. That I wasn't performing. And there I was acting like you. Couldn't let it go like some young fool."

Eddie had criticized me recently on the floor for omitting something that in fact I hadn't omitted. The next morning he caught me heading out the gate to the parking lot and whispered, "I have to fuss at you when I jump on the other managers, or else I'll have hell to pay." It was the closest thing to an apology I'd heard yet.

"I kept badgering Henry that I wanted to see the numbers. I think at one point he thought I was going to come across the desk at him. I wanted to, but I didn't."

I knew that in his own way Eddie was between a rock and a hard place. No one was immune to the plant's politics. Someone wanted me out. Telling me my production was down was his way of pleasing upper management and holding on to his own job. "Did he show them to you?"

He winced. "He didn't have to. The numbers don't make a bit of difference."

"How can you stand being lied to?"

"What are you going to do about it? We might be cut from the same cloth, but I know when to shut up. Mouthing back won't get you anywhere. You've never learned when to back down."

"Why are you doing this? You know it's not fair."

"You're always ready for a fight. You can't let anything go, can you?"

"But you still haven't shown me any proof of your criticisms."

"And I'm not going to." He picked up his unopened folder, stood, and walked away.

I asked him when we'd meet again.

He turned and barked, "You're bad for morale, Lilly. Do us all a favor. Why don't you just retire?"

Soon after, at our morning managers' meeting, once again Jeff's audit downgraded me. He'd reported that I didn't have a lock on one of the machines, but he was the one who was supposed to give it to me. And he never did. My frustration overtook me. I couldn't continue to try to hold my head high or push away my anger. I'd tried before, when Eric was still my supervisor, to speak to him about the mistaken audits. Sometimes when I approached him, he seemed friendly; more often, he was too busy to meet with me. I decided to talk to Jeff myself and followed him into his office at the end of the meeting.

"You got a minute?"

"Sure."

He didn't invite me to sit down.

"I need to know why you continue to downgrade my department when you know good and well my guys wear their safety equipment and my machines are always running." I didn't mention the fact that when the other auditor filed his reports I was in compliance with the guidelines.

"You must have had a bad night. Something go wrong with a machine?"

"Nope, but something's gone wrong with your audits. Each one of them is marked wrong. I've been in my department with you, and you've seen what I've seen, my men dressed in all their safety gear. But that's not what you've written here."

"Whoa, Nelly, simmer down now, Lilly."

"No. You quit doing me this way when I've done nothing

wrong. My guys' safety record is better than most." I shook the paper in the air. "You expect me to keep taking this? Look at it. It's all wrong. How can you even begin to say they're not wearing their gear? And to write that my machines aren't always running when you know they are."

"I mark what I see."

He was as smooth a liar as you'd ever meet. How it came so easy I'll never know.

"Then you need your eyes checked."

Jeff chuckled. "Hell, Lilly, I'm in a tough spot. You see these big old guys. If I write them up, they're going to give me a whooping, push me around, and dog-cuss me."

I knew what he meant. I'd seen the other managers roughhousing with him. He was smaller than the rest, and I doubted he could hold his own with the bigger guys. But that didn't mean he had the right to mess with me.

"Then maybe you need to quit playing golf and take up boxing. But whatever you do, that doesn't have a thing to do with me."

"Sure it does. It's a hell of a lot easier to downgrade you. You're just a little female. You're not going to cuss me back."

I bit my bottom lip hard and thought, *Just a little female? Who would believe this stuff if you told them?* His words were beyond ridiculous.

"Besides, I have to write up *some*body." He scratched the inside of his ear and inspected his forefinger. "Everybody can't look good." He flicked whatever it was off his hand.

NOTHING CHANGED with my audits. Toward the end of that summer Eddie called me into his office again. "Lilly," he said like he always did, as if about to scold me, "we have a technology-engineer opening you need to interview for. I've already recommended you for it." He was starting to gray around the temples and his hair was thinning, but his temper hadn't mellowed.

I had the familiar feeling of being hemmed into a corner. I didn't need to transfer departments. I liked the tire room. "I'm fine where I am," I said, keeping my voice matter-of-fact.

"It's only to your advantage to interview for it and consider taking it."

Quality control, where I'd been moved during the EEOC investigation in the early eighties, wasn't as challenging or interesting to me as supervising tire building. "No, really, I'm good where I am."

"Change is not bad, Lilly. We all resist it, but sometimes it's the best option we have." Behind his small wooden desk, he jotted down notes.

My stomach tightened and a shot of pain ran through my lower body as I sat on the hard metal chair. "You know I enjoy where I am and I have a good crew there," I said. And that was in spite of the fact that now if I disciplined a builder, Eddie wouldn't back me up on my recommendations.

He sat back up, clicked his pen closed, and placed it on his yellow legal pad. Leaning back in his chair, he finally looked at me. He placed the tips of his fingers together, forming a pyramid shape with his hands. "I felt the same way about change myself just a few weeks ago until I was convinced it was in my best interest to make a move. It's only to my advantage to take the advice I was given and move to Lawton, Oklahoma."

For a second, I felt kind of sorry for him, having to move. He'd lived in Gadsden all of his life, working at the plant for the past twenty-six years. "I don't know, Eddie. I've been in the tire room a while now. Like I said, I like it there."

"All I can tell you is what I was told. Change is good for you. Any other option won't be what you want."

What options? I didn't see options. "Who else is moving? Or am I the only one because I'm the only woman?"

He leaned forward and said intently, "You've got to quit

blaming everybody else for your problems, Lilly. You should be thankful your pay stays the same. And if I were you, I'd be glad to have a job. Everybody else around here's getting laid off."

"I've moved a lot, and you know I'll do what I need to, but I'd really like to stay where I am."

I didn't dispute him any further. Rumors about layoffs and demotions continued running wild, but during the previous year, when the plant was supposedly shutting down, there'd been some layoffs of bargaining men but not any managers that I knew of. The scuttlebutt I'd overheard in the break room was that some area managers had gotten raises even though the word was that all salaries were frozen.

"I suspect if you don't take it, you won't have a job either. Chris is waiting for you now to talk about the transfer. I suggest you go see him."

I did go see Chris about the technology opening, as instructed. I waited to be moved, but in typical Goodyear fashion, I stayed where I was for several more months until another person was found to take my place and the company released the position in quality control.

As the Christmas holidays approached once again, I looked forward to the plant going dark for a week, so I could spend time with my family, but the holidays didn't turn out quite as expected. A few days before Christmas, the doctor found a tumor the size of a lemon lodged in Edna's throat. She'd been having trouble breathing for over a year, and she could barely sleep without suffocating, but no one had caught the real reason for her difficulties: lung cancer.

In the doctor's office Edna sat on the examining table in a flimsy gown, her legs dangling, reminding me of a little girl. I re-tied the strings in the back of her gown to keep it from gaping opening as we waited for the doctor.

When the doctor finally arrived, Edna asked him what kind of tumor it was, and he told her that she'd have to wait until after the holidays for more conclusive testing.

"Do you think it's malignant?" She crossed and uncrossed her ankles unconsciously.

"Have you ever smoked?" he asked, still reading his chart.

Her legs became still. "Yes."

He looked her straight in the eye. "Then you've probably answered your own question."

Time felt like it was melting as his words sifted through my mind and buried their weight in my heart. The sounds in the room—Edna's wheezing and the squeaking soles of the nurse's rubber shoes—became distant, and the doctor's words sounded as garbled as the sounds Louise and I made when we used to try to converse underwater.

"I can tell you this," he continued. "If it is cancer, the only way I approach each patient I have is, no matter how advanced any cancer may be, I will do all in my power to cure you, if possible."

Based on what the doctor told me in private afterward, her prognosis wasn't good. Somehow, Edna had missed the last two words, "if possible," and she convinced herself and everyone who listened that she was being cured. Her mind was set, and knowing how she was used to being the one in charge, I knew I was in for a time trying to take care of her.

WE GOT through the holiday the best we could. The new year started and I was officially transferred. In January 1998 I became a technology engineer, just another highfalutin term for someone in quality control. My position as area manager was filled by one of my former tire builders, a man, who'd been promoted.

In quality control, the last stop before the tires are shipped, the inspection area covers about twenty thousand square feet and the ceiling is several stories high, reminding me of an airplane hangar.

My main job was to hand-check 125 Hummer tires. If the offgoing shift neglected to do theirs, that meant another 125 to check. The worst thing an inspector can do is let a bad tire get out the door. Then you have to shut down the machines and scrap the batch of bad tires until someone figures out where on the production line the problem occurred.

The first thing I did on my shift was go to the pits and set up the curing press. Each time I worked on the presses, I thought about the last thing one supervisor said to me after telling me to report to my new job. I was walking out the door when he called my name. I turned around, puzzled by the seriousness in his tone. "Lilly," he said, "whatever you do, don't make a mistake on the curing press." What he left unsaid was: *If you do, you're done.* I had a bad feeling then that I'd been hung out to dry.

The curing press, similar to a giant waffle iron, gives the tire its final shape, engraves it with its tread pattern, and makes the sidewall markings, required by law for identification, that rate the tread wear, traction, and temperature and give other important information about the make and model.

During the production cycle, when different tires are made, there are mold changes, so each shift I'd have at least three mold changes to double-check, making sure all the specifications on the new tire setup had been entered correctly. To do this, I took a computer printout one of the supervisors in final finish had given me outlining the specifications. Then I adjusted the gauges and dials for the length of time, temperature, and level of steam pressure for that particular tire.

Once the tire was cured, after about twenty-five minutes in the press heated to over 300 degrees F, I caught the tire, which was released hydraulically, before it hit the conveyor belt so I could inspect it. I traced the entire tire with a thin waxed paper, comparing the drawing with an illustration in a manual to make sure the two matched exactly.

After my very first shift as a technology engineer, my apprehension about my job only deepened. That shift I'd been left alone and told to call another supervisor if I had questions. When I did, he said he didn't have time to help me, so I did the best I could with what little instruction I had. In all other departments, I'd always been given a job description and a training manual and spent a significant amount of time being trained.

After I finished in the pits, I unloaded and spot-checked Hummer tires. One night as I checked a tire, it spun out of my hands, landing on the concrete floor. I let it sit there a minute while I wiped my forehead with the sleeve of my blue shirt. Then I bent over to prop the tire against my legs. In the dimly lit warehouse, I ran my flashlight over every inch of the tire, looking for lumps or splices burned into the surface when it was cured.

After I checked the tire inside and out, I looked for a hoist to load the large tire onto a handtruck to wheel it to the side of the eighteen-wheeler, where I stacked the tires for the trucker to load onto his truck. A hoist was nowhere to be found. There was no way I could lift the tire onto the handtruck without it, so I rocked the eighty-pound doughnut across the floor to the empty eighteen-wheeler. About that time a young coworker, Bobby, who stayed in the pits, walked by on his way to the area where whitewalls are sprayed blue to keep them from being damaged during shipping. Only three or four of us worked in my department, and I was by myself most of the time, so I tried to catch his eye, but he looked away.

"Hey," I said, "can you help me out a minute? I need a hand stacking this tire."

"Don't think I can help you, I'm afraid. I'm busy right now." Bobby kept walking. The outline of a round Skoal chewing tobacco container created a worn white circle on the back pocket of his Carhartt jeans.

As we say in the South, he acted as sour as a gallbladder. "It won't take a minute," I said a little faster, without raising my voice.

He stopped and turned around. "Look, I got work to do. Besides, everybody says you're a troublemaker and to stay away from you." Glancing over at the tires that the shift before me had not finished unloading, he jerked his head in their direction before he said, "You're on your own." I'd seen that other stack of passenger tires, and it was a daunting sight. I'd also seen the hard look on Bobby's face and heard his blind anger before. I wanted to tell him that I didn't want to be inspecting tires any more than he wanted me there, but there was no point in saying anything.

During the break, I looked for Rodney, one of the quality control area managers overseeing the shipping end of final finish.

"You know, the offgoing shift didn't check their tires again," I told him.

A tall man, Rodney shook his head and clucked his tongue in sympathy. He'd been there as long as I had and had confided in me that when he first started, one of his supervisors was in the Klan. As an African American, he must have found that unnerving, to say the least.

"You know, some of these guys don't know to do anything but keep their feet on your neck. And they can come up with about anything to do that," he said.

"Yeah, I know."

He continued, "One time I was told I was inflating my production numbers. Then the manager who did the investigation discovered that I was actually understating them. I wish I could have seen his face. That's not what they expected to find, but they did."

"You lucked out that time."

"Like I tell the other black supervisors, 'Know your job, do your job, and no one can find fault.' "

"How am I supposed to know my job when I don't even have a job description?" I cringed at the whininess in my voice.

"You have to keep asking."

"I have. Several times now. I'll ask again, but you'd think at this point they'd have already have given me a description."

"Lilly, you've been here as long as I have. When I first started, I was still supposed to be sitting at the back of the bus. Now, how many times have they set up the guillotine for you? And each time, you've never walked through it. You've walked around it, and you might have even thumbed your nose at it a few times. And that makes them even more determined to drop the blade. Don't get me wrong. I know what you're up against better than anybody here. They're pros at this game, and they've set up that guillotine for you again. But remember, you don't have to walk through it."

Someone across the room called for Rodney. He patted me on the back and gave me a quick smile before he left. I needed to quit complaining, pull up my bootstraps, and get the job done, but the past couple of years had worn me out; I was done stuffing down my disappointment and swallowing my anger, throwing myself harder into my work like a good little hedgehog, thinking that if I just worked longer and smarter, my merit would speak for itself. It hadn't and it wouldn't. It had taken me too long to see what had been so transparent for so many years. I needed to earn the best salary possible, yes, but more than that, I needed approval for being someone special. That didn't have a thing to do with money. I had stuck it out so long, to the detriment of myself and my family, in part because I was waiting for acceptance. Even though I'd found comfort and reward in other parts of my life, like dancing and my grandchildren, I never let go of the secret hope that Goodyear would change how it treated me.

Just a few days earlier I'd finally been given my annual evaluation for the previous year. I'd met with Paul, a manager who had supervised me less than a month after I went on leave for my colon surgery. He told me I wouldn't get the raise I had been counting on. Using Jeff's audits, he said my performance was poor, specifically criticizing me for not having team meetings.

I answered right back. "That's right. Eddie froze the overtime pay and the guys won't come in an hour early for a meeting if they're not paid."

I was coming to the horrible realization that I held no real value in the eyes of those I had tried hardest to please. I knew I wouldn't be given the material I needed to perform my duties successfully in my new department. Walking back to where I'd been unloading Hummer tires, I pondered how long I could maneuver the curing presses before I was tripped up unwittingly.

I TOOK a few days off in February so I could take Edna to the doctor to continue the battery of tests as the doctor determined the best chemotherapy and radiation treatment for her; he'd decided not to perform surgery. On the drive to Birmingham, Edna was quieter than usual, her rattled breath and the occasional grumble of my empty stomach the only sounds between us.

"How do you feel today? Were you able to sleep okay last night?" I asked. She had to prop herself up on pillows and barely rested each night.

"I feel about the same as I do every day." I glanced at her as I made a right turn, her tight lips thinner than they used to be, pulled inward as if holding in a disgraceful secret. "I'd feel better if you'd been here on time when you said you would to pick me up. I waited and waited and thought you weren't coming. I was about to call Charles when you drove up."

I turned on the radio. She had no idea how hard it had been to get the week off, and since I hadn't shared my troubles at work with her, she didn't understand the stress I was dealing with. Every minute outside work I'd dedicated to her, and I'd rushed as best as I could to get to her house straight from work. For a minute I fantasized about stopping the car and letting her out on the side of the road, but listening to her struggle to breathe, I kept driving, embarrassed by my ugly thoughts.

"I told you that we sometimes have a managers' meeting and if I didn't get to your house by nine o'clock, the meeting was on and I'd be running an hour late."

"I've never understood why it takes you twelve hours to work an eight-hour shift. No one else works like that."

How many times had I heard her say those exact same words, and how many times had I explained that I had to go in early to prep and stay late for the morning meetings?

My head felt as heavy as a piece of metal, and I snapped, "Has anyone ever told you that you are the hardest person in the world to be nice to?"

She turned her face away from me and stared out the window without a word. I immediately regretted my outburst. She was nit-picking me over being late, but her anger didn't have anything to do with me. She was mad about the cancer, and I was an easy target. I'd overreacted as usual, the same way I did with poor Charles, yelling at him in a flash now. My nerves had gotten so bad that, like Edna, I could no longer sleep.

THE TESTING showed that Edna's cancer was more aggressive than originally diagnosed. Only the approaching spring weather lifted my spirits, and I'd leave work scouring the skyline, the way I used to search for four-leaf clovers as a girl, looking for my favorite bird, the redheaded woodpecker, which I considered a good-luck omen. I'd lose myself for a moment observing something inconsequential like a flock of startled blackbirds swelling from the branches, the oily sheen of their dark wings swirling like ink against the sky. I'd linger and marvel at their simple beauty before I'd pick up Edna and take her to Anniston for her radiation treatments. Before I went home to try to rest before the next shift, I made sure she had enough food and medicine. Each day felt like more of the same until the day a coworker named Ray joined me in final finish.

Walking behind the force grinders, he reached behind him and automatically pulled the lever to shut the gates, which had been let down while he showed me how to operate the machinery. The steel gate caught me, pinned my body to the ground, and pressed my knee down in a vise grip. Pain shot up my leg into my groin. The world became a grainy blur, like the snowy static of a late-night TV screen when the daily programming is over. Unable to speak, I looked over at Ray. He stood for what seemed like a long moment before he flipped the lever. As the gate lifted off of me, I rolled to my side, clutching my knee. He helped me up, and I hobbled to the hospital at the back of the plant.

The Goodyear nurse confirmed that my leg wasn't broken, but my knee was swollen as big as a baseball, the torn cartilage, I'd find out later, balled up under my kneecap like a stubborn wad of rubber caught in a machine. I knew then, more than ever, that I'd need all the luck I could get to avoid the guillotine's sharp edge my final years at Goodyear.

CHAPTER 7

Holding the Tiger by the Tail

||||||||||||||||||||||||||||||||||||||||||||||||||||||||||||||||||||||||||||||||||||||||||||||||||||||

Tiger, Tiger, burning bright
In the forests of the night,
What immortal hand or eye
Could frame thy fearful symmetry?

—WILLIAM BLAKE

I CALLED A specialist to schedule an appointment for my knee but had to wait a couple of weeks before he could fit me in. In the meantime, I kept working as best as I could. Then, before my shift one day, I found the torn piece of paper stuffed with the mail in my cubby listing my name next to the names of the three other area managers in the tire room.

The note showed my salary, down to the dollar, and the male managers' salaries: I was earning thousands less than they were. I earned $44,724 while the highest-paid man earned $59,028 and the other two followed close behind him, earning $58,464 and $58,226. I don't know how I made it through that night. I was scalding on the inside and out, as if someone had thrown a skilletful of hot grease on me. One minute I wanted to give somebody a piece of my mind, wondering how many people knew about this; and the next I wanted to throw up from the anxiety, remembering how much we'd done without as a family. All night, humiliated and devastated, I struggled over what to do. If I ignored it, I wouldn't be able to live with myself. It would gnaw away at me. If I said something, there'd be retaliation, payback far worse than any I'd experienced before.

By the end of my shift that day, I was so tired I could barely walk, and I was sopping wet with the effort it took to keep my emotions at bay. On the way home, I didn't bother to go through the drive-through at Hardee's for my usual bacon biscuit, and I didn't turn on the country music station that never failed to soothe me. Heading back to Jacksonville directly into the morning sun, I let my emotions flow through me—anger, sadness, fear. It wasn't pleasant, but it was something of a relief, like blood returning to your arm or leg when the circulation has been cut off.

The drive that morning in March 1998 seemed like the longest drive I'd ever made. I could feel myself holding the steering wheel so tight that my fingers tingled as I saw my life at Goodyear flash before me. I remembered all the times I brought a cake Edna had baked and the guys almost finished it before I set it on the breakroom table. I thought about more serious moments when the men I supervised, with a simple nod or a few quiet words, thanked me for looking out for them, making sure they were paid properly for overtime or given the right number of vacation days.

What upset me the most was what could have been. If I had ever been accepted by management at Goodyear, I know I could have accomplished more and contributed more—not just made more tires but helped to make the plant a better place to work. I could have made a difference for the women who came after me. Instead, all those years management had been trying to get rid of me, all I'd done was survive.

As those numbers tumbled through my mind again and again, I understood that my belief that hard work pays off was downright naïve, even though I'd been far from naïve when I started. I'd known from the get-go that I'd have to work longer and smarter than the men in order to prove myself. And that's what I did. I came in early and stayed late to make sure my area was prepped properly. I rarely said no, never stopped learning, and never backed down. And I'd done what I was supposed to; over the years my production numbers were high, my scrap low. I kept absenteeism in my department to a minimum. Now I was the first one they called when a machine went down.

There wasn't any logic behind these numbers. I couldn't catch up to their salaries scribbled on that note, and I couldn't start over.

On the drive home, even as I deliberated about what to do, I knew that the only choice I had was to stand up for myself and do what was right. I understood the risk I was taking. I'd seen workers who'd lost so much fighting for years for disability. It surely would be the hardest fight of my life, and there were no guarantees that the man in the white hat would win. I certainly didn't have the money to pay for a lawyer to help me. And I might lose my pension with less than a year left before retirement. But as I ruminated, I realized I had to at least try to prove that the good guy could still win, and that I could still make a difference. It was just my nature. I couldn't help myself. Alone in the car, I ached to get home and try to see my way clear through this situation. I needed to tell Charles what had happened. With him by my side, I could handle whatever I had to.

When I finally made it home, I walked past the banana plant one of the union men who gardened had given me, its green shoots unfurling from the brown stalk we covered in black plastic for the winter. Walking into the house, I smelled coffee. Charles was in the kitchen pouring a fresh cup, standing next to my favorite plaque hanging on the wall that read DON'T LOOK BACK. I stood in the doorway of our small kitchen and didn't even sit down.

"You look beat. You want a cup of coffee?" Charles offered.

I nodded. He reached into the cabinet for the coffee cup I always used, one he'd given me from Fort McClellan.

"I've had a hard night."

He fixed my coffee the way I liked it and motioned for me to sit at the table. Before I sat down, I pulled the note out of my pocket and gave it to him.

"What's this?"

"Read it."

He did, and looked up at me, his eyes wide. "Is this a joke or something?"

"Don't think so." I took a quick sip. "I've already made up my mind. This won't be a quick fix by any stretch of the imagination, but unless you can convince me otherwise, I'm going to Birmingham to file an EEOC complaint." This would be my second time filing. And it would make the first look like a walk in the park.

He looked at me. His hair had turned gray years ago, but his eyes, still a startling blue, sparkled brighter, as they always did when he realized there was something that needed doing. That was a good sign. After a few moments, he put the note on the table between us. "What time would you like to leave?"

I'd never loved him more than in that moment.

THE FOLLOWING morning, on the drive to Birmingham, Charles and I didn't say much. To keep my mind off the task before me, I stared into the woods whizzing by, marveling at the blooming white dogwood trees, hoping to catch a glimpse of a deer. After a couple of wrong turns, we found the EEOC building downtown. Inside, we passed through security and walked into a crowded waiting room. I tried to find a vacant seat in the corner and settled on a spot in the middle of the room. I don't like crowds, but Charles was worse. He didn't sit down at all. "I'm going to get some coffee and a newspaper down the street," he said before he hightailed it out of there.

I couldn't blame him. The somber atmosphere felt the same as a hospital waiting room—everyone fortified for a long wait with newspapers and coffee. I glanced at the girl next to me. She was about Vickie's age. I wondered why she was there. I pretended to read the *Time* magazine I picked up from the stack on a table but peered around the room instead. Each person there was waiting to tell her story. What were the experiences that had brought them all to this point? Were they similar to mine? Did they feel as nervous as I did? I couldn't help but feel that we'd been thrown together by a natural disaster, united by default into a club I had no desire to join.

I flipped through the magazine and tried to read the article about the thirty-third anniversary of the Selma march in Alabama; I couldn't concentrate, discouraged by the fact that Alabama only made national news for negative stories. The only positive press for the state highlighted Heisman trophy winners or national football championships.

Rifling through the magazine stack next to me, I recalled something one of my interviewers had said while I was training at Goodyear. I hadn't thought of it in years, but on the drive into Birmingham it had popped into my thoughts with other bits and pieces of moments at Goodyear. Now his words kept running through my mind, stuck in my head like a bad song. The interviewer, one of the factory council members, wanted to know why I was at Goodyear when I should be home at the kitchen sink. Why was I at Goodyear looking for a job when Goodyear didn't need women working there? he'd asked. That was such a long time ago, and I thought so much had changed in the world—until I found the note.

Over the years, I'd done exactly what the men had done: I'd climbed the two-story buildings in the mill room; knocked down the lampblack from the boxcar into the giant banburies; started the dangerous conveyors, as wide as one-lane roads, in the rain and the sleet. I'd made it alone; the handful of women managers along the way had come and gone, quitting or having nervous breakdowns and seeking professional help. Good men like Bruce, the union representative who'd stood by me when I made the first EEOC claim in 1982, suffered when they stood up for the right thing. His integrity had cost him his position as the union rep; the following year he was defeated. I'd always regretted that had happened to such a decent person.

When my name was finally called, I met in a cramped cubicle with Ollie Crooms, the EEOC officer, an attractive, pleasant woman. In this confined office with a stranger, I relived my darkest moments at Goodyear. Over the course of several hours, without lunch or a restroom break, I recounted being blamed for a tire hold the day I returned from the week off in February when I took Edna for testing. I was never shown the actual tires or the printout with the wrong specifications. I was simply informed that I had made a $10,000 mistake, that they were deciding what to do about it, and that I'd probably be suspended. I knew there'd been one hold that year—someone had let the wrong lampblack get mixed in a batch of tires, which resulted in the scrapping of more than 76,000 tires—and that no one had been suspended for that.

Much of the time I talked, I was struck by the ugliness I was describing. Then that poor woman had to pull the more embarrassing details from me—the conversation was as painfully slow and halting as plucking a stubborn splinter deeply embedded in the flesh.

She needed to know the other details, like the unbelievable fact that when I challenged Jeff about his unfair audits, after so much that had happened so long ago, he'd actually asked me to go get a drink after work, starting up the same nasty behavior he'd demonstrated at my very first evaluation, when he asked me to meet him at the Ramada Inn. In our brief conversations with Eddie about my performance, I had intimated that Jeff's remarks were inappropriate because my audit scores continued to drop after my refusal. Eddie ignored me and I didn't push the matter—I had enough of a challenge to try to make him see that I was being evaluated unfairly. Relaying these awkward and sordid details, saying out loud the incidents and remarks I had kept to myself for so long, I couldn't help but feel like I had done something wrong to provoke the mistreatment. It was twisted, but I kept worrying that the EEOC officer would somehow think I had deserved my treatment at Goodyear. I guess that's the nature of trauma: In order to make sense of it all, you tend to blame yourself.

At the close of the interview, Ollie was more upset than I was. "You do realize, don't you, those guys were just messing with you all that time?"

I gathered my purse and stood up to shake her hand. "Yes, ma'am, I do. They've been messing with me for almost twenty years."

ONCE I filled out the EEOC questionnaire, I didn't feel any better about the whole situation. I was more anxious than I'd been before I had the interview. I'd felt compelled to take my stand, but now I was consumed by the same jumpy feeling that possessed me when I was in the house alone at night and I let my fears run away from me, convinced someone was hiding in the bushes outside the window about to break in. It was irrational, but I had a mixture of feelings, vacillating from anger to fear to worry that I'd opened a Pandora's box. Mainly, I was resigned to the fact that there was nothing to do now but wait for the EEOC to investigate. That would take months. No matter what happened, I had to make it another year until retirement age when I was sixty-two and eligible for Social Security, though the actual thought of trying to work again overwhelmed me.

The long journey I'd embarked on that day in late March 1998 would be a lesson in the intricacies and convolutions of a complex justice system steeped in politics and inconsistencies. I had entered

the labyrinth, and I would be approaching my seventy-first birthday, more than a decade later, before I found my way out.

SINCE MY injury, I'd felt like I had a knife stuck in my leg. Shortly
after my meeting with the EEOC, I was able to see the specialist.
He performed an MRI that day and scheduled arthroscopic surgery the very next day. I took some time off work to heal and attend
physical therapy. In a matter of a couple of weeks after my knee
surgery, I was able to move around and walk with crutches. During
those weeks at home recovering, I kept smelling something rancid
in the house. I thought maybe a rat had died outside in the yard.
I also couldn't focus when I was reading the newspaper; I tried to
work the crossword puzzles, but I forgot how to spell simple words.
I couldn't sleep at night, and when I did, I had nightmares. I kept
dreaming that I was standing at the edge of a tall building, looking
down weak with fear, knowing I was about to fall off. I woke up,
my heart racing, unable to go back to sleep.

Then one morning I decided to get dressed and get out of the
house. I felt someone staring at me as I ran a brush through my
hair. I looked behind me. Charles was standing in the doorway
of our bedroom, the book he was reading, *Left Behind*, still in his
hand. He had a quizzical look on his face.

"What?" I said. "Why are you looking at me that way? Is there
something wrong? Did I leave the coffeepot on again?" I kept forgetting to turn it off, along with leaving the garage door open at
night.

He hesitated. Then he looked me up and down, from head to
toe. "Is that what you're wearing today?"

I took a quick look down at the navy sweat suit Vickie had
bought me when she knew I needed something comfortable to
wear after surgery. It had a couple of stains on it. I hadn't felt like
doing laundry, and I couldn't remember the last time I'd washed it.

I tried to brush the stains off with my hand. "I'll wash it to-night," I said.

"Lilly, how many days in a row have you worn that?"

His words gave me a zap, like the static shock I'd get from walking across the carpet in stocking feet and then touching the metal handle on the refrigerator door.

I sat down on the edge of the bed. He sat beside me.

"I'm worried about you, Lilly," he said. "You're not yourself lately."

I looked down at my hands, rubbing the tips of my fingers where the skin was worn so smooth I no longer had fingerprints, something I'd discovered recently when updating my military pass. "It's just going to take me a while to get back to my normal self."

He shook his head. "No, I'm afraid it's not that simple."

I studied the cover of Charles's new book, which he'd placed beside him on the bed. He'd told me a little bit about it, how the Rapture had occurred, and people had disappeared from the face of the earth as a result. I didn't like the ominous cover, a picture of the planet surrounded by darkness. I didn't like Charles's own doomsday tone either when he forced me to recognize that I wasn't acting like my usual self, but I knew he was right. I couldn't con-tinue to function like I was, and he could only do so much to help me. It was time to ask for real help. I'd tinkered with the idea; a lot of people I knew went to see one particular psychiatrist in Gads-den, known as "the Goodyear psychiatrist." When Charles and I finished talking, he reached below the bedside table and handed me the yellow pages. I looked up her phone number and scheduled a meeting with her as soon as I could.

SINCE I'D found the note, I'd been overwhelmed by a kind of shame I'd never felt before. In the safety and calm of Dr. Judy Cook's office, for the first time in my life, I was able to talk about my deepest thoughts and feelings. While my knee continued to heal slowly on my extended medical leave, I started to work on all the emotional damage I'd incurred.

At first, pieces of myself flaked away as easily as silver slices of mica, and I was afraid that in the end nothing would be left of me. Talking to a psychiatrist, another stranger, was unsettling, and for a couple of days after visiting her, I was convinced I felt worse, not better. But I'd bottled up my problems for so long, and once I'd said out loud to the EEOC officer the things I had experienced, I couldn't return to sealing all those emotions away anymore. They'd overtaken me with a vengeance, and it was a relief to be heard. Bit by bit, I began to see how off-kilter my life had become, how cut off from myself I was. I faced the painful fact that I'd let Goodyear become the family I kept trying to please, neglecting my real family. I found that realization devastating, and I knew I needed to make amends to Charles and Vickie and Phillip.

ABLE TO drive again, I shuttled Edna back and forth to her radiation and chemotherapy at the hospital in Anniston. Edna, of course, was stubborn when it came to listening to the doctor. He'd warned her that getting out in the sun would harm her, but there she was, not long after he fussed at her for doing too much, standing outside in the middle of the yard in the blazing heat.

While Edna gave instructions about the grass, the yardman nodded, leaning against his silent lawn mower. The collar of Edna's housecoat gaped open, her chest covered in burn blisters from the radiation. If I hadn't been so disturbed by the sight of her once-beautiful olive skin charred as if from rubber poisoning, I would have laughed a little, remembering how aggravated she made Charles when he tried to cut her grass after we were first married. He finally quit.

On the way to her treatment, I tried to tell her that she was going to make herself sick. "You have to do what the doctor says, or you'll make yourself worse," I insisted.

"Hush talking now. You're giving me a headache."

No, the sun had given her the headache, but Edna was used to being the caregiver, not the patient. I didn't expect her to listen, because she always did things her way.

In just a few months Edna's cancer had spread quickly, her health deteriorating at a disconcerting pace. In May she was hospitalized for pneumonia, and once she settled in at home again, I started spending the night with her. After a week, needing a break from sleeping on a lumpy sofa (better than the hard mattress in the guest bedroom), I decided to spend the night at home. I wanted to get some rest and clear my head. I'd gotten another call from Goodyear. They didn't understand why I was taking so long to return, and indicated that the longer I stayed out, the more problematic my absence became. I knew I needed to get back into the swing of things, but I was worried about the doctor's concerns—he'd warned me that if I returned to what I was doing, I'd be crippled in two years and need an entire knee replacement—and about asking for a lighter work schedule. I didn't want to jeopardize my position by staying out too long, but I also didn't want to return before I could handle what I was expected to do.

Before I could put my bag down in my kitchen, the phone rang. Edna said her temperature was 103. I rushed back to her house, thinking we were headed to the hospital for another long visit. In her bedroom, I shook the glass thermometer and then took her temperature. The red mercury line read normal.

"Edna, you're okay. Everything is fine. It's kind of stuffy in here. Maybe if I open a window, you'll feel better," I said, pulling back the curtains she'd drawn.

She grimaced a little as the sunlight flooded her bed. "You know I don't like it so bright in here."

"I know, but this breeze will cool you off. I'm going to go now, but I'll turn on the TV before I leave so you can watch the news."

"Don't forget to water my pear tree. You forgot again. If it doesn't get watered, it will die." She'd had the yardman plant a fruit tree that spring, and all she could talk about was how much she looked forward to making pear preserves. I, on the other hand, was so wary about what was around the next corner, I didn't even subscribe to magazines. Who knew what could happen in a year? "The watering can is in the garage," she said. "What time are you coming back?" she asked as I fiddled with the TV.

I'd begged her to let someone else help me with her care, but she refused to have a stranger in her house.

"This afternoon," I said, satisfied that the volume was adjusted correctly. "I'll be back this afternoon to check on you," I repeated, leaving.

"Don't forget the pear tree, now, you hear?"

"I won't."

Watering the spindly tree, I realized that as Edna's demands increased, I could not be pulled automatically into every real or manufactured crisis anymore. I could not drop everything and go into high-functioning overdrive. I had to establish some real boundaries. I had an important obligation to fulfill, but to what degree was I going to disappear into this crisis?

MY DOCTOR continued to extend my medical leave, insistent that I find a more appropriate job or I'd ruin my knee for good. In the meantime, for the entire month of June Edna was in and out of the hospital. She'd developed a blood disorder that required close monitoring and frequent blood transfusions. I did my best to take care of myself, but I became entirely wrapped up in looking after her.

At the hospital one afternoon, I waited with Edna for her to receive a blood transfusion. Uncomfortable with any form of silence, she started in about how she had cared for her mother night and day.

"I didn't leave her side. Not once," she said, lying in bed, staring at the ceiling. "I did everything for her."

My heart ached for her when I thought about her losing her mother as a young girl only to become a mother when she was still a child herself, but I couldn't respond to her unspoken charge. The last time she was given blood, I'd left to run an errand and returned to find her alone in the room choking on her own vomit. I'd run down the hall to alert the nurses, who were gathered chit-chatting, completely unaware of the situation. I wouldn't let that happen again.

Listening to Edna complaining, I hoped she wasn't planning to pull another stunt like she had a few days earlier. She'd protested because I didn't stay with her one night. She quit drinking liquids, got dehydrated, and slipped her frail body underneath an electric blanket turned on high. We had to rush her to the hospital. Then she'd gone as far as telling her neighbors that no one was taking care of her. I couldn't let that bother me because I knew everyone saw Charles and me coming and going.

Now I managed to maintain my composure until she brought up my having left her alone to stay with Vickie for the birth of her third son, Alex. Against my better judgment, I jumped in to defend myself.

"Mama, we've been over this. You know I wouldn't have left for anything else. I came back as soon as I could. Anyway, I'm here now, so let's just forget about that."

The nurse finally came in to tell us that they were ready to give Edna the transfusion and wheeled her out of the room. I waited in the sterile, quiet room grappling with the fact that everything I did, no matter how important or insignificant, made her mad. My sleeping on the couch upset her, and she'd berate me for not using the guest bedroom. *There's no way I will ever please her*, I told myself. Then I said something I'd never said to myself before. *Edna hates me. My mother actually hates me.* She'd tell me she wanted me to have her dining room set, and the next thing I knew she'd have given it to another relative. Looking for an outfit for her a few days earlier, I'd chosen a dress she liked when I felt a lump in one of the pockets. I stuck my hand in and discovered my sock, the one I'd been missing for months, the one I'd turned the house upside down looking for when I stayed with her so many nights. The entire time Edna had had it in her pocket.

I'd never understand this strange spitefulness. Recently I'd discovered box upon box of brand-new books in her attic, each one inscribed on the crisp front page in her neat script with "Edna McDaniel" and the date the book was purchased. I knew she'd joined a book-of-the-month club after my father died, but talking to her, I realized she didn't understand that she could have chosen one or two books, not the entire monthly selection. What I couldn't reconcile when I saw so many boxes filling her attic was the fact that my entire childhood she'd refused to allow my father or me to buy books.

As if the nurses and doctors could actually hear what I was thinking, I stood up and closed the door, then leaned back against it, closing my eyes. Why did I think her behavior would change at this point in her life? Trying to please her was just setting myself up for constant disappointment, and she would only become more unreasonable as the cancer wreaked havoc on her body. The only way she could deal with her own fear of death was to lash out at the world, and I'd always been the nearest punching bag. I was the one who had to change my expectations. I would continue to take care of her, but I would no longer take her criticisms personally. I wasn't the bad person she insisted I was.

Letting this realization spread through my body, I stood there until Edna was wheeled back into the room, her arms bruised and bandaged from so many transfusions.

|||||||||||

I RETURNED to work in late July, assigned to a lighter workload. I worried about what I was facing, considering that Rodney and the union man had been given a three-day suspension without pay for the tire hold the three of us had been blamed for in February. As I'd relayed to the EEOC officer, that last day I worked before taking a week off for Edna's testing, we'd supposedly scrapped four hundred tires.

At the time that tire hold occurred, a lot of blame had been going around—there'd been more than one hundred holds the previous year, including large batches of tires with upside-down sidewalls or the wrong tread getting out the door. Most of the time, the problem is discovered after the tires have been released; other times, if the problem is caught early enough, a change in code during the processing can correct the situation, particularly if it's something simple like the incorrect serial number. If not, a knife is stuck in the tire and it becomes scrap. Those tires are then displayed on a flat with a large sign indicating the problem and serving as a warning not to make the same mistake.

I was told the day I returned in February that the plant manager was deciding what course of disciplinary action to take. Every day after that, before I was actually suspended, one of my supervisors, a short, overweight man named David, told me in one form or fashion that I'd probably be suspended without pay. He'd play out different possible punishments until I'd say, "You really need a procedure in place when these things occur. That way you treat everybody the same." I was unaware of anyone being suspended for a tire hold, and I'd ask him why others hadn't been punished in this manner, citing the specific tire holds we all knew about at the plant. "I'm sorry, Lilly," he said in a not-so-sorry tone. "You're right. We don't have a consistent disciplinary program for salaried people."

Preparing for my first day back in July, I knew something was up when David instructed me to come in at 7:00 A.M. rather than at 6:00, when the regular managers' meeting was held after the night shift. I attended that 6:00 meeting anyway. No one looked at me or talked to me. It seemed strange that one of the other technology engineers, who worked an opposite shift, was there. David directed me to his office afterward.

"I really apologize," he said. "I know you've been through a lot, and I hate to do this, but I must suspend you for three days without pay."

I couldn't get away from the stigma of a mistake that I wasn't convinced I was responsible for, and I now understood that he'd wanted to tell me about my suspension after the meeting and send me home then. He didn't want me at the meeting because my replacement was already there. I imagine he'd also planned to announce my unpaid layoff as a warning to the others.

David slid a piece of paper across the desk at me.

"What's this?"

"It indicates we've had this discussion. I need you to sign your name at the bottom."

Nothing was written on it. I could tell he wasn't going to let me go until I signed the paper, which I did.

After the meeting, I walked past a straggling group of managers getting ready for the day shift. I held my head high and didn't answer the questions they threw my way: Where are you going? Aren't you supposed to be working? Who've you pissed off now? When I passed the guards, one of them asked me, "Wait, didn't you just go in? Why are you leaving now?" I was humiliated.

I took the unpaid three-day suspension and filed an incident report with the EEOC.

ONLY A short time later, in mid-August, while I was still on light work duty, one of my supervisors said, "If you don't return to your regular job, I won't have anything for you." Not long after his warning, an e-mail popped up in my in-box saying that four technology engineer positions were being eliminated and encouraging all employees to take an early buyout effective November 1. Rereading the e-mail, I had to ask myself what was stopping me from retiring. Clicking it closed, I stretched out my stiff knee underneath the desk. Fear, of course. If I stayed for twenty years until my retirement date, February 1 of the following year, I'd receive a higher compensation and would be eligible for Social Security. That way I could knock down some of my debt faster. I had been with the company nineteen years and ten months. Couldn't I just hang on three short months from the early buyout offer until February? I wished I hadn't been moved; if I'd stayed where I was as an area manager in the tire-building room, I wouldn't have to consider this possibility. Those jobs weren't being cut.

And how was it that I was facing the loss of my mother better than letting go of Goodyear? Maybe because I couldn't control her cancer, and I'd come to terms with the fact that I'd never fulfill her demands. Since I'd found the note, it was clear that I'd never been accepted at Goodyear either, so the only way I could really win was to take control of the rest of my life. If I didn't let go, the ways things seemed to be going, I'd get laid off or fired and lose what little I had accumulated in retirement. The truth was, I couldn't hold that tiger by the tail any longer.

For two years, everywhere I turned, I'd felt pressured to leave Goodyear. Determined to keep going, I ignored my doctor and Charles when they expressed their concerns about my physical health. Just as Edna refused to see that she was dying, I was not able to accept that my career was over. When I found the note showing that my salary was so much lower than that of my male counterparts, I finally understood that I had no choice but to leave. They'd finally gotten to me, but not in the way they'd intended.

The only thing they left me after they pushed me out was an anger as invasive as the cancer I watched destroy my mother's life, 80 percent of my salary, and a crystal clock with an emerald winged foot set with my service time: nineteen years.

||||||||||||

Once I put in my retirement notice, I was given the assignment of training the two men replacing me. I had worked twelve days straight and had taken a day off, planning to work another twelve days before my last day in October, when Edna became critically ill with more tumors and fluid in her lungs. She spent the rest of the month in the hospital, so I used my vacation to be with her. By the end of October, although Edna wanted to start new treatments, there was nothing else the doctors could do for her. All that was left was to make her as comfortable as possible, and I moved her into a nursing home.

On the first day of my retirement, I sat alone with Edna in her room, bare except for the two-foot card some union guys had sent her several months earlier, addressed to "the cakemaker," standing open on the table. I sipped my cold coffee, the lipstick that had stained the edge of the Styrofoam cup now worn off my chapped lips. I didn't care if the coffee was cold. I wasn't leaving Edna's bedside. I'd stayed with her around the clock, sleeping in the chair. She had barely opened her eyes for days, and if she spoke, it was only to call me "Mama."

I scooted my chair close to her and rested her small hand in mine, amazed at how light it felt. It shook a little, her skin brushing mine as lightly as the fluttering of a butterfly's wing. With my other hand I smoothed the hair above her forehead like I used to do to Vickie when she was sleeping. I was amazed that Edna's expression seemed so sweet and was reminded of when I was a child and she would wrap my feet with blankets warmed by the stove. How I would long for her to stay on my bed and talk to me. She didn't linger once her job was done. During my entire life, I'd waited for her in those quiet moments before bed or the unsure seconds before I stepped on the school bus to tell me, "I love you." But something about me must have disappointed her so deeply, she couldn't bring herself to say those three simple words.

Lost in my thoughts and memories, it took me a minute to feel the stillness in my hand. I leaned toward Edna's face to listen closely. Her rattled breath was quiet. I sat, afraid to let go, afraid to shatter the stillness with the inevitable, numbing details of practical action, my sadness deepened by my shame: Not once had I ever told her that I loved her, either.

CHAPTER 8

Protecting My Good Name

||||||||||||||||||||||||||||||||||||||||||||||||||||||||||||||||||||||||||||||||||||||||||||||||||||||||||||||||||||||||||||||||||||||||||

Protect Our Good Name.

—Goodyear motto

S OON AFTER I took the early buyout October, 31, 1998, I was contacted by a Goodyear attorney. The company was offering me a small sum of money to settle the EEOC complaint I had filed. It seemed that the constant upheaval in my life would never end, and I was ready to put the past couple of years behind me—finding the note and filing the complaint, undergoing knee surgery, nursing Edna, being told my position was being eliminated, and coming to terms with retiring early had added up to a never-ending ordeal. Glad about the idea of moving on and eager to focus on Charles and my grandchildren, I made a counteroffer, agreeing to accept two years' back pay as the next-lowest-paid person in the department. I never received a response from Goodyear.

Shortly afterward, in October 1999, I was issued the right to sue by the EEOC for the claim I'd made the year before. I lost no time contacting a young attorney I'd heard about, Jon Goldfarb, who'd been practicing for seven years, specializing in employment discrimination. The word was that he took pro bono cases, and I was hopeful he'd represent me.

We met at his office in Birmingham. As I told my story, he listened, taking notes, stopping me to ask questions, sometimes asking me to repeat an incident, his dark brown eyes flashing with a hint of anger. Jon didn't mince words, and he immediately gave me a feeling of confidence. Though he had a natural sense of authority, it was the intensity in his eyes that assured me I'd found the right person to argue my case, to stand up for what was right.

To my great relief Jon agreed to take my case that very day. Sometimes I wonder if he would have made the same decision if he'd known what the process would entail and the ultimate outcome. By the end of the trial, if all of the documents were vertically stacked, they would create a fifty-foot tower, tall as a three-story building. To make matters more challenging, this process involved twentieth-century technology—briefs, complaints, and appeals were either faxed, mailed, or hand-delivered. Today everything is filed electronically.

The time between the filing of the lawsuit on November 24, 1999, and the actual trial on January 21, 2003, was more than three years of my life. I can't tell you how many miles I drove on the road to and from Birmingham, skirting strips of blown-out tires (known as "gators") littering the highway, fighting construction delays, and avoiding wrecks. By the time of the trial, Jon, who had only two children when I met him, would be a father of four.

The number of hours and days translated into over half a million dollars in the law firm's time and out-of-pocket expenses. I depleted our 401(k) account just to make ends meet. Charles assured me that we'd started out with nothing and survived, and if we ended up with nothing in order to fight this battle, well then, we'd take care of ourselves one way or another. Even though I'd worked my entire life, motivated by fear, ambition, love for my family, and a desire to keep from slipping back into poverty, when you've lived with cracks between the floorboards so large a cat could fit through them, it's not so scary to imagine being destitute. And I would rather be financially devastated than live the rest of my life feeling victimized.

I'm not sure how to calculate the emotional toll suing a multibillion-dollar corporation takes. From the day I filed the lawsuit, I opened my eyes every morning to the knowledge that I had no control over the outcome, and it's what gnawed at me until I closed my eyes at night.

I struggled to relax, to breathe deeply. I was imprisoned by each long moment leading to the trial; I wanted to fast-forward time, to wake up the day after the trial. But I had to force myself not to become lost in my musings about a future I couldn't predict. I focused on what I could control: my preparation.

My greatest joy came from spending time with Charles. For the first time since we'd been married and had children, Charles and I were at home together. He puttered around in his workshop making elaborate, whimsical birdhouses, battling the squirrels as he tested out different bird feeders, filling them till they brimmed over with the gourmet birdseed he liked to buy. I'd hear him in the living room calling my name, as urgent and persistent as a fire alarm. I'd run to see what the emergency was, and there he'd be looking through the window, muttering as a crafty squirrel swung on top of the bird feeder he'd thought for sure was squirrel-proof. They thwarted his best efforts each time. Often, I'd go bargain hunting when he was gardening. While I watched TV, he read biographies about men such as Ted Turner, Billy Graham, and Bear Bryant. He went through every book in the *Left Behind* series.

Many nights we watched his favorite show, *Law & Order*, but we had no idea how justice unfolded in real life. I could not even begin to comprehend the depth and breadth of what a lawsuit actually involved, and how hard it would be, even under the best of circumstances, to prove my case. Suing Goodyear was like giving birth: There's no way to know what it feels like until you're smack-dab in the middle of pushing that baby into the world. I soon became familiar with legal terms and phrases, most of which I'd heard on TV: depositions, affidavits, subpoenas, exhibits, briefs, mediation, witness lists, exhibit lists. Many I'd never heard, such as Motions to Compel, Summary Judgments, cat's paw,* and quid pro quo harassment. The list seemed endless.

Goodyear stalled, of course, at every possible turn, refusing to deliver documents. They stalled so handily that in the fall of 2000, after months of preparation and multiple requests for employee records and other key documentation, Jon was forced to file a Motion to Compel, asking the court to order Goodyear to produce the information it had refused to turn over to him, such as the rates of pay of my male coworkers. Thankfully, the court granted the motion and ordered Goodyear to produce the requested information.

To see the real pay disparity there on paper and to see how cheap I was compared to my male coworkers made me realize that I must have been just a joke to Goodyear's human resources department. Seeing the difference in front of me confirming what I'd long suspected hurt more than my wondering thoughts. It was clear that Goodyear didn't play fair, never had, and never would as far as I was concerned; this, along with my painful memories, fired me up even more during this long phase of preparation.

To PREPARE for my deposition, I'd spent numerous hours discussing with Jon what had happened and when. A deposition, Jon explained, is like your life in a book in the most negative light. Goodyear's lawyer would ask me the most minute details from

---

*The theory of employer liability under which employers are liable for discrimination where lower-level supervisors with discriminatory motives influence adverse employment decisions made by higher-level managers, thereby greatly increasing employer accountability for the actions and recommendations of lower-level supervisors.

every phase of my career at Goodyear, knowing how easy it could be to confuse me when I was trying to remember and recount events and conversations that happened long ago.

I was nervous before the day I was to be deposed, but I was willing to walk through fire and brimstone to do what I needed to do, and I didn't throw up like Jon had warned me many people do.

My deposition was a ten-hour ordeal.

The defense attorney who took the deposition was a seasoned corporate defense litigator from the law firm Bradley Arant Rose & White. At first Jay St. Clair, a middle-aged man dressed in a perfectly tailored suit, asked basic questions. He joked a little with me about football and seemed like a regular guy. But as the day wore on, he started picking apart my answers in an increasingly insinuating tone. The last several hours, he'd repeat the same questions over and over again, his open, friendly manner replaced by rapid-fire questioning.

My head spinning and my heart beating so fast I felt nauseous, I knew what he was doing. He was trying to beat me down, confuse me, make me stumble and trap myself in a web of words. I stuck to the truth. I sweated so much that day that even the dry cleaner couldn't eliminate the dark crescent stains of nervous perspiration in the armpits of my jacket. I never wore that blue suit again.

After my own deposition, I attended every deposition of the Goodyear men, about ten all together. I sat across the table, stiff, my emotions glazed, listening to their defensive account of our working life at Goodyear. One plant manager got so mad, ranting and raving at Jon, that he had to be excused, his attorney claiming that his heart wouldn't be able to stand the stress of a trial. His outburst didn't surprise me one bit; this time he couldn't intimidate me, and he acted out with impotent rage when he lost control of the situation.

After another deposition, from a former plant manager who

had been vicious toward me for a long time, the man shook my hand and said, "I'm sorry. I hope it goes well, and I do hope you get what you deserve." I was shocked by this unexpected change of heart. He'd retired by then. Maybe being away from the performance pressure and outside the internal politics of the plant had given him a different perspective.

WHEN JON filed my complaint, the four counts in my claim fell under three separate laws: the Equal Pay Act, Title VII of the Civil Rights Act of 1964, and the Age Discrimination in Employment Act.

The first count came under the Equal Pay Act of 1963,* which makes it illegal to pay men and women different wages for equal work on jobs that require equal skill, effort, and responsibility and are performed under similar working conditions. My suit contended that I was "similarly situated" (that is, I had similar qualifications, experience, and tenure with Goodyear) and was doing the same work as my male coworkers but was paid less. After my transfer to the technology engineer position, I was again paid a lower rate than the other, male technical engineers in a "willful and malicious" (acting with full knowledge of the consequences of the action) manner because of my sex.

Under this act, if I'd only experienced pay discrimination, I could have hired an attorney and filed a lawsuit two years from the day I received my last discriminatory paycheck, skipping the step of filing an EEOC charge to obtain a "right to sue" notice.

But the Equal Pay Act (EPA) only ensures that employers can't deny equal pay for equal work, while Title VII encompasses sex discrimination more broadly to ensure that employers can't deny women transfers, promotions, or raises; manipulate evaluations to

---

*Equal Pay Act: http://www.eeoc.gov/policy/epa.html.

reduce pay; or segregate employees according to their gender. All of these situations I'd encountered, so under Title VII, I was required by law to start the legal proceedings through the EEOC office.

Count two, which claimed "disparate treatment," fell under Title VII of the Civil Rights Act.* I was discriminated against in wages. I performed work "equal or substantially equal" to that of the male area managers but received less pay for a "substantially similar" job. Despite my expressed interest in overtime, I was offered overtime last, only after the other, male managers had been offered it. I was also discriminated against in evaluation and terms and conditions of employment, in which I received a low score while men performing the same job in the same manner received a higher score; I was excluded from meetings and involuntarily transferred from a supervisory position, which reduced my pay and benefits. Out of the sixteen managers, I was the only area manager transferred, and the position I vacated was filled by a man. Once I left as a supervisor, there were no other women in management. Despite receiving no training, procedure manual, or job description, I did my job, a grueling assignment. I was also suspended for supposedly making an error, while men who had made similar mistakes had not been.

Also part of Title VII is the provision known as the Paycheck Accrual Act, which defines the starting point for discriminatory behavior as the last discriminatory paycheck issued. In other words, each new paycheck is a new starting point for the discriminatory act. This provision would become an important element of my case as it progressed.

Count three came under the Age Discrimination in Employment Act[†] and also claimed disparate treatment. I was discriminated

---

*Title VII: http://www.eeoc.gov/laws/statues/titlevii.cfm.

[†]Age Discrimination in Employment Act: http://www.eeoc.gov/laws/statutes/adea.cfm.

against because of my age by being transferred and replaced by a younger coworker. A male in his twenties filled this vacant position. Significantly younger, male area managers made substantially higher salaries for equal work. At the time these events occurred, I was over the age of forty, the oldest manager. After complaining to my supervisor about being discriminated against, I was instructed that it was in my own best interest to accept the transfer. I was further retaliated against when I applied to be rehired and was told that Goodyear was not rehiring, when in fact five area-manager positions were available and one person was rehired.

Because my work environment was hostile and abusive, we decided to file a constructive-discharge complaint under Title VII as count four, which meant that the intolerable working conditions I experienced as a technology engineer were intended to force me to quit. The environment was so hostile and abusive that I suffered depression and underwent medical treatment. Eventually, the conditions of being a technology engineer and the unwarranted discipline forced me to resign against my will.

I belabor these dry, often tedious points because the judicial process would become for me a quagmire of interpreting and reinterpreting the intricacies of these laws. It's also important to note the ripple effect sex discrimination had on my career and the devastating consequences for my income and quality of life. Goodyear effectively relegated me to being a second-class citizen for the rest of my life.

AFTER DISCOVERY ended, Goodyear filed a Motion for Summary Judgment to dismiss the lawsuit on all claims; this, Jon assured me, was typical in discrimination cases. Our case was before a magistrate judge, John Ott. Judge Ott issued a Report and Recommendation that recommended granting Summary Judgment on all claims except the three-day suspension for the tire hold. He reasoned that on this claim I'd offered sufficient evidence by citing several incidents in which other employees who were responsible for tire holds weren't suspended as I was. We appealed the rest of his ruling to an Article III judge and caught our first break.

Judge U. W. Clemon was Alabama's first African American federal judge and had a long history as a civil rights activist. He was randomly selected to review the magistrate judge's report and try the case. On July 31, 2002, Judge Clemon upheld some of our objections to Judge Ott's Report and Recommendation. He kept the Title VII discriminatory pay claim that I was discriminated against for being a woman, the age discrimination claim, the retaliatory refusal to rehire claim, and the unfair suspension claim. He agreed with the magistrate judge's recommendation to throw out the retaliatory evaluation and transfer claim, the constructive discharge claim, the lack-of-training claim, and the pay-discrimination claim falling under the Equal Pay Act. Later, after all was said and done, there would be criticism that this case wasn't handled properly because the pay claim under the Equal Pay Act wasn't included. Judge Clemon upheld Judge Ott's ruling to throw it out, but we had a pay claim under Title VII that allowed us to move forward.

The trial date was set for January 21, 2003, Jon's thirty-ninth birthday, and after his fourth child's due date.

The majority of cases like mine settle out of court, a situation that can occur at any point in the process. Three weeks before the trial date, we met with the Goodyear attorney, Jay St. Clair, to mediate the case. Fern Singer, a well-known employment attorney who'd mediated hundreds of cases, attempted to mediate a negotiated settlement. To no avail.

Goodyear offered what my counsel deemed an insufficient amount. They also offered to rehire me two days a week for two years, working with a human resources manager named Thomas they knew I liked. I suspected those two days would amount to my sweeping lampblack in the mill room on Saturday and Sunday.

I also knew that Thomas was due for a transfer, which happened shortly after the mediation.

At one point during our preparation for the mediation, Fern commented, "The law is frequently an ass." I didn't quite know what she meant, but I assure you, by the time I reached the end of this long road, I understood it well. All I knew after the mediation was that I wanted what I'd already earned, not the pittance they'd offered.

BY THE time the trial rolled around, I'd called more than one hundred people to ask them to testify on my behalf. Mostly I was turned down. The reasons varied: They couldn't afford to lose their jobs, they wanted to avoid controversy, they were afraid of placing themselves and their families at risk in a town where Goodyear was the nerve center. We scrounged up four witnesses: Sharon; Rodney; Karen, a former manager; and Joe, a union pipefitter. All but Karen still worked at the plant, so they were taking a huge personal risk by testifying, and I knew way back then I couldn't ever repay them for their commitment to this case. I worried after they testified they'd all be forced to quit, but that didn't stop them from agreeing. There was no hesitation on their part, no abrupt no, no hanging up in my face, no "I'll think about it."

Jon's task was to prove through both direct and circumstantial evidence that my claims were true. Direct evidence could be documents, what people said, actual salary differences; circumstantial evidence required the jurors to infer that something was indeed a fact, and usually required eliminating all other possible explanations of the question: Why was I, one of the only female managers in Goodyear's history with hundreds of male employees, making so much less?

Jon figured that Goodyear would argue that I was making less because I was a poor performer. On this issue we had the burden of proof; we had to show that I was discriminated against through the evidence we gathered in discovery.

For several weeks before the trial, I spent every day with Jon at his office preparing. He explained in great detail the significance of each exhibit and made sure I understood the legal language pertaining to the damages. We would run through the witness list discussing who might say what. We practiced what it would be like when I was on the witness stand by rehearsing questions he would ask me as well as what the defense could throw at me. "Stick to the truth," he reminded me, "and you'll do fine."

But many nights before the trial I stayed awake worrying. If I lost in court, I had no idea whether or not Goodyear could hold me accountable for the cost of litigation. I was scared we'd lose our house, and the fear inside me sat heavy and thick. During those sleepless nights, Charles would hear me rustling around in the den, flipping channels. He'd come in and sit next to me on the sofa. He'd wrap his arm around me, asking, "Are you sure you know what you're doing?"

I'd involuntarily pull away from him. I'm not much of a physically affectionate person to begin with, but when I'm agitated—the reason I was up in the middle of the night in the first place was that I'd gotten us into such a mess—I need some breathing room. "No. I have no idea what I've gotten myself into."

He'd move back next to me, ignoring the careful distance I tried to maintain between myself and the world. "You don't have to go through all of this."

"We're too far into it, and too many people are counting on us. I have to go through with it. I can't let it go. We can't let people do me, do us, like that." I kept clicking the TV remote held rigidly in front of me as I searched for something to distract me in the flickering light of late-night TV.

Charles would get up and fix his bowl of Frosted Flakes, and we'd switch between the two shopping channels until we went back to bed. I can't imagine another man in the world who would have stood by me like Charles did.

THE DAY of the trial was finally upon us. How would my experience at Goodyear be summarized in a few days in the courtroom? It seemed as impossible as squeezing someone's life into a newspaper snippet on the obituary page. The night before the trial, I prayed and reviewed my five-hundred-page deposition. All that mattered, I reminded myself, was what I knew in my heart was true—what was right. I remembered what I had been through. I knew that whatever would happen in court would be nothing like what I'd dealt with before.

That morning I dressed in black slacks and a blue shirt as if I was going to work, with the one addition of a black jacket, in deference to Jon's request that I dress up. Jon wanted me to wear a skirt and heels to trial, but I dressed like I did every day as an area manager in the tire room. I always wore black pants, to hide the grease stains, and on most days, a blue shirt. During the trial, I wasn't trying to be someone else. I was simply trying to get back what I'd rightfully earned doing the job I'd been hired to do.

ON A bitterly cold January 21, 2003, after we drank an entire pot of coffee, Charles and I drove to the Anniston courthouse.

After parking in front of the two-story stone-and-brick courthouse on Noble Street, Charles paused inside the car a minute, letting the engine run, the heat still blowing on us.

He turned to me. "Well, this is it. This is what we've been working toward for a long time."

I nodded and rubbed my hands together. "It's here now," I said, putting on my warm gloves. The courthouse's white Corinthian columns loomed before us.

He leaned over and kissed my forehead, then turned off the engine and gave me a quick pat on the back.

"It's time to see how it goes." He opened his door, and a blast of cold air smelling like the car's exhaust fumes enveloped us.

When Charles and I went inside the courtroom, we sat on the benches behind the table where Jon was sitting; the sleekly dressed defense attorneys, Jay St. Clair and Ronald Kent, had staked out the table next to the jury box. Suited for battle, his leather shoes shining, Mr. St. Clair looked through his notes. Mr. Kent, a young, clean-cut man, chatted with the human resources manager at Goodyear, a man I liked and got along with, who sat between them at their table.

Earlier, Jon had wheeled in several flimsy brown boxes spilling over with documents. They looked a bit tattered. He had also arranged several large charts near the shaky easel. I hoped it wouldn't topple over in the small courtroom. To our relief, Jon's partner Mike Quinn showed up at the very last minute.

One thing we had going for us was the fact that Jon and Mike made such a good team; they complemented each other well. A short man in his sixties, Mike was a veteran attorney with an open manner. He spoke with extraordinary ease, and I got the impression that, as gregarious as he was, he was comfortable talking to people from all walks of life. He seemed like he would be as much at home shooting the breeze with a neighbor on the front porch as he would dealing with corporate heads in the boardroom. Jon was more reserved, and the most driven, hardworking individual I'd ever met. He was relentless in his focus and pursuit of justice. If anybody could win this case, I believed it was Jon, though he was worried that the jury wouldn't take too kindly to a Jewish lawyer— in the heart of a rural county he could be seen as just another liberal do-gooder from out of town telling the locals how to run their business.

Before jury selection, Judge Clemon urged Mr. St. Clair and Mr. Kent to settle the case. They made an offer, but it was too low.

Once the jury selection began, men and women from the surrounding counties filed into the courtroom. One woman who was around my age looked like she could be my sister—the defense eventually eliminated her as one of their three strikes. The group was asked questions you would expect—whether anyone knew me or my family or had worked at Goodyear. Then the questions ranged from what their favorite TV shows were to whether they owned businesses, held management positions, and believed men should be paid more than women. An hour later a jury of seven was struck. The course of the remaining years of my life rested in the hands of seven strangers. Jury duty was probably the last thing in the world they wanted to do. Until now I'd always viewed it as an inconvenience. Never again.

Trying not to stare at them, I wondered what opinions they'd already formed of me, of Jon and Mike, of the Goodyear team. At first glance, I was most intrigued by the young man in his forties who was a nurse. I wondered if the young, heavyset woman and the middle-aged working woman—the only two women in the group—had had any experiences similar to mine. An older man who'd retired recently from a paper company looked like he could have been buddies with some of the Goodyear men outside in the hallway. There was no way to know how and what they might think and feel about me or my testimony.

ONCE THE jury settled into the jury box, I was called as the first witness. Stepping onto the stand, I faced Mr. St. Clair and his team on my immediate left. I was as far away as I could be from Jon and Mike. The empty balcony across from me, the high vaulted ceilings, and the wood paneling reminded me of the courtroom in the movie *To Kill a Mockingbird*. A lot had changed in the South since 1936, when that story took place; this time it was the judge, not the defendant, who was an African American. We would soon find out whether attitudes about women had changed significantly in north Alabama.

Opening first, Jon stood before me to begin his questioning. For a brief moment, I was flooded with a terrible foreboding, the sense that I'd made an awful mistake, done something foolish like lighting a cigarette next to a gas pump. Once Jon started asking me questions, my sense of doom slowly lifted. I kept my gaze steady on him pacing the room, every once in a while running his hand over the top of his cropped hair when he paused, thinking, before another question. Anchored by his confidence and determination, I answered him.

Jon first asked me to discuss the progression of positions I'd held throughout my career in general and at Goodyear. In the course of this description, he established that I was a high achiever, noting the objective ranking as the second-highest out of almost one hundred employees who'd taken an electrical and mechanical test in 1985 when the scope of the area manager's duties broadened at the plant. He also wanted to know about the end of my career when I was supervised by the plant manager who had said the plant didn't need women because we caused problems.

He let those words linger for a moment before he asked if anything else was said. Mr. St. Clair, who throughout the trial would jump up unexpectedly like a jack-in-the-box to object, made his first objection but was overruled.

"One of my former bosses who had been a business-center manager told me that he asked Eddie, 'When are you going to get rid of the drunk and that damn woman?'" I answered.

After Jon asked how many other women managers were at Goodyear when I was working at the end—I knew of none—he offered as his first exhibit a pay chart for my beginning salary; it showed my salary along with those of the five men I started with in 1979. Mr. St. Clair tried to object, stating that the pay chart wasn't relevant because those salary decisions were made so long ago, but again he was overruled. Jon stood next to the chart, blown up so everyone could see the numbers, while the jury was given a sheet of paper with the same information.

As the chart indicated, we'd all made the same amount on April 1, 1979, and continued to earn the same salaries, $18,216.96, a few months later in October, after we'd all received a raise.

Jon continued to ask me questions about my experiences over nineteen years at Goodyear. He showed that when I complained at the end of my career about the memo addressed to "Boys," it was shortly afterward that I was told that I needed to apply for the technology engineer opening. After I was transferred to technology engineer, I was replaced by a young man who was promoted from being a union tire builder. The exhibit Jon offered outlined the difference in our pay.

This young man, still in his twenties, had started in 1994, and less than ten years later his salary was almost double mine, at over $81,000; after almost twenty years, when I retired, I was making $44,724.

Jon wound down his direct examination, asking me how it felt to be paid less, to be punished for the tire hold, to be transferred to a physically grueling job. He ended his questioning by inquiring whether I'd gone over the back-pay calculations with the paralegal, comparing my salary with that of the other folks I worked with. I had.

"Who was ranked lower than you on many occasions?"

"Matt Brown." He'd been hired at the same time I was, and though he was ranked lower, he was paid significantly more.

AT THE end of Jon's questioning, I wondered how in the world the jury could keep up with all of the information. We had jumped from one department to another and one manager to another, skipping all over the place. The pieces of this puzzle seemed too hard to fit together, but I knew Jon had to cover all areas of evidence supporting our position. I hoped the jurors could make the right connections because I could barely sort through it all, and I was the one who'd lived it.

Then Mr. St. Clair stood up and walked toward me smiling. I took a deep breath.

He began by asking me if I was as qualified as a man who had been called back as an area manager after the 1998 buyout.

He was trying to get me to say I was as qualified so he could prove all the ways I wasn't. "I could do my job," I answered.

Then he asked me to define a tire hold and asked didn't I scrap $10,000 worth of tires?

He wanted yes or no answers, so I could not offer an explanation to establish the context of the situation. I felt like I was playing a game of dodge, not dodging the truth but avoiding setting myself up for him to distort my truth. "I don't know. I didn't see the tires. I didn't see the paperwork. They didn't show them to me."

"You don't deny that?"

"I can't admit to it, because I didn't see the paperwork. See, that's what scared me so much. You know, when we had—when I had builders that had scrap, especially if it was ten thousand dollars' worth—even if it was two tires, four hundred dollars' worth—I'd carry them out on the dock or carry them to shipping, we would examine them, see why it's scrap and what we need to do to correct it."

Next he jumped to my transfer: Weren't you told you were on a long list of layoffs? The implication being that I was lucky to be transferred at all.

I replied, "I didn't hear 'long list.'"

In an exaggerated, indignant voice, he picked up my deposition. "Don't you remember I took your deposition?" He flipped to a page. "And do you recall you were placed under oath?"

"Yes, sir."

He turned to a page and made me read out loud what I'd said, which was that I was on a long list of layoffs in 1997. But that's not what he'd asked me. He'd asked me whether I'd been told by Eddie that I was on a long list. I hadn't been told that in those exact words. He was playing games, twisting things just enough to make it so confusing that I looked like I was lying. He did this the entire time. He wanted the jury to think I was making things up. When he berated me so intensely about the details of the 1986 and 1997 layoffs, Judge Clemon finally said, "Are you about finished along this line?"

By the end of the first day, I was ready to step off the stand. Before I could help myself, I'd gotten testy with Mr. St. Clair too many times. It was hard to tell from anyone's expressions how things were going. Charles and Phillip sat behind Jon and Mike (Vickie would come the next day), but they didn't register much emotion as we all endured the punishing atmosphere of that initial day in court.

That night when Charles and I walked into the kitchen after a long, quiet ride home, I flipped on the light, glancing at the clock. It was time for our show to come on.

"Hey, *Law & Order* is on tonight," I automatically reminded him like I always did.

He gave me a halfhearted smile. "No, thanks. I've had enough of courtroom drama for one day, thank you very much."

Unable to go to bed right away, we watched an old dance video instead.

THE FIRST thing the next morning I returned to the stand and that sly Mr. St. Clair focused immediately on the tire hold again.

"You admit to making an error in regards to the tire hold, don't you, Mrs. Ledbetter?"

The words stumbled from my mouth as I tried to make him understand my point: When I said that I couldn't answer, my words were based on what I was told, not on what I believed I had done. Judge Clemon stopped me with a simple "All right." I looked over at Charles. His expression didn't change, but he gave me a slight nod as if to reassure me and encourage me to stay strong. I recrossed my legs to regain my composure.

Mr. St. Clair moved on, referring to Eddie. "You can't say he didn't like you because of what happened twenty years ago—he sent you a nice note in 1992, didn't he?" he asked. Yes, it was a congratulatory note. Then in a tone one uses when trying to explain a very simple idea to a confused child, Mr. St. Clair continued his questioning, implying that in 1997, when Eddie could have laid me off, in a magnanimous gesture he transferred me to the technology engineer position. In other words, this generous, kind man was really looking out for my best interests, and I was too dumb to see it.

"Many people think this technology engineer job is a good job, don't they? Now, I know you said that you didn't think it was a good job, but that's not what everyone in the plant thought, was it?" he continued. "There were people who wanted those jobs." He picked up my deposition as if brandishing a weapon. He plucked a single line from the impossibly thick book and read my observation to the jury that one man thought my job as technology engineer was better than his job working in the pits; he'd remarked to me one day that it was a great injustice to him that I had gotten the position.

I was getting aggravated again. "I don't think so. I think he's the only one."

He wielded my deposition again. "Look with me, please, ma'am, at page 243 of your deposition." He stopped to remind the jury that I had said these words "under oath" before he read that I said that a lot of people who had harder jobs in that department viewed the position I had as better; it was a promotion in their eyes, not a demotion as it had been for me.

Satisfied with his point, he turned to the pay chart and started nitpicking about the fact that all the men with higher salaries did not start at the exact same time I did, as I'd said. He showed their employee records and their start dates. What he was saying didn't make sense, though. These men all started in management around the same time I did. He was going to ridiculous means to prove that my claims were not based in the truth. And the truth, I worried, was only what the defense attorneys, as charming as snake-oil salesmen, convinced the jury to believe.

During Mr. St. Clair's harangue about the exact start dates, Judge Clemon finally interrupted to ask, "Isn't the relevant history when they were hired in the supervisory position?"

So Mr. St. Clair switched his focus to the year 1981, when Goodyear implemented a merit-based program to replace the cost-of-living raises they'd given in prior years. I didn't know it at the time, but it was only after this program was implemented that my pay and that of the other managers began to diverge. But now, through the discovery process, I'd seen my peers' raises and compared them with mine.

Mr. St. Clair proceeded to explain each of my raises over the years, trying to show there wasn't any discrimination involved, but I disputed his conclusion each time. I knew, in doing so, that I was being combative and probably alienating the jury, but I was compelled to correct his distortion.

Skipping to the 1998 EEOC complaint, he inquired why nothing about Jeff's sexual harassment was included, insisting that the current lawsuit was the first time I'd mentioned Jeff's renewed harassment.

"And do you know why Jeff wasn't in court today?" he asked.

I knew.

"And why can't he be here?" he said slowly, as if I had done something to prevent him from appearing.

"He died of lung cancer."

"That's all I have."

He was clearly trying to make it look like I fabricated this harassment charge because Jeff wasn't there to defend himself. What he failed to inform the jury was that Jeff had died shortly before the trial; Goodyear had had plenty of time to take his deposition but chose not to.

MR. ST. Clair's examination had opened the door for Jon to address the details surrounding my 1982 EEOC complaint. The defense attorney had let his guard down, and all the information blacked out on that 1982 EEOC exhibit now came to light. In Jon's short redirect he explained the reasons for the EEOC charge and why, fearing repercussions, I didn't go into detail about Jeff's recent misbehavior in 1996. He recounted Dennis's behavior and Jeff's poor evaluation of me when I wouldn't go to the Ramada Inn with him. Even though it had happened a long time earlier, hearing Jon describe it made me feel as if it had just happened.

Jon entered the initial EEOC complaint as an exhibit and pointed out how my raises before the 1982 complaint were higher than any other raises I received in my Goodyear career. He also clarified what Mr. St. Clair had tried to distort: that the Top Performance Award was, according to the employee handbook, an award, not just a raise. Goodyear couldn't justify its position that I was such a poor performer, since I'd received this award. I wondered if they would call my former workers to the stand to claim that I was a bad manager.

MIKE QUINN called Dr. Judy Cook to testify on my behalf. I was used to seeing Dr. Cook in one setting, her small office, and here, a short, older woman, she looked out of place. When she addressed the stigma often attached to seeking psychological counsel, I felt the stigma, all right. I stared straight ahead, embarrassed when she said she'd diagnosed me with depression and prescribed medication for it.

Dr. Cook indicated how stressed I was from work, that my stress came from working in isolation, from my knee injury, and from my mother's illness and difficult nature. I'd never talked about Edna to anyone but Charles and Dr. Cook. As frustrating as Edna could be, she was still my mother, and it was painful to sit there while a room full of strangers heard about my tangled relationship with her. In the privacy of Dr. Cook's office, the anxieties and fears I'd revealed had seemed contained and examined in a respectful manner. Now they were public record, and I was ashamed.

With Dr. Cook's notes from our counseling sessions in hand, Mr. St. Clair asked her if I'd had a choice about transferring to the technology engineer job.

She said I hadn't.

Hadn't I had headaches all my life, Mr. St. Clair pushed, and been diagnosed with depression before? I guessed he was trying to show through his punishing scrutiny that I was unstable. He must have read in Dr. Cook's notes what I'd told her when she asked about my medical history: that I'd had blinding headaches as a child, and the headaches had cropped up again early in my marriage when Charles and I had struggled to get by, right before I decided to start working again. The only other time I'd taken medication besides the antidepressant Dr. Cook temporarily prescribed me was when I'd been prescribed Prozac in the late eighties after starting back to Goodyear.

Mr. St. Clair did his best to say I'd given conflicting stories to Dr. Cook about my Goodyear history. She shook her head. No, the threads of my story were simply hard to piece together, she said.

That was an understatement.

Referring to the point when I'd started seeing her in the spring of 1998, after being transferred to the technology engineer position, she commented, "I would say that at that point in time, she was so stressed she was a little like a cat that just had its tail stuck in a 220 socket."

Not a real pretty description but, unfortunately, an accurate one, and it explained the reason for the uncontrollable screaming rages that I'd started experiencing my last few years at Goodyear.

But not so, Mr. St. Clair insisted; I was glad to be laid off. He elaborated this point at great length, reading from Dr. Cook's notes about my feelings and struggles with my mother. Listening to this, I wished I'd never gone down this path. During a trial, there's no time to absorb what's happening because the momentum of questioning rushes forward as furiously and inevitably as a swollen river after a hard rain. And I didn't understand what Mr. St. Clair was trying to accomplish—that is, until he asked if all my feelings about Goodyear weren't really just a transference of my feelings about my mother.

Dr. Cook disagreed.

Mr. St. Clair wrapped up with a final grand gesture, directing Dr. Cook to read the last sentence in her notes from my visit following Edna's death—I'd seen her only a few more times after I retired. He handed Dr. Cook the notes she'd typed three years earlier. She took a minute to find the sentence before she read: "She realizes her mother was even harder to please than Goodyear."

KAREN, A woman in her late fifties who'd been hired at Goodyear in 1976, walked toward the stand. She'd worked briefly, from 1993 to 1995, as an area manager at the plant before she left for good. She was now a supervisor at Honda. Her immediate testimony confirmed my similar experience when she explained that her evaluations "stunk." Far from a pushover, Karen had complained about the evaluations but was told, "That's just the way it is."

After the usual drawn-out back and forth at the beginning of each new witness's testimony, Jon asked her what her understanding was concerning why she was graded lower than the men who worked alongside her.

"The way they put it," Karen said, "I was not doing the job

100 percent of what they expected of me. And I was doing my job exactly like everybody else was. I was doing exactly what they told me to do."

"And you were working the same as the men?"

"Yes, sir."

"Did you reach an understanding why your evaluation was lower?"

"It just seemed that the women were, for some reason, rated lower than the men. They didn't think they could do the job that men could do."

After questioning Karen about her last raise, which she was given because her salary was "way below the level she was supposed to be at," Jon produced an exhibit showing her what she'd never seen: her pay in comparison to that of the other, male managers. She made $2,728 a month, while the men's monthly pay ranged from $3,960 to $4,662. I looked at the defense team and jury to measure their expression. It seemed everyone had been schooled in keeping a blank face.

"Did you know they were paid that much more than you?"

"You always hear rumors, and I've heard it out of several people's mouths that they made quite a bit more than I did."

As Jon read out each man's pay in comparison with hers, he asked her what her understanding of this difference was.

Her final conclusion: "Just being a female in a man's world."

"Did you ever complain you were being paid less because of your gender?"

"No, sir, I didn't complain, because I was a single mother with a handicapped child, and I knew my job would be in jeopardy if I started complaining about the pay."

WHEN SHARON testified next, I had a hard time watching. I could tell she was nervous. She'd had a tough time, losing so much weight that she looked downright pitiful; it broke my heart.

Sharon recounted what she'd told me while we'd worked together in the office for a short while. She'd been hired in 1971,
and being a single mother, she had to quit her position as a night
supervisor when the woman who cared for her child died. She
became a supervisor again in the 1990s and was promised a pay
raise. After asking twice about the promised raise, she returned
to being a secretary when she was told again the third time she
inquired that they were still working on it. When she said she was
returning to her job as a secretary, she was informed that the best
that could be done was a 20 percent increase in her salary. Jon also
introduced to the jury the EEOC charge she had recently filed for
pay discrimination.

During Sharon's testimony, she hesitated once or twice, focusing her gaze on the back of the courtroom. She was distracted by
the crowd of Goodyear workers, all men, and many of them my
former coworkers, taking turns peering through the windows of
the courtroom doors. One after another, their faces would appear
in the doorway—reminding me of the circus act where clowns keep
tumbling out of a small car. They also filled the hallway, sitting on
the benches and milling around in groups.

On a break that first day, Sharon had told me what she'd overheard in the hall as she walked past the gang. Apparently, when one
of the guys asked Matt why he was there, he shrugged and grinned
underneath his blond handlebar mustache, saying, "Hell, I don't
know. Goodyear just called and said get your ass dressed and get
down to the courthouse."

When I saw Matt in the hall later, the first thought that came
to my mind was how, during his shift, he used to like to hop
Goodyear's steel fence to go into town and drink at a local restaurant until it was time to hop back over and punch out. On the
weekends, he and some of the guys hunted and fished together in a
club Goodyear sponsored for its employees, so we called them "the
hunting and fishing club." Neither Matt's attitude nor his com-

ment surprised me or Sharon, who knew the club's sorry ways better than anyone.

I figured she was agitated by the fact that she would face these same men at work when the trial ended. I hated to think about the price she'd have to pay for speaking out.

WHEN JON sat down, Mr. St. Clair took immediate aim at Sharon, asking about her lower pay: "What makes you think that had anything to do with the fact that you're a woman?"

Sharon didn't miss a beat. There was no other male area manager who was making the small amount of money she was—her secretary's salary—but her supervisor expected her to accept this pay difference without question.

AFTER LUNCH Mike called to the stand Janet Essix, the paralegal who calculated my back pay, to outline how back pay worked. The back-pay claim fell under the pay-discrimination claim related to the involuntary transfer—we were attempting to determine how much I would have made had I not been transferred and stayed in my position as area manager to that day. Back pay is calculated according to standards created by the National Labor Relations Board, Janet explained. Her calculation reflected my rate of pay from when I retired to the present day, January 21, 2003.

Mike displayed the exhibit, which told the additional amount I would have made had I continued working as an area manager (excluding overtime): $236,791.72.

Mike compared my pay, which according to the law could only be two years prior to when I filed the EEOC charge, which was March 25, 1996, to that of another area manager who was similar in ranking to me, showing on a pay chart the difference between our salaries.

"What is the difference in their pay?" Mike asked.

"$328,597.93."

The next exhibit showed the back pay if I were to have received the same pay as the young man who replaced me as an area manager: $321,453.03.

The back pay for another area manager who retired at the same time I did and was recalled to work was $344,153.54.

The white chart, with its black-and-white numbers showing stark differences, spoke for itself. There wasn't much Mr. St. Clair could say except that I'd received a lump sum and retirement benefits when I retired, *which weren't reflected in the calculations and were long gone*, I thought to myself. It was also noted that if I received back pay, I'd have to pay back my retirement.

On redirect, Mike propped on the easel a chart highlighting the glaring contrast between the actual earnings of three area managers compared with what I'd have been earning if I'd continued in the technology engineer position from 1998 to the present.

The most dramatic chart was the comparison in pay between me and six other area managers. They were making $59,028, $55,679, $57,696, $58,226, and $58,464, when I was making only $44,724.

WITH THE differences in numbers fresh in everyone's minds, the defense took its turn to present its witnesses. Paul, a business-center manager and my supervisor for a month when I was in the ARF section in 1997, had flown all the way from the Goodyear operations in Brazil. He went first, probably because Jon had not had a chance to depose him during the discovery.

Mr. St. Clair submitted my 1997 performance evaluation so Paul could explain that evaluations were based on scorecards, which combined managers' audits and observations. Paul elaborated on the spreadsheet he'd created to rank all of the managers, weighting each person differently according to the complexity of the job. When he'd taken all of my performance data and fed it into the computer, I was "tied for worst" because I needed better results from my crew, didn't attend safety meetings, and didn't hold team meetings, he claimed. Mr. St. Clair lingered in great detail on each of these points, while Paul commented that I didn't protest his criticisms, except the one about not holding team meetings due to overtime being frozen—these meetings were always held in the morning after the night shift, and my guys had to be paid overtime to attend them. But I had protested every wrong thing he had said about my performance.

If I thought I'd been uncomfortable listening to Mr. St. Clair try to portray me as an emotionally unstable liar, it was even harder to hear him paint me as such a poor performer. I guess if you give a company twenty of the best years of your life, that's a hard pill to swallow.

Mr. St. Clair made Paul read from his notes on my evaluation. I'd said my new job as a technology engineer was "great and a better fit" when Paul had asked me about it in our conversation. I hoped the jury would have sense enough to understand that I was trying to remain nonconfrontational during that meeting. What good would it have done at that time to tell him that I was miserable?

Paul concluded with his thoughts about my being a technical engineer: "It was a better job for Lilly because she was better at managing herself."

Sure, moving two hundred 80-pound tires daily was a better fit for me than managing people.

DURING CROSS-EXAMINATION, Jon immediately jumped to the heart of the matter by asking for the original documents and audits with the actual production numbers used to feed the data into the computer in the first place. Paul couldn't tell him where they were.

JON: But you destroyed those documents, didn't you?
PAUL: I didn't destroy anything.
JON: They're destroyed, aren't they?

PAUL: I don't know.

JON: Well, you'd have them here today if they weren't
       destroyed, wouldn't you?

Jon turned to face the jury at the end of his question before he
continued in this same vein.

It's a law that when an EEOC charge is filed, a company has to
retain all of its records. By September, when Goodyear was notified of the charge and the EEOC inquired about personnel records,
the documents were already missing. If Goodyear wanted to prove
how bad my performance was, then the actual production numbers
could verify it. The original documents disappeared, Jon argued,
because they didn't support Goodyear's case. And as Jon later discovered when questioning Paul, the process by which Paul weighted
the evaluation wasn't an objective, computer-generated score; it was
a subjective evaluation.

To add to the mix, Eddie had shared with Paul his performance notes from the prior year. Paul insisted that these negative
notes were not taken into account for my evaluation, and that he
did not keep them. But they were not among the documents that
Goodyear turned over to Jon during the discovery phase. Jon also
pointed out that Paul had kept his own detailed notes about my
performance behavior based on our discussions, conversations Paul
had commented were like "a counseling session." Paul could not
recall having those same sessions with anyone else.

Jon brought forth the evaluation ranking that put me next to
the bottom with one underneath; the man underneath me earned
significantly more than I did. He paused for a long moment before
he asked, "Who are the two lowest-paid on the list?"

The answer: the only two women on the list, Sharon and me.

For the first time, I felt the tide was turning a bit. With the
women's testimony, the drastic differences in pay, and the missing

documents, the facts were building to create an accurate picture of Goodyear.

MY HEART started beating faster when Eddie took the stand. Mike started out easy, addressing the memo Eddie distributed to "Boys," which I had deemed sexist. Eddie tried to pass this off as humor, though his tone toward me had never been lighthearted. My shoulders tensed hearing his version of events, especially when he couldn't recall that I'd been given the Top Performance Award. His testimony was what I'd dreaded about going to trial, knowing how smooth and convincing he could be to people who didn't know him like I did. I wasn't surprised when he denied calling me a troublemaker and telling me to retire.

Just the sound of his voice evoked the familiar feelings of frustration and fear I'd lived with daily at Goodyear, and everything around me in the courtroom created heightened sensations. The sounds of Jon's pen scribbling furiously on his legal pad, light scratches similar to a mouse skittering inside the walls at night, unsettled me. I was distracted when he occasionally leaned over to whisper something important to Mike, who'd propped his elbows on the table and rested his chin on his folded hands, while his focus never left Mr. St. Clair's questioning.

I remembered how angry Eddie had become that last year when I'd questioned him about my treatment and later my transfer. Eddie had never forgiven me for enduring so long when he believed I didn't belong there in the first place, and as Goodyear's efforts to get rid of me once and for all escalated those last two years, Eddie had gladly helped deliver the last blows.

In the following testimony my attorneys brought up many issues surrounding the Top Performance Award and questioned why I received a merit award if I was such a poor performer. Eric, who had given me the award, struggled to explain this. In a faltering voice he surmised why the original documents to support my poor ranking were missing: They were thrown away because everyone thought the plant was closing and the offices were cleaned out to sell the furnishings. But why, then, were the only copies salvaged from the discarded file cabinets the ones supporting Goodyear's side?

Not only that. How twisted, then, was it for Eric to award me the largest raise I'd received since the merit-based program was enacted when I was such a bad employee? To answer that, Eric began by saying that I was a hard worker and dependable, and I worked well with people. His tone changed abruptly, as if he realized he'd made a mistake by telling the truth, and he started talking about my performance not being up to standards.

Strangely, Eric's memory began to fail him, and he couldn't recall what he'd told me when he gave me the award. But his words just didn't add up. I had an unimpressive record, yet he awarded me raises three years in a row, adding the Top Performance Award the last year, not for superior performance but "to make sure Lilly was not at the bottom of the pay range or under the minimum."

The men's salaries, supposedly, didn't come into play at all; the raise was strictly because I was below the minimum.

"All right," Mike continued. "Then let me ask you this: If it didn't have anything to do with the men's salaries, but it had to do strictly with the fact that she was below the minimum, why did you lie to her and tell her it was because of her performance? Why didn't you just tell her, it's because you're below the minimum?"

"I can't recall. You know, maybe I did. Maybe I didn't. I can't recall what I told Mrs. Ledbetter. You have my deposition."

"You just can't admit that this lady was never paid like the men because you still work at the company."

"No, sir."

"And you didn't think it was right."

"No, sir."

"But you couldn't tell her that, because if you told her the real reason, you'd be admitting that Goodyear had not been paying this woman what she deserved."

The minute Mike made that statement, my state of awareness heightened. The courtroom became very still, interrupted only by Eric's exasperated "No, sir. That's not correct."

Judge Clemon interjected, "Well, are you saying that she was being paid what she deserved?"

"Sir, with her job rate, there's a maximum and a minimum. Okay. It's my responsibility to keep anyone working in my area above the minimum, and that's what I was doing. And I—"

"So she was being paid below the minimum?" Judge Clemon asked, his voice vibrating across the room.

"Sir, the only thing I can tell you is, I thought the right thing to do was to make sure I raised Lilly Ledbetter's salary. And I violated that Top Performance Award policy to make certain that I increased her salary, but I still think that was the right thing to do. And that's the only thing I can tell you."

When Eric finished, the defense rested its case.

Leaving the courtroom, I looked everyone standing in that hallway in the eye. In my mind, it was clear that Goodyear never called any of the workers under my supervision to testify that I was a bad manager because I'd treated them fairly all those years, they knew I'd done a good job, and they weren't willing to lie.

I tossed and turned all night, my empty stomach growling. I had barely eaten all week.

THE CLOSING arguments were short, thirty minutes total for both lawyers on each side.

Jon spoke first. Why didn't Goodyear call any witnesses to rebut what I said? Where was the witness to deny the remarks about "the drunk and the damn woman"? This wasn't the only hidden evidence, he stated emphatically; the hard-core data, as we'd seen, was nowhere to be found. It existed in February 1998, right before I filed the EEOC charge, and disappeared shortly thereafter. Where were the union workers on my shift to say that I was a poor manager? Why was I chosen to start up the radial light-truck division if I was such a bad employee?

When Jon sat down, I was grateful for everything he had done for me over the previous four years. We'd developed a close friendship, and I viewed him as family. I knew that no matter what the verdict was, Jon would always be an important part of my life.

THEN MR. KENT, the younger defense lawyer, took his turn. He repeated that I was not involuntarily transferred due to my age or gender, or as retaliation. He maintained that I wasn't paid the same simply because I wasn't as good a manager as the others.

Up next, Mr. St. Clair began his speech by talking about driving to the courthouse that very morning and passing a construction crew on the highway, a typically male job until recently. Then he went on about sometimes you might see a woman flagging traffic and a man running the jackhammer, and the next day they might switch positions. He carried on about how women have to pull their own weight when they take jobs traditionally held by men. I was baffled by his analogy and glanced at the jury to see their expressions. He then focused on the time line for awarding damages, which confused me, so it had to have confused the jury.

When Mike began talking, he corrected the time line, pointed out that Goodyear was responsible for my deteriorating mental state, reiterated that I had been involuntarily transferred, and asserted that it was ridiculous to believe I'd be happy lifting Hummer tires. As for the differences in salary, that was a result of the "good old boy" mentality.

The closing arguments finalized, Judge Clemon gave the jury instructions about their deliberations. He informed them that they couldn't be influenced by sympathy or prejudice. They should consider only the evidence but could make reasonable deductions. They also needed to disregard anything he said during the trial concerning the facts because they were the only judges of the facts. He went into great detail about how to decide whether to believe a witness, outlining questions to ask themselves about each one. He talked about the plaintiff's responsibility to prove each of the claims by a "preponderance of evidence," also known as the "burden of proof" or "burden of persuasion." Unlike a criminal case, where there has to be proof beyond a reasonable doubt, a civil case requires a sufficient amount of evidence that the claim is more likely true than not true.

After he discussed each of my claims and the laws associated with them, he explained that compensatory damages should restore a plaintiff to the same position the individual would be in if he hadn't been discriminated or retaliated against. This number shouldn't be based on guesswork but should be limited to actual damages: in my case the lost wages and benefits beginning six months from the day I filed charges, if the jury found that my employment would have continued to that day or another date on which the jury determined my employment would have lawfully ended. Compensatory damages also covered emotional and mental anguish arising from sex discrimination and weren't restricted to actual losses. Punitive damages were different. They were meant to punish and discourage a corporation from acting in such a manner again. They were awarded when sex discrimination and retaliation were done with malice and reckless indifference to my federally protected rights. The jury needed to consider how egregious was the wrong, what my financial resources were, and what relationship the punitive damages have to the compensatory damages.

Under my age-discrimination claim, I was entitled to what is called liquidated damages if the jury found that Goodyear had willfully violated the Age Discrimination Act. The liquidated damages would be twice the amount of back pay.

Once Judge Clemon finished explaining the meaning of damages, he instructed the jury to go to the jury room. Now there was nothing left to do but wait for them to decide who was telling the truth.

THAT NIGHT I again slept fitfully. I was called to the courtroom late the following morning, the fourth and final day of the trial. The trial had lasted only three days, when I'd expected it to last at least a couple of weeks. When the jury filed into the courtroom, no one looked in my direction. Here I was, almost twenty-five years after starting at Goodyear, having stuck my neck out as far as it could go, waiting to hear the verdict on each of the four claims I'd filed against the company I'd called home for so long.

After the jury settled in their chairs, the foreman stood. I pressed my lips together and felt the raw skin on my bottom lip where I'd been gnawing on it without realizing it during the entire trial. I looked down at my black loafers.

As I waited to hear the verdicts, I felt the nervous flush making its way across my face. Hard to believe that all this brouhaha had started out with one tiny anonymous note tucked into my cubby five years earlier. When I opened it and saw those scrawled numbers and realized I'd been denied the same money as my male equals, by 40 percent no less, I knew in an instant that there was nothing to do but fight. And now I was about to find out either that it had all been worth it or that the boys from Goodyear had pulled off yet another discriminatory feat, keeping their boys' club intact.

Judge Clemon asked the jury if they'd reached a verdict. The jury foreman said they had. Judge Clemon then stated, "The court will receive the verdict," and the foreman handed the verdict to the courtroom clerk, who took it to Judge Clemon, who started to read it silently, flipping each page. He stopped at one page, and I heard Mike whisper to Jon as he grabbed his arm, "We lost." Judge

Clemon continued flipping until he reached the last page, where apparently the damages were listed.

Finally he began to read the verdict. To the first charge of being transferred against my will from area manager to technology engineer my last year because I was a woman, the foreman answered, "No." My stomach drew up in a knot.

Then the foreman said no to the second claim that I'd been transferred because of my age. I spread my fingers as far out as they would go and held them frozen that way, as if to distract myself. I didn't dare turn and look at Jon and Mike.

I tensed to hear the third claim and held my breath, not letting myself think about the previous four years of sleepless nights, worrying and wondering how it would all end. I'd always imagined that when I retired, Charles and I would be playing with the grandchildren and going on church trips. I'd thought I had the best years of my life ahead of me. I had no idea I'd spend my retirement battling the place where I'd spent most of my working life, with the simple hope of building a more comfortable lifestyle for my children than I'd had. When I heard the foreman read, "Do you find it more likely than not that the defendant paid plaintiff an unequal salary because of her sex?" I heard the answer "Yes," and I finally took a breath. I whispered to myself, "Thank you, God," and almost didn't hear the answer "No" to the fourth claim of being transferred as retaliation for complaining about being discriminated against.

The next thing I heard was "To what amount of back pay is the plaintiff entitled?"

"$328,597.93."

"To what amount of damages is plaintiff entitled on her disparate salary claim?"

"$223,776."

"To what amount of damages is plaintiff entitled for mental anguish?"

"$4,662."

"What amount of punitive damages, if any, do you award?"

"$3,285,979."

When I heard the amount, over $3 million, I was flabbergasted. I couldn't have been more shocked than if I'd been sitting on an airplane and the top of the plane peeled off to reveal blue sky. Then I was elated, and so deeply thankful that the jury got it.

In those first moments of hearing the jury's verdict, something unclenched inside of me. Believing that all my worries were over and even that the women working at Goodyear and other places would be safe from being harassed and underpaid, I felt a lightness in spirit that I hadn't felt in a very long time.

CHAPTER 9

Ms. Ledbetter Goes to Washington

||||||||||||||||||||||||||||||||||||||||||||||||||||||||||||||||||||||||||||||||||||||||||||||||||||||

In our view, the court does not comprehend, or is indifferent to, the insidious way in which women can be victims of pay discrimination.

—RUTH BADER GINSBURG

I NEVER WOULD see that $3.8 million jury award. Goodyear appealed, of course. In any event, by law, the damages were capped at $360,000. According to the 1991 law, compensatory and punitive damages under Title VII are subject to caps dictated by the company's size. For a company with more than five hundred employees, the amount is $300,000, in addition to back pay, which is not included, bringing the total to $360,000. Race claims under Section 1981 of Title VII are not subject to limitations on damages.

The local and national media immediately swirled around me: A verdict this large was unheard-of in a pay-discrimination case anywhere in the country. The foreman, the nurse, told Jon after the trial that there were a few on the jury, including both women, who at first didn't believe I was discriminated against but were convinced otherwise by the rest, who "wanted to give Goodyear a bee sting" as far as punitive damages were concerned. Regarding compensatory damages, my stoic demeanor, the "emotional blunting"

I conveyed, convinced the jury that I hadn't suffered much emotionally when, ironically, this flattening effect on expressiveness is
often one of trauma's side effects. It's also just my nature to hide
my vulnerability, which I'm well aware can be interpreted as an
inscrutable coldness; it's really just a way of protecting myself from
pain.

Goodyear's appeal put me in a holding pattern, a place the company left me often over the years. I resumed my daily life. Charles
and I were happier than we'd ever been, spending time with Vickie's three boys and Phillip's new baby from his second marriage,
Grace. Charles was also helping Phillip run his businesses.

MORE THAN two years after the trial, I stayed home for the appeal
hearing in Atlanta, since protocol dictated that only the lawyers
appear before the judge to argue the briefs they'd already filed—
Jon had another lawyer argue the case, since the date of the oral
argument fell on a Jewish holiday. By the fall of 2005, the Eleventh
Circuit Court of Appeals, one of the most conservative courts in
the country, reversed the jury verdict, stating that my case was filed
too late—even though I continued to receive discriminatory pay
throughout my career—because Goodyear's original decision to
pay me discriminatorily had been made years earlier, in the 1980s.

I was speechless. It wasn't the fact that I lost the money. For
some reason it had never felt real to me in the first place—it might
as well have been Monopoly money. What felt real, what disturbed
me deeply, was the fact that Goodyear was exonerated for its
wrongdoing, simply because Goodyear had been doing me wrong
long enough to make it legal, like certain African traditions mu-
tilating young women. If it's part of the company culture to discriminate in pay, then that company is free to continue business as
usual.

And all the good people who'd worked so hard to do the right
thing had been mistreated as well. Worse, women in workplaces

everywhere remained vulnerable to pay inequity. An employee still had 180 days from the discriminatory act, such as a firing or demotion, to file a discrimination claim, but with this decision the Eleventh Circuit Court had reversed what the EEOC and nine of the ten courts of appeals had applied in pay-discrimination cases under Title VII. Known as the paycheck accrual rule, this long-standing precedent ruled that repeated payments of discriminatory paychecks can be challenged as long as one paycheck occurred within the charge-filing period. In other words, each new paycheck was treated as a separate discriminatory act that started a new 180-day clock. By holding instead that all charges of pay discrimination must be filed within 180 days of the employer's *original discriminatory decision*, the Eleventh Circuit Court reversed this accepted practice and left victims of pay discrimination with no recourse against pay discrimination they don't immediately challenge. Under this new rule, employers are immunized from accountability for their discrimination once 180 days have passed.

This decision also ignored prior court precedents such as the *Bazemore* ruling, which upheld the "continuing violation" doctrine of my unequal pay claim. Simply put, each time I received a lower paycheck based on discriminatory reasons, the law under Title VII was violated. But this ruling had now reversed that precedent.

I assumed that my fight with Goodyear was over. There was nothing left to do. But I was wrong. In one way or another the fight is never over, at least when it comes to women's rights, which are human rights. Before I knew it, Jon and his partner Bob Wiggins filed a cert petition, a request to review the Eleventh Circuit Court of Appeals' decision to the Supreme Court. Another attorney, Kevin Russell, based in Washington, D.C., was called in to help with the petition.

My case was a long shot. The Supreme Court declines review in about 99 percent of the cases presented to it—only about seventy are granted from around eight thousand submitted annually.

While this appeal worked its way through the passages of the justice system at a glacial pace, I was focused on what was happening at home with Charles.

THAT SUMMER of 2005, right before the court of appeals ruling, Charles and I had gone on a trip with Vickie and her family to our favorite beach on the Gulf Coast, pristine and as yet untouched by the ravages of Hurricane Katrina that would soon devastate the city of New Orleans and the communities of the nearby Gulf Coast. The entire drive to the beach, Charles was agitated by the strong sun bearing down on one side of his face through the driver's side window—as painful as shards of glass pricking his skin, he insisted. Once we arrived at the condominium we were renting, he stayed in bed most of the time, only mustering enough energy to watch our favorite new show, *Dancing with the Stars*. Back home, the ENT doctor discovered a few blisters in his mouth but nothing else out of the ordinary.

That trip to the doctor was the starting point of a long, difficult health ordeal for Charles. He was already combating back issues and high blood pressure. Still lethargic after the beach trip, he underwent more extensive testing, and the doctors found a cyst in his lower back. He had a second back surgery—the first had been about a year earlier, after the epidurals that had given him relief stopped working—to alleviate the chronic pain he'd been experiencing.

While Charles recovered from the back surgery, which, all told, took another year, I tried to carry on as usual. One morning, after I'd collected my mail as I did every morning, I stood at the counter in the small post office just down the street from my house and sifted through the bills and junk mail. I opened an envelope from Jon's law firm and found a letter from Goodyear. What in heaven's name would they be sending me? I bristled when I read the demand letter for over three thousand dollars to pay their court-related fees. I wanted to tear the bill to pieces, but I restrained myself.

I didn't have time to dwell on Goodyear when, the next summer after Charles's back surgery, the doctor found skin cancer on his ear on the same side of his face that had been so sensitive on the way to the beach. In the heart of a July heat wave the cancer was removed, the surgery more difficult and more extensive than the doctor first anticipated due to the malignancy having spread much deeper than we'd thought.

A couple of months later, a strange growth popped out of nowhere on the damaged side of Charles's face. The doctor took one look at this bony mass jutting out of his cheek and refused to let him leave until he performed a biopsy. A few days later, as we waited at the office to hear the results, the nurse came in. She couldn't contain herself. "I have good news," she whispered before the doctor made it official. "It's benign."

Now Charles only had to have the bizarre protrusion removed. Around Halloween the doctor performed the face surgery and another biopsy. I was sickened by how butchered Charles looked. His face might as well have been a side of roast beef someone had sliced open. When the doctor called with the results, he had devastating news: "The growth was malignant. I've already scheduled him for surgery on Monday. He's got the worst possible cancer in the worst possible location."

My heart froze. *No, not Charles. Please, not Charles.*

The doctor continued. Charles had a deadly type of cancer known as squamous cell carcinoma. The procedure would require a skin graft from his leg, and he'd remove any lymph nodes or glands infected by the cancer. In disbelief, I mashed the phone harder into my ear. The doctor rattled off what else needed to be done, how to prep for surgery, the type of treatment he recommended following recovery from the operation.

After I hung up, I sat with the phone still in my hand. We were fighters. We could beat this. But the day of Edna's last diagnosis came back to me, how she had only heard that the doctor could cure her. I couldn't ignore the reality of this situation: We were facing a battle for Charles's life. The sound of the operator broke through my reverie as her disembodied voice repeated for me to please hang up the phone; then the incessant buzzing of the dead connection really jerked me to attention. I hung up. Now I had to tell Charles the news, both of us acknowledging the fact that there was a good chance he was dying while dancing around those exact words.

EARLIER THAT summer, the Supreme Court had agreed to hear my appeal, setting the date for November 27, 2006.

After a subdued Thanksgiving dinner with just Charles and me—he just wasn't up to a big family gathering—I boarded the plane for Washington on a gray November Saturday to attend the Supreme Court hearing on Monday, only a year after Goodyear won its appeal in the Eleventh Circuit Court. I was concerned about the final outcome of my legal journey, which had started almost ten years before. Vickie sat next to me on the plane, while Charles stayed home with the help of home health care to recover from his latest radical face surgery and the wound on his leg where the top layer of his skin had been shaved off. He would begin chemotherapy and radiation treatment after the Christmas holidays. Seeing my reflection in the window of the plane, I thought that I didn't even look like myself anymore. Vickie had taken me to a new hairdresser, who'd given me a coiffed blond bob, and I wore a navy skirt and a silk blouse I'd scouted at the discount outlet.

In Washington that evening, I met Kevin Russell, whom I'd talked to numerous times over the phone, for the first time. He'd worked on my case for over a year, with the help of a group of Stanford Law students associated with the Stanford Supreme Court

Litigation Clinic, which helps prepare pro bono cases. Kevin had also been aided by the National Women's Law Center and the National Employment Lawyers Association, both of which had written amicus briefs for the court.

On the third-floor mezzanine of the posh hotel, Kevin appeared in jeans and a sweatshirt, sporting a red beard. I was expecting an older man, and for a minute I thought he was one of the college students. The moment he started talking, I got excited listening to him articulate the ins and outs of the legal proceedings with such expertise. This would be his first time before the Supreme Court. He explained the situation: There were four conservative justices and four who would probably lean in our favor. Justice Anthony Kennedy was somewhere in the middle, but not necessarily when it concerned employment cases, so Kevin thought we had to focus on convincing another justice.

Since I'd filed the lawsuit in 1998, there had been many baffling twists and turns, so much out of my control. Then President Bill Clinton had been in office. By the time my case had made it to the highest court in the land, I'd seen firsthand how the fickle nature of politics impacted the delivery of justice. Now that President George W. Bush was in office, the Justice Department, as an agency of the federal government, leaned toward Goodyear's defense even though the EEOC was on my side. This development upset me, but I'd seen how people will turn away from the truth to keep their boss (or the person who hired them) happy, as payment for giving them the job opportunity, or to maintain stability and a steady paycheck.

ON THAT brisk Monday morning, men and women bustled down the sidewalk, large lattes in one hand and black briefcases in the other, all headed to the Capitol to conduct their business on the Hill. I hurried past them up the steep white steps of the Supreme Court Building, flanked on one side by *Contemplation of Justice*, a statue of a woman holding in one hand a book of law and in the other a figure of the guardian of justice, which holds a set of balanced scales; and on the other side by *Guardian of Law*, a male figure. Jon, Vickie, and I walked under the solemn Corinthian columns that seemed to reach to the sky and entered the building, constructed of white marble—some of it mined from Alabama. Passing through the Great Hall to the hushed courtroom, Vickie and I sat two rows from the front, facing the elevated mahogany bench where the justices presided. In the cavernous room with its forty-four-foot-high ceilings, invulnerable marble columns (I counted twenty-four), and plush red carpet, the podium stood only a few feet from the justices. The hearing had the feel of an intimate conversation. But there was nothing cozy about the occasion in the mausoleum-like atmosphere where we waited to hear the two competing narratives presented to the most powerful justices in the land.

Kevin presented our side in the twenty-seven of the thirty minutes allotted to him, answering the justice's questions in a respectful, precise manner. One of the young Stanford students sitting beside me kept whispering before the case started, "It's only right; the law is on our side. This has to go forward." I sure hoped he was right.

In twenty short minutes, Goodyear followed and argued its side, with ten minutes allotted to the attorney from the solicitor general's office—Jon and Kevin had met with the Justice Department before the hearing to see if it would take my side, but it took Goodyear's side instead. Kevin then gave his three-minute rebuttal. After all that preparation, the hearing lasted only an hour.

As I watched Justice Ruth Bader Ginsburg, perched in her black robe, the lone woman among the nine justices, pose questions to both sides, I thought about how her mother had gone to work as a bookkeeper in the New York City garment district; her earnings helped support her oldest brother's college studies. Only a generation later Ginsburg was one of the nine female law students out of an entering class of five hundred at Harvard Law School; many years later she became the first tenured woman professor at Columbia Law School.

We were around the same age, and she too had been one of the first women to break into her profession. I might have been on the factory floor as she walked the hallowed halls of the American justice system, but I imagined that men in ties and men in jeans can act just the same.

A FULL six months after the hearing, in May 2007, I heard the Supreme Court judgment. By then Charles had started treatment for his cancer. He insisted on driving himself to Gadsden every weekday, shooing me away when I tried to accompany him for his chemotherapy shot followed by radiation half an hour later. I would act nonchalant, telling him that I really needed to get out of the house. Only then did he let me go with him. After all these years, he was still trying to protect me.

That day Charles and I were on our way to Fort McClellan to eat lunch with the senior group at our church. Even though he'd lost his sense of taste, he felt better that morning and wanted to get out and about on the invigorating spring day. There were only a couple of weeks of cool weather left before the relentless summer sun would make us want to stay indoors for good.

We had just pulled out of the driveway when my cell phone rang. I retrieved it from among the scattered contents in my purse. Mike Quinn was on the other end; Jon was out of town, and he had some news to tell me. I motioned for Charles to pull back into the driveway.

My connection was bad, and I strained to hear Mike. "Let me call you right back," I said. I told Charles to wait and ran inside to the den to use the landline.

"Lilly, I have to let you know the decision," Mike said in an awful rush of words once we'd reconnected. "We lost. The Supreme Court ruled against us. I'm sorry."

I was quiet for a moment, letting the disheartening news seep into my bones. I had really held out hope that justice would prevail. "I'm sorry, too," I finally said.

I thanked him for all he and Jon and everyone else had done. He told me I might get a few media calls. "Don't get too caught up in the temporary frenzy. It will die out soon enough," he assured me.

I set the phone on the table. I noticed the spot where the charred wood paneling had been replaced from a fire long ago, and I remembered the blizzard of 1993, when we'd experienced a freak snowstorm in March. Several feet of snow had blanketed the area, and the power had gone out. I'd fallen asleep on the sofa with a candle burning on the table close to my head. The flame had licked the top of my bleached-blond head lacquered with hairspray resting on the arm of the sofa. I woke up with my hair on fire. Later, I was convinced I'd been spared for a special reason, but I had yet to figure out why; and for a selfish, childish moment after hearing the decision, I'm ashamed to say this, especially when Charles was suffering so, I wished I hadn't been spared in that fire.

I looked up. Charles had followed me inside and caught the end of the conversation.

"We lost," I told him, watching him take the news, stabbed for a frozen moment like he'd swallowed a cold drink too fast and was overtaken by an ice headache.

"I'm so sorry," he said.

But I was the one who was sorry, sorry I'd put him through so much. Vickie and Phillip's school pictures still hung on our den wall. I looked at a picture of Vickie in college, her long, light-brown hair parted in the middle, the style in the late seventies, around the time I started at Goodyear. The first thing the secretary had told me when I started working was that if I wanted to succeed at

Goodyear, I'd do two things: I'd contribute to United Way every year, and I wouldn't discuss my paycheck. The way she said it made me feel like I'd disappear into the night if I didn't do exactly what she said.

Charles, who'd lost so much weight that his shirt fell slack from his once-broad shoulders, sat down on the sofa. "What are you going to do now?" he asked, the side of his face marbled with the dark purple scar, zigzagging like the jagged edge of a lightning strike down the side of a pine tree.

"It's not what I wanted to hear, but we can't stop living. We had the best attorney, and we did the best we could. There's nothing to be ashamed of. There's nothing else left to do but go to lunch."

I couldn't hide now that it was over; I had more important things to tend to for the time being. And for the moment, that was enough. Despite the deep disappointment, I needed to focus on Charles and my own life now. I'd done what I could. Goodyear was simply a greater force than I could overcome. That was clear as day.

CHARLES AND I never finished our meal the day of the decision. At lunch we had kept the news to ourselves, not wanting to dampen anyone else's spirits. But in the middle of my moving my chicken salad from one side of my plate to the other, my cell phone rang again. I reached for my purse, almost knocking the arm of the waitress who was refilling my glass of tea.

It was NBC. Could they send a film crew to my house to do an interview for the nightly news with Brian Williams? I agreed, and when I finished talking to the producer, we had to tell our group of friends, since we had to leave quickly—my house was a mess and we needed to clean up a little.

The film crew arrived and rearranged all my furniture. That night I answered the phone and a man's voice said, "This is Norman Lear. Do you know who I am?" Of course I knew who he was;

I watched *All in the Family* and *The Jeffersons*. How did *he* know who *I* was? He wanted to film a video to run on YouTube.

Then CNN called. The next day the CNN film crew came and rearranged the house again. I kept expecting my phone to stop ringing, but the public outcry was deafening and media from around the world appeared on my doorstep. One of the first newspaper reporters to contact me was Linda Greenhouse from the *New York Times*. She wanted to know whether I had heard Justice Ginsburg's dissent. No, actually, I hadn't.

In a rare moment, Justice Ginsburg had voiced her dissent, joined by three other justices—John Paul Stevens, David Souter, and Stephen Breyer—from the bench, addressing their dissatisfaction with the outcome of the case and the effects on employment laws. Only six times before, in thirteen terms on the Court, had Justice Ginsburg found it appropriate to underscore her dissent by reading a summary of it aloud in the courtroom.

"The Court's insistence on immediate contest overlooks common characteristics of pay discrimination," Justice Ginsburg declared. "Pay disparities often occur, as they did in Ledbetter's case, in small increments; cause to suspect that discrimination is at work develops only over time. . . . Small initial discrepancies may not be seen as grounds for a federal case, particularly when the employee, trying to succeed in a nontraditional environment, is averse to making waves." Her dissenting opinion stated:

> *Ledbetter's petition presents a question important to the sound application of Title VII: What activity qualifies as an unlawful employment practice in cases of discrimination with respect to compensation? One answer identifies the pay-setting decision, and that decision alone, as the unlawful practice. Under this view, each particular salary-setting decision is discrete from prior and subsequent decisions, and must be challenged within 180*

days on pain of forfeiture. Another response counts both the pay-setting decision and the actual payment of a discriminatory wage as unlawful practices. Under this approach, each payment of a wage or salary infected by sex-based discrimination constitutes an unlawful employment practice; prior decisions, outside the 180-day charge-filing period, are not themselves actionable, but they are relevant in determining the lawfulness of conduct within the period. The Court adopts the first view, but the second is more faithful to precedent, more in tune with the realities of the work-place, and more respectful of Title VII's remedial purpose.

Justice Ginsburg hit the nail on the head when she said that the majority's decision didn't make sense in the real world. People don't go around asking their colleagues how much money they make; in most workplaces, you get fired for discussing one another's sala-ries. Anyway, even if you know that some people are being paid more than you, that's not necessarily a good reason to immediately suspect discrimination. Most people assume they work for an em-ployer who does the right thing.

JUSTICE SAMUEL ALITO's written opinion for the five member majority suggested that I should have complained every time I re-ceived a smaller raise than the men, even if I didn't know what the men were making and even if I had no way to prove that these pay decisions were discrimination. The Court ruled that once 180 days have passed from the initial pay decision, the worker is stuck with unequal pay for equal work for the rest of her career and there is nothing illegal about it. Basically, the Supreme Court had ruled that if you don't clue in right away, the company can treat you like a second-class citizen for your entire career. Now I wasn't the only one who had to swallow the consequences of pay discrimination—every other working woman in America was being forced into the same corner. But the majority didn't understand that, or didn't care. How they could have thought Congress would have intended the law to be so unfair, I'll never know.

Another thing I've never understood about the ruling is how in the world Justice Thomas voted against me. Growing up in the South, he, too, must have experienced discrimination. For goodness sakes, he grew up in a county poor like mine. And I knew from what I'd seen at Goodyear that women were treated with kid gloves compared to the way some people acted when it came to working with African Americans. (Whenever I contemplate this, I remember how, when I was a child, Papa would cross the street whenever he saw a black person and how I'd try to catch the eye of the person to smile in sympathy. The rural South wasn't an easy place to live for African Americans, to say the least.)

What I did understand when Justice Ginsburg voiced her dissent as the only female voice on the Court is that the importance of women being appointed to the Court cannot be underestimated. My case shows that those individuals who are appointed to the Supreme Court really make a difference. If one more person like Justice Ginsburg or Justice Stevens had been on the Court—one more person who understood what it's like for ordinary people living in the real world—then my case would have turned out differently. Most people I've talked to simply can't believe what happened to me and want to ensure that something like this doesn't happen again. They don't care if the justices are Democrats or Republicans, or which president appointed them, or which senators voted for them. They want justices who understand that the law must serve regular hardworking folks who are just trying to do right and make a better life for their families. And when the law isn't clear, justices need to use some common sense and remember that the people who write laws are usually trying to make a law that's fair and sensible. This isn't a game. Real people's lives are at stake.

I won't lie; I was pretty devastated by the Court's decision. The ruling had severely limited the ability of victims of pay discrimination to vindicate their rights under Title VII.

In one fell swoop, I lost my case and became the poster child for *un*equal pay for equal work. And the real clincher is, as I've said before, Goodyear continues to treat me like a second-class citizen because my pension and Social Security are based on the amount I earned—Goodyear gets to keep my extra pension as a reward for breaking the law.

Instead of taking what happened quietly, swept up by the current of outrage from numerous organizations such as the National Women's Law Center (NWLC), the American Association of University Women (AAUW), the American Civil Liberties Union (ACLU), the AFL-CIO, the National Employment Lawyers Association (NELA), and the National Council of Jewish Women (NCJW), to name only a few, I decided to fight back. For the sake of my granddaughter and future generations of women and their families, I refused to take this unjust ruling lying down. I owed that much not just to myself but to all of America's women and girls, who deserved a fighting chance.

Ready to stand with me every step of the way were passionate women: Jocelyn Samuels, an early advocate for Title IX, which leveled the playing field for girls and women in sports; Marcia Greenberger, founder and copresident of the National Women's Law Center; and Lisa Maatz, from the American Association of University Women. These women showed me that Justice Ginsburg, her dissenting colleagues, and I weren't the only ones who thought the ruling was crazy. As these women, now my lifelong friends, marched me before their members, I became filled with a sense of mission. Pay equity wasn't my personal problem; it wasn't a southern problem or even a national issue. Pay inequity was an international epidemic that needed to be remedied. What was required now was a simple legislative fix to restore the law to how it was applied by the EEOC and the lower courts prior to that crazy Supreme Court ruling.

INSPIRED BY Justice Ginsburg's dissent and dressed in the black Talbot jacket and skirt Vickie bought me, I spent the next two years traversing the halls of Congress telling my story. I lived to fulfill a greater purpose. Though I may have lost the case—and my $3.8 million verdict—I was made a figurehead of pay inequality from that day forward. The ruling, and Justice Ginsburg's dissent, put me at the helm of a civil rights issue larger than myself. Perhaps naïvely, I hoped that Congress would recognize the urgent importance of women's equality in the workplace and pass a bill to prevent future cases like mine.

This bill would reverse the Supreme Court's decision, helping to ensure that individuals subjected to unlawful pay discrimination had an effective recourse to assert their rights under the federal antidiscrimination laws. The bill would reinstate prior law and adopt the paycheck-accrual rule, making each discriminatory paycheck, rather than the original decision to discriminate, the starting point for a new claim-filing period. The paycheck-accrual rule provides sufficient time for employees to evaluate and confirm that they have been subject to discrimination.

Ultimately, what would become the Lilly Ledbetter Fair Pay Restoration Act would protect workers from workplace discrimination as Congress intended.

The House Democrats immediately heeded Justice Ginsburg's clarion call for Congress to amend the law. Jon and I flew to Washington together to meet with House Education and Workforce Committee chairman George Miller, a tall, white-haired man from California, to discuss the proposed bill, HR 11. After we returned to Alabama, Representative Miller called Jon to ask about naming the bill after me. When Jon told me this, I said, "Well, that would be fine by me."

"It's a great honor," he remarked.

"It certainly is," I said, amazed at this turn of events. "And now Goodyear will never forget me."

Only a month after the Supreme Court verdict, in June 2007, House majority leader Steny Hoyer and Representative Miller announced that a bill would be passed to prevent future court rulings in line with mine. Republicans including Howard "Buck" McKeon, a ranking member of the Education and Workforce Committee, opposed the bill, contending that it made companies vulnerable to disgruntled employees seeking damages years later when the company couldn't offer a meaningful defense.

Starting that humid summer after the Supreme Court verdict in May, I spent at least two weeks out of each month in Washington, depending on Charles's doctor appointments, treatment, and hospital stays. A typical day started at 5:00 A.M. with a call-in talk-radio show, followed by meetings with congressional staff members on the Hill, press conferences, and more media interviews.

During one of my very first press conferences, I tripped over the electrical cords snaking like overgrown tree roots around my feet when I was walking to the podium, almost causing the entire sea of microphones to tumble down. I learned to step with care when I approached any podium. At first, I didn't know who this woman was standing inside the congressional building with a field of microphones, reporters, and cameras thrust before her. Sometimes, after telling my story so many times in the same day, I had fitful nights, dreaming that I still worked at Goodyear.

More often than not, I met with staffers who couldn't or wouldn't commit to supporting Senate Bill 1843. Only a few times did I actually meet with a member of Congress. During my meeting with Alaska senator Lisa Murkowski's young aide, she jumped up. "I'll be right back," the aide said. Next thing I knew, there was Senator Murkowski standing before me ready to listen. I started over. At the end of my story, she walked to the door, turned, and said, "You have a compelling story, but I can't support you." Then she left.

I was crushed. As we gathered ourselves for our next meeting, she came right back and asked if I would like to have a photograph taken. Deep inside I was too demoralized for a photo opportunity, but I smiled for the pictures anyway, hoping she would change her mind.

On our way to the next meeting, I told myself, *Well, we didn't get that one, but maybe the next one will be different.*

PASSING A bill in Congress can be tricky, to put it mildly. In order for a bill to be passed, a member of Congress must submit it for consideration. In the House, a copy of the bill is literally dropped into a box called "the hopper." In the Senate, a member recognized by the presiding officer may introduce a bill. Once a bill is introduced, it is assigned to a committee for study—the committees in the Senate and the House do basically the same thing. The bill is then assigned to a subcommittee and scheduled for hearings, at which time witnesses may be called to testify as to why a bill is needed. Once the hearings are held, the committee and subcommittee members vote on whether the bill should proceed to the full House or Senate, where it is placed on the calendar for action. The House and Senate then debate the bill and vote on whether to pass or reject it. Most bills die in committee.

Twice that June, just weeks after the Supreme Court's ruling was delivered, I testified before the House Judiciary Committee. I'd watched the Watergate hearings on TV and had been especially riveted to the Anita Hill hearings many years later. Now here I was sitting at a long wooden table, the seats behind me packed with people, the table cluttered with papers and water bottles while the thin microphone arched in front of me. I faced questions from the most powerful decision makers in our country, photographers kneeling in front of their table, their cameras clicking. I occupied a place I could have never imagined being in. I have to say, these hearings felt like an out-of-body experience, but all I had to do was think of how unfair the ruling was and my indignation fueled the words that flowed from me.

During the hearing before the House Subcommittee on the Constitution, Civil Rights, and Civil Liberties of the Committee on the Judiciary, Neal Mollen, the lawyer representing the U.S. Chamber of Commerce, accused me of waiting to retire before suing. He claimed that I'd known all along about my lower salary. That set me off like a firecracker.

I interrupted his lies, shaking my finger at him, telling him what really happened. Did he really believe that I would choose to work for almost twenty years knowing I was being discriminated against in pay and then wait to sue? What kind of sense did that make?

After this testimony, Mr. Mollen assured me that he never wanted to go up against me again.

The next month the Ledbetter Act passed the House.

Sponsored by Education and Workforce Committee chairman George Miller from California and Congresswoman Rosa De-Lauro from Connecticut, the bill, which amended the Civil Rights Act of 1964 by reinstating that the 180-day statute of limitations for filing a pay-discrimination lawsuit resets with each new discriminatory paycheck, squeaked by in a close vote of 225–199 on the last day of July.

Twice I testified before the Senate as well. The first time was in January 2008, before the Committee on Health, Education, Labor and Pensions.

A few months later, sponsored by Senators Ted Kennedy from Massachusetts and Patrick Leahy from Vermont, the bill was voted on during the 110th Senate in April 2008. The Democrats had no idea what was going to happen, especially since we only had fifty-seven votes and sixty were required, and they waited to convene until 5:00 P.M. so presidential candidates Senators Hillary Rodham Clinton and Barack Obama could return from the campaign trail. Senator John McCain chose not to return, not that his vote would have made a difference. In reference to the bill, he'd already made the ridiculous comment to reporters that what women really needed was more education and training. He had the same mindset as most Republicans: that this bill was a trial lawyer's dream come true and would ignite a firestorm of frivolous lawsuits.

During this vote, I watched from the Senate gallery as Senate majority leader Harry Reid purposefully voted against the bill. That way, the bill could be reopened for consideration if it lacked enough votes to pass. After the vote, I waited outside the Senate door, thanking the senators who voted for it and asking those who opposed it why they did. I'd already unsuccessfully cornered Senator Richard Shelby from Alabama when I ran into him at the airport and asked him to support the bill. If I thought calling people to testify against Goodyear was tough, trying to get support from representatives from my own state was even tougher. The only one who supported the bill was Congressman Artur Davis.

That day I also had the privilege of meeting Hillary Clinton. When she asked me to endorse her, I hated to say no, but I wanted to stay neutral for the sake of passing the bill. I met Senator Obama for the very first time as well, and a photograph of us together ran in the *Washington Post* the next day.

The next time I testified in the Senate was in the early fall in the midst of election fervor. Emboldened by the desire for change I'd heard from so many across the country, I stood before the Senate Committee on the Judiciary in the Senate Chambers as they discussed the merits of equal pay for equal work in their debates leading up to a vote on the bill.

Navigating the ins and outs of politics on the Hill, I'd learned about the unpredictable and uncontrollable process of trying to get a bill passed. With the "Great Recession" hitting the country, banks failing, the housing market plummeting, and the financial markets teetering, focusing on pay equity in a world that had turned upside down was even more challenging. Not to mention the trade-offs representatives felt compelled to make when, say, considering the practical needs of their constituents recently ravaged by hurricanes. The uncertainty of the outcome and the chaotic nature of the passage of a bill unfolding reminded me of the time I ran around, slipping and sliding in the pouring rain and slick mud, trying to capture frightened chickens when a flooded building collapsed at Tyson.

Nevertheless, this was one of the most exciting times of my life as I was affirmed by thousands of people. It was a time of social empowerment for me, yet in my personal life I felt helpless. Charles's cancer was eating away at him as surely as the vinegar dissolving the shell of an egg in the science experiment my grandson showed me. At first after both Charles and I had retired (despite the fact that we were dealing with the stress of the trial), we were so happy together. But then his cancer blindsided all of us.

While I traveled back and forth to and from Washington, I did my best to care for Charles as he suffered through his painful ordeal. As the momentum of my new public role carried me forward, I was also pulled home by my heartache over Charles's cancer, unable to face the fact that he might really be dying. I might as well have tried to look straight into the sun without blinking. As it was, my heart already felt scorched.

CHAPTER 10

Becoming the Grandmother
of Equal Pay

|||||||||||||||||||||||||||||||||||||||||||||||||||||||||||||||||||||||||||||||||||||||||||||||||||||||||||||||||

*The work goes on, the cause endures, the hope still lives,
and the dream shall never die.*

—SENATOR TED KENNEDY

B EFORE I started giving speeches, my grandson assured me
that if I didn't know what to say, my Alabama accent would
at least be entertaining enough to keep most people listening. The
first time I spoke before a large audience, I was being honored,
along with Nancy Pelosi, by the National Women's Law Center
in Washington, D.C. After I finished speaking to the audience of
twelve hundred people, they gave me a standing ovation. In that
moment, I remembered my despair during the dark nights the year
before the trial. I felt giddy and even a little dizzy from the power
of the reversal. Before long, I became pretty comfortable speaking
to groups.

Nothing compared to the 2008 Democratic National Convention in Denver. The Obama campaign had contacted the National
Women's Law Center to ask me to deliver a five-minute speech
during prime time on Tuesday evening. My heart almost stopped

just thinking about it. Throughout the election campaign, in an effort to seek bipartisan support for the bill, I'd shied away from endorsing a candidate. But Marcia Greenberger explained how Ronald Reagan Jr. had spoken at the Democratic National Convention in support of John Kerry, who was an advocate for stem-cell research like the Reagans—and he did so without endorsing Kerry. Likewise, I could also speak without endorsing anyone. I agreed, knowing I had an incredible opportunity to raise awareness about the issue of fair pay.

Security at the stadium was tight, and I was whisked through several checkpoints before I spoke. Waiting, I almost gnawed my bottom lip in two, I was so worried about making a mistake. As I told my story to eighty-four thousand people in the stadium and millions more through the broadcast, I felt my nervousness replaced by the crowd's extraordinary energy. Above me, gigantic screens flashed images from the stage and stadium; below me women cried. Tears streaming down their faces, men yelled, "Yes, we can!" as they waved their signs, while the crowd chanted my name. I could feel the power of thousands of voices, thousands of individuals aspiring to a greater good, rising through the bottom of my feet and coursing through my body like an electrical current. Charged by the intensity of that moment, I felt part of something far more significant than myself.

When I walked off that stage, a reporter asked me when I'd endorsed Obama. I intuitively said, "Right now."

I knew in that moment that I had to wake up America to the injustice happening to American families, and the best path for doing so was to join Barack Obama's campaign.

A few months later I flew into Philadelphia to campaign for Obama in the last push before election night. From morning until evening I was driven across the state, stopping to speak at colleges, campaign headquarters, and union halls. At the Steelworkers

Union headquarters, a man in the audience asked me if what I was doing was worthwhile. Wasn't I just preaching to the choir when I spoke before my fellow Democrats? "Yes, sir," I answered him. "I'd be in Alabama, but it's a die-hard Republican state. If I had any possibility of changing anybody's mind, I'd be there. They're some stubborn folks, and I know better than to waste my breath."

IN OCTOBER I met Michelle Obama for the first time as I joined her and Jill Biden in Virginia. I had never experienced anything like Ms. Obama's sincerity and compassion. And after we all spoke at a college in Virginia and she and Dr. Biden told me to follow them as they stepped offstage to greet the crowd, I was, for a moment, bewildered. I didn't belong in the same category as these two accomplished women I'd come to admire. Every once in a while during an event or speech, I had these moments, overcome by how surreal my life had become. But there I was as people hugged my neck and snapped a picture of us on their cell phones.

Daily, I was inspired by the women I met, women of all ages from all different backgrounds. Their stories always resonated for me. We were all the same—young women struggling to pay for a decent education, widowed women struggling to buy medicine, military spouses, all hardworking people living paycheck to paycheck, a situation I understood well. When lying awake in a strange hotel room by myself worrying about passing the bill and Charles's and my own dwindling finances, I saw these women's faces and heard their voices. They carried me on my journey.

BY THE fall of 2008 Charles could no longer hold out for an entire day in his woodworking shop like he used to. He took a nap in the morning, one in the afternoon, and another before he went to bed. He remained religious about attending his Tuesday-morning men's prayer meeting at the church. But he'd gotten to the point that when he was driving he had to pull over on the side of the road and rack his brain to remember where he was going. As I continued to travel in support of the passage of the bill and Obama's campaign for president, my heart ached for Charles.

On election night I sat with him in the den and watched the returns. Throughout my life, I'd rather have voted for a blue dog, as they say in the South, than vote Republican, so I'd kept my politics to myself, especially at Goodyear. As usual, on any local or national election day, management at the plant got off early to go to the polls to make sure their Republican vote was cast. I'd pick up my purse and leave early along with everyone else in management, only pulling a different lever in the voting booth.

As long as I'd known Charles, he might vote in the local races for a Democrat, but when it came to the president, he'd always voted Republican.

That night, for the first time in five decades of marriage, our votes hadn't canceled each other out.

The day in December 2008 that I left for New York to be interviewed on *20/20* about the campaign for pay equity, I knew in my gut that I shouldn't go. By that time Charles was feeling too sick to see the grandchildren when they wanted to visit us. Right before I left, he told me he'd had enough of life, but I pushed aside his comment like I always did. Charles used to tell me, "I'm gonna die early. My body's just gonna wear out." I told him to quit talking like that because if you visualize something, it will happen. I really believe that. When he'd first been diagnosed with cancer, he immediately started telling me, "You know I'm gonna die before you do, and you're gonna be left to your own devices." I'd say, "Then you need to show me how to do the outdoor lights," to hush him up.

The morning I was supposed to leave I sat in the den reading the paper. Charles was making coffee in the kitchen. When he brought me a cup, he asked me what I was doing.

"I'm reading the newspaper."

"You mean you're not going to New York?"

"No."

"Why not?"

I didn't answer and pretended to keep reading an article.

"Lilly, go on. You've already changed the date twice. Go on. Get it done, and that way they won't call you anymore. You'll be back tomorrow, and then it'll be the holidays."

I thought about what he said. Things seemed to have stabilized since the doctor had changed his medicine. I could get the interview done, come right back, and then we could have a quiet Christmas together with the family.

"Promise me you will call someone if you don't feel well," I said before I threw some clothes into a suitcase.

On my way out the door, he stood watching. I started to kiss him good-bye, but he stopped me.

"I've got a sore throat."

I kissed him lightly on his scarred cheek.

"Don't forget to get the cough syrup that you can take with high blood pressure when you get your decongestant medicine," I reminded him.

At the Atlanta airport, I called to check on him, but no one answered. I figured he might still be at the drugstore. When I called him once I landed, he still didn't answer; I reasoned that he'd gone to bed early like he'd been doing for some time.

Before the interview I tried once more. No answer. I thought maybe he'd gone to the post office or run to get a biscuit. Once I did the segment, I went straight to the airport to try to get an earlier flight. I really started worrying in the car on my way home from the airport when there was still no answer.

The minute I drove up to the house, I knew something was wrong. The garage door was standing wide open, but it was raining lightly. Maybe Charles had left the door open so I wouldn't have to get wet. Only what were the white plastic bags full of groceries doing sitting at the back door? When I walked into the house, every light in every room was on. I smelled something burning and found a scorched pan sitting on the hot eye of the stove.

I discovered Charles lying on the floor by the bed, his hand over his heart, blood all around him. I knelt beside him. All I wanted to do was put my head on his chest to comfort him like I'd always done. I wanted to go with him so badly. And I was suffused with regret. I covered his body with the bedspread and told him, "I'm sorry." Sorry he'd suffered so much and profoundly sorry that he was alone when he died. I finally got up, the knees of my pants damp and stained red from the blood-soaked carpet. I needed to call Vickie. As I picked up the phone, it occurred to me that the next week would have been our fifty-third wedding anniversary.

In the coming months, as I tried to accept Charles's death, I also tried to come to terms with the nature of my relationship with him over so many years—as well as my guilt about leaving him alone at home so often. He was always afraid I'd leave him for good, and in the end, in a sense, I felt like I had. I'll probably never forgive myself for not being there with him when he died. But I also tell myself that he might have known how close he was to the end when he urged me to go New York. Maybe he didn't want me there. Maybe he knew my own heart would have stopped from the shock of my loss had I been there with him. And in a way that would have been fine with me.

The morning after Charles's funeral, I answered the phone, which had been ringing with calls from upset family and friends. A voice I didn't recognize said, "Would you please hold for Senator Clinton." Vickie was sitting beside me, and when I said I'd hold for the senator, her eyes got wide. On the phone Senator Clinton told me how sorry she was. I couldn't help but mention that it was our anniversary, and then I lost my composure.

Before I knew it, another call came. Could I please hold for the president-elect? He, too, was thoughtful and concerned, and again I became emotional.

Early in the morning, two days after the funeral, I answered the phone not expecting to hear "What would be a good time for Mrs. Obama to call you?"

"Anytime she'd like to," I answered, sitting still on that spot on the sofa until she called not too long afterward.

I don't mention these phone calls to name-drop. I mention them because it was remarkable to me that these individuals took the time and effort to do this when they had more pressing affairs to attend to, but somehow, despite the fact that they were transitioning to a new office, they managed to maintain a real connection with real people.

I never would have gotten through that sad time had it not been for the outpouring of kindness from so many people. My living room looked like a florist shop. I was so grateful. My grief had made me restless, unable to settle down, reluctant to sit still in the house Charles and I had shared for so long. In my heart, I was uninterested in the world that I found myself muddling through. Even though Charles had battled cancer for two years, enduring radical surgeries and toxic treatments, I was unprepared for his death. I hadn't seen what was coming, swept away like those rafters on the Colorado River I'd read about in a newspaper account. They'd been drifting calmly down the river on what they thought was a good day. Before they knew it, they were swept up in a torrential current from a thunderstorm in the mountains many miles above them whose deluge, out of nowhere, had overpowered them. My own grief almost drowned me.

And what took me most by surprise was the sense of fear that consumed me. When I was little and the sunset illuminated the sky a fiery red, my grandfather told me that the world was about to end. I'd stare at the setting ball of fire, facing the awful realization that I had no control over the fact that my life was about to be over. That's how I felt on a daily basis with Charles gone.

After Charles died, I found some stories he'd written in his unsure handwriting on lined notebook paper. He talked about his childhood in Asberry. He wrote, "History will tell you the Depression is over but no one told us. I am not in the mood to tell all about the hard times we had. We did survive. I'd much rather take stock of my blessings and tell you what I'm thankful for. The birds and that first ray of sunshine every day. I'm thankful I have a good wife beside me, that I can trust her and depend on her in a lot of ways. I am grateful we can talk to each other sometimes without even speaking and have an understanding on a lot of things."

Reading his words, I relived our early years together. Charles showed me the best in what man can be. It's so strange how it's the small things your mind latches on to as grand gestures of love. When we first got married, he ate my first upside-down pineapple cake—the worst thing you've ever tasted—without so much as a word. I had to spit it out, it tasted so bad. I sorely missed the simple fact that he made and brought me a cup of coffee every morning.

He was a good man. If someone needed something, Charles would help any way he knew how. He was just the type of person who family and friends turned to in need. At church he started a bus ministry, picking up children who had no way to Sunday school. He overextended himself so badly, working long hours during the week and on Saturdays around the house, that by the time Sunday came he was plagued with migraine headaches. The doctor told him he was doing too much, that he had to learn to say no. He never did.

I smiled through my tears remembering the time he dressed up as the country pop star Billy Ray Cyrus, imitating him and dancing to the tune of "Achy Breaky Heart" for a competition. I can't imagine how long he must have spent convincing himself to do this. This was the man who was as sober as his military uniform most of the time.

The only way I survived my darkest times dealing with Goodyear was through Charles's kindness and clean heart. And when I was traveling so much over the previous two years, the person Charles leaned on the most was our preacher. They talked together for hours, and I felt some peace believing that Charles, a deeply spiritual man, was supported and sustained by God's love through his journey, one we all face when our death comes.

I was thankful that he left his stories that he must have written while I was away. As I read and reread them, I felt some measure of comfort to hear his voice again through his written words.

BECAUSE OF Charles's health, I hadn't planned on going to the inauguration. I guess the White House felt sorry for me, because I was invited shortly after Charles's funeral. The whirlwind week began in Philadelphia, where Vickie and I met up with a group of forty-one ordinary folks like me invited to accompany the Obamas and Bidens on the inaugural train ride, a 137-mile journey, covering part of the route President-Elect Abraham Lincoln made to his own inauguration in 1861. Over the course of one day, the inaugural train, nine gleaming silver cars with a blue vintage caboose draped in red, white, and blue bunting, whizzed from Philadelphia to Washington, D.C.

In Wilmington, Delaware, we stopped to pick up Vice President–Elect Joe Biden. The Amtrak conductor Biden befriended on his daily trips to Washington spoke to the ebullient crowd, who sang "Happy Birthday" to Michelle Obama for her forty-fifth birthday. (I couldn't help but reflect that when I was that age in the mid-1980s, I was just about to be laid off for almost a year and work in the chicken plant.)

It was here that the president-elect commented about the guests he'd invited, remarking, "These are the quiet heroes who have made this country great. They work hard, they look after their families, they sacrifice for their children and their grandchildren, and they deserve a government that represents the same enduring values that they live out in their own lives." When he spoke those words, I forgot the bitter cold for a moment and thought with pride about all that had happened since the Supreme Court ruling. I had thought I'd come to the end with that crazy verdict.

Along the train route, people lined roads, holding cameras and waving signs reading WE DID IT. They bundled up to survive the arctic blasts, huddled shoulder to shoulder on highway overpasses. They even hung from trees or stood waving their hats and arms, grinning from ear to ear, on rooftops, on porches, and in barren fields. I'd never seen or felt anything like it; the sense of hope was palpable. In Baltimore, around forty thousand people, whose toes and fingers must have been frozen, stood in single-digit temperatures to greet the president-elect. At the whistlestop rallies, the flush-faced crowds had waited for hours in the unforgiving winter weather for the train's arrival. When President-Elect Obama spoke of the ordinary Americans whose voices he would carry with him to the White House, the audience waved their American flags, cheered, and wept all at the same time.

During the entire trip I wore a microphone for my interview with ABC News. Most people who came up to me took one look at it and said, "I'll be talking to you later when that thing is gone," but I kept it turned off most of the time, periodically turning it back on to comment on what I was seeing and feeling.

Early on, President-Elect Obama and Michelle and Vice President–Elect Biden and Dr. Jill Biden came through our car to say hello. They hugged me, and behind me Vickie sat by the window. She was so quiet that I looked over my shoulder to check on her. She had tears slipping down her face. She'd just lost her father, and the experience of seeing so many people, their expectant faces, all of them, no matter their race or class or gender, at heart the same, simply wanting something better for the future and placing that hope in this man standing before us, who was acknowledging *us* of all the millions of people in America, had gotten to her. As they moved away from us down the aisle, I asked Vickie, "Are you okay?"

"Yes." She wiped her eyes. "But you're right. They're amazing people."

Vickie and I differed when it came to politics. Not on the topic of pay equity, mind you, but we politely agreed to disagree, as the saying goes, on other matters, party affiliation being one of them.

As we approached Washington, the crowds grew larger. The train arrived in Union Station at night as crowds waited along Pennsylvania Avenue to watch the president-elect make his way with his family to his temporary residence.

At the swearing-in on the steps of the Capitol, the crowd was unbelievable. Looking at the kaleidoscope of faces, I marveled at the beauty and diversity all around me, soaking in the fact that it hadn't been so long ago that only miles away from my hometown the infamous Scottsboro trial had taken place. So much had changed within my lifetime. Yes, so much more had to be done, but for that historic moment, I could celebrate progress. It was with wonder and great excitement that I watched the first African American president being sworn into office. Truly, it's not an event I thought I'd ever see.

Afterward, with the north wind bearing down on us, Vickie and I grabbed a hot dog from a street vendor and limped in our boots back to the hotel, where we thawed out and watched the parade on television.

You would think that winning a national championship in ballroom dancing would prepare you to dance with just about anybody. Well, I thought I was quite the hotshot dancer until I danced with the president at the Neighborhood Ball the evening after the inauguration. A small group of us were whisked to the elevated stage, where the president was dancing his first dance with Michelle. I was pleased to be wearing my favorite silver sequined skirt from my dancing days, but I was so thirsty I couldn't stand it. I was told that if I left the stage, I couldn't come back, so I ignored my scratchy, dry throat and started dancing along with everyone else in high spirits.

We were all moving to the music when a nice young man who had been on the inaugural train ride tapped me on my shoulder, grabbed my hand, and said, "Come with me." Next thing I knew, he marched right up to the president.

"Mr. President, here's someone you need to dance with," he said like they were the best of friends.

The president smiled his electric smile, took my arm, and off we went. I was concentrating so hard on making my body move the right way, I couldn't say much. As he guided me on the dance floor, I heard someone below the elevated stage say my name. I glanced down. It was Kevin Russell, who'd argued my case before the Supreme Court, and his fiancée. I smiled at them.

As I tried to make my stubborn feet act right, the president assured me, "We're going to do this."

My tongue felt like stone and my words were blunted, but I thought to myself, *Now, I know he's not talking about dancing. He's talking about the Ledbetter bill.*

ON JANUARY 15, the bill had passed the House, and only two days after the inauguration, it passed the Senate. I was elated, but when Secretary of State Hillary Clinton came to congratulate me, she pulled me aside and asked me, "How are you doing?" clearly wanting the honest truth about my state of mind after the loss of Charles.

Frankly, I was more than a bit of a mess inside. But I said, "Fine, just fine." I just couldn't go there, to my core, in that moment.

The day President Obama signed the Lilly Ledbetter Fair Pay Restoration Act into law, I walked with him on the red carpet to the East Room of the White House. As I settled into place to hear the president's remarks, I missed Charles more than I ever had. Listening to President Obama talk about my struggles and the hardships so many families face, I appreciated his remarks about his grandmother, thinking of my own grandmother Lillie, who died of cancer at such a young age and left such a crippling legacy for my own mother to bear.

After he finished his remarks, the people in the packed room stood and applauded as he returned to his desk for the signing. I saw Vickie and her family sitting next to Michelle Obama. Jon sat behind them. Even though I knew he wasn't there, I scanned the room, looking for Charles's piercing blue eyes and wide smile. In that moment, I felt the unbearable emptiness of that place beside me I'd leaned into for as long as I could remember. The crowd's applause lessened. President Obama looked at me, and I stepped forward to say a few words. I thanked God for all the good people around me who had worked so hard to pass the law, but sorrow sifted through my happiness all during that day as I did my best to hold my shoulders high and smile a hundred smiles.

Right after the bill had passed the Senate, I'd flown to New Jersey to speak at an American Association of University Women meeting. As I ate my breakfast that morning in a hotel in the middle of nowhere, I was reading an article about me in the *Wall Street Journal*. When the waitress poured me some more coffee, she noticed the article about the bill and the picture of me. She looked at me and then at the paper and back at me. And I said, "Yes, I'm Lilly Ledbetter." I finished my breakfast and the paper and kept waiting for my bill. It never came, so finally I asked the young woman, and she said it was covered. I said, "No, no. You don't need to do that." She said, "All the waitresses wanted to thank you for what you've done." The next morning, the waitresses covered my bill again. These unexpected gestures, along with the incredible passage of the bill, helped me slowly find my way through my sadness.

As I finish telling you the story behind the legislation that carries my name, at the age of seventy-three, I travel the world, speaking to law schools, high schools, women's professional groups and organizations, government agencies, and political groups on the state and national level, as well as at military bases and Democratic fundraisers. I often speak at universities, something I especially enjoy.

I'll never forget the day I spoke at Harvard. I'd scooted out to go to the ladies' room before my speech. I hurried into the stall, afraid I'd be late. Fumbling with the lock, at first I didn't notice the poster plastered on the stall door. It was my picture staring right back at me on the announcement for the lecture. I smiled back at myself, and even laughed out loud a little. Here I was, unable to go to college myself, speaking to the brightest young minds in the country. I just prayed that in these difficult economic times these young folks would have the power, voice, and passion to create a truly equitable workforce for all working families.

I told the Harvard undergraduates what I tell all of my audiences. For almost two decades, I was cheated. That's the way I see it. In 1979, when I began my career as one of the first women ever to work at Goodyear, my pay was equal to that of my male supervisors. But in 1981, shortly after I finally came forward about being sexually harassed and was consequentially labeled a "troublemaker," Goodyear implemented a merit-based program to award annual salary increases based on performance. My salary started slipping, despite positive performance reviews. By the end of 1997, I was being paid as much as 40 percent less than the male managers, taking home $3,727 each month while the lowest-paid male area manager received $4,286 and the highest-paid pocketed $5,236 per month. Of course, I had no idea. After giving almost twenty of the best years of my life to Goodyear, in the end I lost more than $224,000 in salary and even more in overtime and retirement money.

But what really enrages me is that my experience is not uncommon. Today, 71 million women work to support themselves and their families but continue to make seventy-eight cents for every dollar a man takes home. The Institute for Women's Policy Research calculated that a typical twenty-five-year-old woman who graduated from college in 1984 and who was in her mid-forties in 2004 has lost more than $440,000. In 2004, the median annual earnings of women aged fifteen and older was $31,223, compared with $40,798 for men. If women in the workforce earned the same as men who work the same number of hours; have the same education, age, and union status; and live in the same area of the country, their annual income would rise about $4,000, and their poverty rates would be cut at least in half.

When I set out on my Goodyear career in 1979, it wasn't part of my grand plan to someday have my name be on a Supreme Court case or an act of Congress. I simply wanted to work hard and support my family. The rest, I believed, would take care of itself.

Clearly, fate had other plans for this Alabama girl. After all, I started out as a supervisor at a tire plant. Thirty years later, I've been a litigant, an advocate, a lobbyist, an author, and a public speaker. Sometimes, life throws us curveballs. We may not have asked for them, we may not have even expected them, but we still have to deal with them.

After all that's happened to me, I've realized that the true test of an individual is not so much *what* happens to her, but *how* she reacts to it. When we see an injustice, do we sit and do nothing, or do we fight back? When we experience failure, do we passively accept it, or do we learn from it and do better the next time? When we get knocked down, do we stay down, or do we get back up? Each of us, every day, breaks through barriers for women and girls simply because we choose to believe the future can be better.

It's important to recognize that there's still much that needs to be accomplished to achieve true pay equity for women. To help end wage discrimination based on gender, the Paycheck Fairness Act still needs to be made into law. It has passed the House but was filibustered by the Republicans in the Senate in November 2010; it lacked two of the sixty votes necessary to end the debate and proceed to a vote. It has now been reintroduced to Congress by the indomitable Senator Barbara Mikulski and Congresswoman Rosa DeLauro, both champions of my bill. This act strengthens and updates the Equal Pay Act passed by President Kennedy in 1963. Among other things, it will bar retaliation against workers for discussing salary and facilitate class-action Equal Pay Act claims.

Those young waitresses who recognized me the day after the bill had passed and all those bright-faced young folks I speak to across the country might bear the fruit of the Lilly Ledbetter Fair Pay Restoration Act. But more than that, I'm hopeful that the Ledbetter Act will impact future generations, generations of women and men I will not live to see but my granddaughter and greatgranddaughter will.

Granny Mac was right. The day I heard the whippoorwill call on my way to work, a death occurred. When I found the note, life as I knew it ended. All I'd ever dreamed of as a young girl was escaping the hot, dusty cotton fields, leaving behind the long sack dragging around my neck that I never could fill. But those endless rows of cotton that pricked my hands until they bled were my saving grace on the journey I began that spring day so long ago. My transformation from an unknown tire manager facing an all-toocommon injustice to a woman people now recognize as "the grandmother of equal pay" took every ounce of grit I'd gained picking cotton on my grandfather's farm in Possum Trot, Alabama.

MY SPEECH at the 2008 DEMOCRATIC
NATIONAL CONVENTION

G OOD EVENING. Many of you are probably asking: Who is that grandmother from Alabama at the podium? I can assure you, nobody is more surprised, or humbled, than I am. I'm here to talk about America's commitment to fairness and equality, and how people like me—and like you—suffer when that commitment is betrayed.

How fitting that I speak to you on Women's Equality Day, when we celebrate ratification of the amendment that gave women the right to vote. Even as we celebrate, let's also remind ourselves: The fight for equality is not over. I know that from personal experience. I was a trailblazer when I went to work as a female supervisor at a Goodyear tire plant in Gadsden, Alabama.

My job demanded a lot, and I gave it 100 percent. I kept up with every one of my male co-workers. But toward the end of my nineteen years at Goodyear, I began to suspect that I wasn't getting paid as much as men doing the same job. An anonymous note in my mailbox confirmed that I was right. Despite praising me for my work, Goodyear gave me smaller raises than my male co-managers, over and over.

Those differences affected my family's quality of life then, and they affect my retirement now. When I discovered the injustice, I thought about moving on. But in the end, I couldn't ignore the discrimination. So I went to court. A jury agreed with me. They found that my employer had violated the law and awarded me what I was owed.

I hoped the verdict would make my company feel the sting,

learn a lesson and never again treat women unfairly. But they appealed, all the way to the Supreme Court, and in a 5-to-4 decision our highest court sided with big business. They said I should have filed my complaint within six months of Goodyear's first decision to pay me less, even though I didn't know that's what they were doing.

In dissent, Justice Ruth Bader Ginsburg wrote that the ruling made no sense in the real world. She was right. The House of Representatives passed a bill that would make sure what was done to me couldn't happen again. But when it got to the Senate, enough Republicans opposed it to prevent a vote.

We can't afford more of the same votes that deny women their equal rights. Barack Obama is on our side. He is fighting to fix this terrible ruling, and as president, he has promised to appoint justices who will enforce laws that protect everyday people like me. But this isn't a Democratic or a Republican issue. It's a fairness issue. And fortunately, there are some Republicans—and a lot of Democrats—who are on our side.

My case is over. I will never receive the pay I deserve. But there will be a far richer reward if we secure fair pay. For our children and grandchildren, so that no one will ever again experience the discrimination that I did. Equal pay for equal work is a fundamental American principle. We need leaders in this country who will fight for it. With all of us working together, we can have the change we need and the opportunity we all deserve.

BENCH ANNOUNCEMENT

Ledbetter v. Goodyear Tire & Rubber Co., 05-1074
Tuesday, May 29, 2007

F OUR MEMBERS of this Court, Justices Stevens, Souter, Breyer and I, dissent from today's decision. In our view, the Court does not comprehend, or is indifferent to, the insidious way in which women can be victims of pay discrimination. Today's decision counsels: Sue early on, when it is uncertain whether discrimination accounts for the pay disparity you are beginning to experience. Indeed, initially you may not know that men are receiving more for substantially similar work. (Of course, you are likely to lose such a less-than-fully baked case.) If you sue only when the pay disparity becomes steady and large enough to enable you to mount a winnable case, you will be cut off at the court's threshold for suing too late. That situation cannot be what Congress intended when, in Title VII, it outlawed discrimination based on race, color, religion, sex, or national origin in our Nation's workplaces.

Lilly Ledbetter, the plaintiff in this case, was engaged as an area manager at a Goodyear Tire and Rubber plant in Alabama in 1979. Her starting salary was in line with the salaries of men performing similar work. But over time, her pay slipped in comparison to the pay of male employees with equal or less seniority. By the end of 1997, Ledbetter was the only woman left working as an area manager and the pay discrepancy between Ledbetter and her 15 male counterparts was stark: Ledbetter's pay was *15 to 40 percent less* than every other area manager.

Ledbetter complained to the Equal Employment Opportunity

Commission in March 1998. She charged that, in violation of Title VII, Goodyear paid her a discriminatorily low salary because of her sex. The charge was eventually brought to court and tried to a jury. The jury found it "more likely than not that [Goodyear] paid [Ledbetter] a[n] unequal salary because of her sex." The Court today nullifies that verdict, holding that Ledbetter's claim is time barred.

Title VII provides that a charge of discrimination "shall be filed within [180] days after the alleged unlawful employment practice occurred." Ledbetter charged, and proved at trial, that the paychecks she received within the 180-day filing period were substantially lower than the paychecks received by men doing the same work. Further, she introduced substantial evidence showing that discrimination accounted for the pay differential, indeed, that discrimination against women as supervisors was pervasive at Goodyear's plant. That evidence was unavailing, the Court holds, because it was incumbent on Ledbetter to file charges of discrimination year-by-year, each time Goodyear failed to increase her salary commensurate with the salaries of her male peers. Any annual pay decision not contested promptly (within 180 days), the Court affirms, becomes grandfathered, beyond the province of Title VII ever to repair.

Title VII was meant to govern real-world employment practices, and that world is what the Court today ignores. Pay disparities often occur, as they did in Ledbetter's case, in small increments; only over time is there strong cause to suspect that discrimination is at work. Comparative pay information is not routinely communicated to employees. Instead, it is often hidden from the employee's view. Small initial discrepancies, even if the employee knows they exist, may not be seen as grounds for a federal case. An employee like Ledbetter, trying to succeed in a male-dominated workplace, in a job filled only by men before she was hired, understandably may be anxious to avoid making waves.

Pay discrimination that recurs and swells in impact, is significantly different from discrete adverse actions promptly communicated and "easy to identify" as discriminatory. Events in that category include firing, denial of a promotion, or refusal to hire. In contrast to those unambiguous actions, until a pay disparity becomes apparent and sizable, an employee is unlikely to comprehend her plight and, therefore, to complain about it. Ledbetter's initial readiness to give her employer the benefit of the doubt should not preclude her from later seeking redress for the continuing payment to her of a salary depressed because of her sex.

Yet, as the Court reads Title VII, each and every pay decision Ledbetter did not promptly challenge wiped the slate clean. Nevermind the cumulative effect of a series of decisions that, together, set her pay well below that of every male area manager. Knowingly carrying past pay discrimination forward must be treated as lawful. Ledbetter may not be compensated under Title VII for the lower pay she was in fact receiving when she complained to the EEOC. Notably, the same denial of relief would occur had Ledbetter encountered pay discrimination based on race, religion, age, national origin, or disability.

This is not the first time the Court has ordered a cramped interpretation of Title VII, incompatible with the statute's broad remedial purpose. In 1991, Congress passed a Civil Rights Act that effectively overruled several of this Court's similarly restrictive decisions. Today, the ball again lies in Congress' court. As in 1991, the Legislature has cause to note and correct this Court's parsimonious reading of Title VII.

PRESIDENT OBAMA'S SPEECH upon the signing of THE LILLY LEDBETTER FAIR PAY RESTORATION ACT, January 29, 2009

I T is fitting that with the very first bill I sign—the Lilly Ledbetter Fair Pay Restoration Act—we are upholding one of this nation's first principles: that we are all created equal and each deserve a chance to pursue our own version of happiness.

It is also fitting that we are joined today by the woman after whom this bill is named—someone Michelle and I have had the privilege of getting to know for ourselves. Lilly Ledbetter did not set out to be a trailblazer or a household name. She was just a good hard worker who did her job—and did it well—for nearly two decades before discovering that, for years, she was paid less than her male colleagues for the very same work. Over the course of her career, she lost more than $200,000 in salary, and even more in pension and Social Security benefits—losses she still feels today.

Now, Lilly could have accepted her lot and moved on. She could have decided that it wasn't worth the hassle and the harassment that would inevitably come with speaking up for what she deserved. But instead, she decided that there was a principle at stake, something worth fighting for. So she set out on a journey that would take more than ten years, take her all the way to the Supreme Court of the United States, and lead to this day and this bill which will help others get the justice she was denied.

Because while this bill bears her name, Lilly knows this story isn't just about her. It's the story of women across this country still earning just seventy-eight cents for every dollar men earn— women of color even less—which means that today, in the year 2009, countless women are still losing thousands of dollars in salary, income and retirement savings over the course of a lifetime.

But equal pay is by no means just a women's issue—it's a family issue. It's about parents who find themselves with less money for tuition and child care; couples who wind up with less to retire on; households where, when one breadwinner is paid less than she deserves, that's the difference between affording the mortgage—or not; between keeping the heat on, or paying the doctor's bills—or not. And in this economy, when so many folks are already working harder for less and struggling to get by, the last thing they can afford is losing part of each month's paycheck to simple and plain discrimination.

So signing this bill today is to send a clear message: that making our economy work means making sure it works for everybody. That there are no second-class citizens in our workplaces, and that it's not just unfair and illegal—it's bad for business—to pay somebody less because of their gender, or their age, or their race, or their ethnicity, religion, or disability. And that justice isn't about some abstract legal theory, or footnote in a casebook—it's about how our laws affect the daily realities of people: their ability to make a living and care for their families and achieve their goals.

Ultimately, equal pay isn't just an economic issue for millions of Americans and their families, it's a question of who we are—and whether we're truly living up to our fundamental ideals. Whether we'll do our part, as generations before us, to ensure those words put on paper some two hundred years ago really mean something—to breathe new life into them with the more enlightened understanding that is appropriate for our time.

That is what Lilly Ledbetter challenged us to do. And today, I sign this bill not just in her honor, but in honor of those who came before her. Women like my grandmother, who worked in a bank all her life, and even after she hit that glass ceiling, kept getting up and giving her best every day, without complaint, because she wanted something better for me and my sister.

And I sign this bill for my daughters, and all those who will come after us, because I want them to grow up in a nation that values their contributions, where there are no limits to their dreams and they have opportunities their mothers and grandmothers never could have imagined.

In the end, that's why Lilly stayed the course. She knew it was too late for her—that this bill wouldn't undo the years of injustice she faced or restore the earnings she was denied. But this grandmother from Alabama kept on fighting, because she was thinking about the next generation. It's what we've always done in America—set our sights high for ourselves, but even higher for our children and our grandchildren.

And now it's up to us to continue this work. This bill is an important step—a simple fix to ensure fundamental fairness for American workers—and I want to thank this remarkable and bipartisan group of legislators who worked so hard to get it passed.

And I want to thank all the advocates who are in the audience who worked so hard to get it passed. And this is only the beginning. I know that if we stay focused, as Lilly did—and keep standing for what's right, as Lilly did—we will close that pay gap and we will make sure that our daughters have the same rights, the same chances, and the same freedom to pursue their dreams as our sons.

THE LILLY LEDBETTER FAIR PAY

RESTORATION ACT

Public Law 111-2
111th Congress
1st Session

An Act

To amend title VII of the Civil Rights Act of 1964 and the Age Discrimination in Employment Act of 1967, and to modify the operation of the Americans with Disabilities Act of 1990 and the Rehabilitation Act of 1973, to clarify that a discriminatory compensation decision or other practice that is unlawful under such Acts occurs each time compensation is paid pursuant to the discriminatory compensation decision or other practice, and for other purposes.

Be it enacted by the Senate and House of Representatives of the United States of America in Congress assembled,

SECTION 1. SHORT TITLE.

This Act may be cited as the "Lilly Ledbetter Fair Pay Act of 2009".

SEC. 2. FINDINGS.

Congress finds the following:

(1) The Supreme Court in Ledbetter v. Goodyear Tire & Rubber Co., 550 U.S. 618 (2007), significantly impairs statutory protections against discrimination in compensation that Congress established and that have been bedrock principles of American law for decades. The Ledbetter decision undermines those statutory protections by unduly restricting the time period in which victims of discrimination can challenge and recover for discriminatory compensation decisions or other practices, contrary to the intent of Congress.

(2) The limitation imposed by the Court on the filing of discriminatory compensation claims ignores the reality of wage dis-

crimination and is at odds with the robust application of the civil rights laws that Congress intended.

(3) With regard to any charge of discrimination under any law, nothing in this Act is intended to preclude or limit an aggrieved person's right to introduce evidence of an unlawful employment practice that has occurred outside the time for filing a charge of discrimination.

(4) Nothing in this Act is intended to change current law treatment of when pension distributions are considered paid.

SEC. 3. DISCRIMINATION IN COMPENSATION BECAUSE OF RACE, COLOR, RELIGION, SEX, OR NATIONAL ORIGIN.

Section 706(e) of the Civil Rights Act of 1964 (42 U.S.C. 2000e-5(e)) is amended by adding at the end the following:

"(3)(A) For purposes of this section, an unlawful employment practice occurs, with respect to discrimination in compensation in violation of this title, when a discriminatory compensation decision or other practice is adopted, when an individual becomes subject to a discriminatory compensation decision or other practice, or when an individual is affected by application of a discriminatory compensation decision or other practice, including each time wages, benefits, or other compensation is paid, resulting in whole or in part from such a decision or other practice.

"(B) In addition to any relief authorized by section 1977A of the Revised Statutes (42 U.S.C. 1981a), liability may accrue and an aggrieved person may obtain relief as provided in subsection (g)(1), including recovery of back pay for up to two years preceding the filing of the charge, where the unlawful employment practices that have occurred during the charge filing period are similar or related to unlawful employment practices with regard to discrimination in compensation that occurred outside the time for filing a charge.".

SEC. 4. DISCRIMINATION IN COMPENSATION BECAUSE OF AGE.

Section 7(d) of the Age Discrimination in Employment Act of 1967 (29 U.S.C. 626(d)) is amended—

(1) in the first sentence—

(A) by redesignating paragraphs (1) and (2) as subparagraphs (A) and (B), respectively; and

(B) by striking "(d)" and inserting "(d)(1)";

(2) in the third sentence, by striking "Upon" and inserting the following:

"(2) Upon"; and

(3) by adding at the end the following:

"(3) For purposes of this section, an unlawful practice occurs, with respect to discrimination in compensation in violation of this Act, when a discriminatory compensation decision or other practice is adopted, when a person becomes subject to a discriminatory compensation decision or other practice, or when a person is affected by application of a discriminatory compensation decision or other practice, including each time wages, benefits, or other compensation is paid, resulting in whole or in part from such a decision or other practice.".

SEC. 5. APPLICATION TO OTHER LAWS.

(a) AMERICANS WITH DISABILITIES ACT OF 1990.—The amendments made by section 3 shall apply to claims of discrimination in compensation brought under title I and section 503 of the Americans with Disabilities Act of 1990 (42 U.S.C. 1211 et seq., 12203), pursuant to section 107(a) of such Act (42 U.S.C. 12117(a)), which adopts the powers, remedies, and procedures set forth in section 706 of the Civil Rights Act of 1964 (42 U.S.C. 2000e-5).

(b) REHABILITATION ACT OF 1973.—The amendments made by section 3 shall apply to claims of discrimination in compensation brought under sections 501 and 504 of the Rehabilitation Act of 1973 (29 U.S.C. 791, 794), pursuant to—

(1) sections 501(g) and 504(d) of such Act (29 U.S.C. 791(g), 794(d)), respectively, which adopt the standards applied under title I of the Americans with Disabilities Act of 1990 for determining whether a violation has occurred in a complaint alleging employment discrimination; and

(2) paragraphs (1) and (2) of section 505(a) of such Act (29 U.S.C. 794a(a)) (as amended by subsection (c)).

(c) Conforming Amendments.—

(1) REHABILITATION ACT OF 1973.—Section 505(a) of the Rehabilitation Act of 1973 (29 U.S.C. 794a(a)) is amended—

(A) in paragraph (1), by inserting after "(42 U.S.C. 2000e-5 (f) through (k))" the following: "(and the application of section

706(e)(3) (42 U.S.C. 2000e-5(e)(3)) to claims of discrimination in compensation)"; and

(B) in paragraph (2), by inserting after "1964" the following: "(42 U.S.C. 2000d et seq.) (and in subsection (e)(3) of section 706 of such Act (42 U.S.C. 2000e-5), applied to claims of discrimination in compensation)".

(2) CIVIL RIGHTS ACT OF 1964—Section 717 of the Civil Rights Act of 1964 (42 U.S.C. 2000e-16) is amended by adding at the end the following:

"(f) Section 706(e)(3) shall apply to complaints of discrimination in compensation under this section.".

(3) AGE DISCRIMINATION IN EMPLOYMENT ACT OF 1967.— Section 15(f) of the Age Discrimination in Employment Act of 1967 (29 U.S.C. 633a(f)) is amended by striking "of section" and inserting "of sections 7(d)(3) and".

SEC. 6. EFFECTIVE DATE.

This Act, and the amendments made by this Act, take effect as if enacted on May 28, 2007 and apply to all claims of discrimination in compensation under title VII of the Civil Rights Act of 1964 (42 U.S.C. 2000e et seq.), the Age Discrimination in Employment Act of 1967 (29 U.S.C. 621 et seq.), title I and section 503 of the Americans with Disabilities Act of 1990, and sections 501 and 504 of the Rehabilitation Act of 1973, that are pending on or after that date.

Approved January 29, 2009.

LEGISLATIVE HISTORY—S. 181 (H.R. 11):

CONGRESSIONAL RECORD, Vol. 155 (2009):
    Jan. 15, 21, 22, considered and passed Senate.
    Jan. 27, considered and passed House.
DAILY COMPILATION OF PRESIDENTIAL DOCUMENTS (2009):
    Jan. 29, Presidential remarks.
Washington, D.C., U.S. Government Printing Office,
DOCID: f:publ002.111, p. 123 STAT. 5.

THE PAYCHECK FAIRNESS ACT

Excerpted testimony of Lisa M. Maatz, Director of Public Policy and Government Relations, American Association of University Women, Hearing by Joint Economic Committee, United States Congress, "Equal Pay for Equal Work? New Evidence on the Persistence of the Gender Pay Gap," April 28, 2009

WHAT WILL THE PAYCHECK FAIRNESS ACT DO?

THE PAYCHECK Fairness Act is a comprehensive bill that strengthens the Equal Pay Act by taking meaningful steps to create incentives for employers to follow the law, empower women to negotiate for equal pay, and strengthen federal outreach and enforcement efforts. The bill would also deter wage discrimination by strengthening penalties for equal pay violations, and by prohibiting retaliation against workers who inquire about employers' wage practices or disclose their own wages.

THE PAYCHECK FAIRNESS ACT WOULD

- **Close a Loophole in Affirmative Defenses for Employers.** The legislation clarifies acceptable reasons for differences in pay by requiring employers to demonstrate that wage gaps between men and women doing the same work have a business justification and are truly a result of factors other than sex.
- **Fix the "Establishment" Requirement.** The bill would clarify the establishment provision under the Equal Pay Act, which would allow for reasonable comparisons between employees within clearly defined geographical areas to determine fair wages. This

provision is based on a similar plan successfully used in the state of Illinois.

- **Prohibit Employer Retaliation.** The legislation would deter wage discrimination by prohibiting retaliation against workers who inquire about employers' wage practices or disclose their own wages. *(Note: Employees with access to colleagues' wage information in the course of their work, such as human resources employees, may still be prohibited from sharing that information.)* This non-retaliation provision would have been particularly helpful to Lilly Ledbetter, because Goodyear prohibited employees from discussing or sharing their wages. This policy delayed her discovery of the discrimination against her by more than a decade.

- **Improve Equal Pay Remedies.** The bill would deter wage discrimination by strengthening penalties for equal pay violations by providing women with a fair option to proceed in an opt-out class action suit under the Equal Pay Act, and allowing women to receive punitive and compensatory damages for pay discrimination. The bill's measured approach levels the playing field by ensuring that women can obtain the same remedies as those subject to discrimination on the basis of race or national origin.

- **Increase Training, Research and Education.** The legislation would authorize additional training for Equal Employment Opportunity Commission staff to better identify and handle wage disputes. It would also aid in the efficient and effective enforcement of federal anti–pay discrimination laws by requiring the EEOC to develop regulations directing employers to collect wage data, reported by the race, sex, and national origin of employees. The bill would also require the U.S. Department of Labor to reinstate activities that promote equal pay, such as: directing educational programs, providing technical assistance to employers, recognizing businesses that address the wage gap, and conducting and promoting research about pay disparities between men and women.

- **Establish Salary Negotiation Skills Training.** The bill would create a competitive grant program to develop salary negotiation training for women and girls.

- **Improve Collection of Pay Information.** The bill would also reinstate the Equal Opportunity Survey, to enable targeting of the Labor Department's enforcement efforts by requiring all federal contractors to submit data on employment practices such as hiring, promotions, terminations and pay. This survey was developed over two decades and three presidential administrations, was first used in 2000, but was rescinded by the Department of Labor in 2006.

The Paycheck Fairness Act maintains the protections currently provided to small businesses under the Equal Pay Act, and updates its remedies and protections using familiar principles and concepts from other civil rights laws. These new provisions are not onerous and are well-known to employers, the legal community, and the courts. As a result, the legislation will enhance women's civil rights protections while simultaneously protecting the job-creating capacity of small businesses.

THE PAYCHECK FAIRNESS ACT

111th Congress
1st Session
H.R. 12

A Bill

To amend the Fair Labor Standards Act of 1938 to provide more effective remedies to victims of discrimination in the payment of wages on the basis of sex, and for other purposes.

Be it enacted by the Senate and House of Representatives of the United States of America in Congress assembled,

SECTION 1. SHORT TITLE.

This Act may be cited as the "Paycheck Fairness Act".

SEC. 2. FINDINGS.

Congress finds the following:

(1) Women have entered the workforce in record numbers over the past 50 years.

(2) Despite the enactment of the Equal Pay Act in 1963, many women continue to earn significantly lower pay than men for equal work. These pay disparities exist in both the private and governmental sectors. In many instances, the pay disparities can only be due to continued intentional discrimination or the lingering effects of past discrimination.

(3) The existence of such pay disparities—

(A) depresses the wages of working families who rely on the wages of all members of the family to make ends meet;

(B) undermines women's retirement security, which is often based on earnings while in the workforce;

(C) prevents the optimum utilization of available labor resources;

(D) has been spread and perpetuated, through commerce and the channels and instrumentalities of commerce, among the workers of the several States;

(E) burdens commerce and the free flow of goods in commerce;

(F) constitutes an unfair method of competition in commerce;

(G) leads to labor disputes burdening and obstructing commerce and the free flow of goods in commerce;

(H) interferes with the orderly and fair marketing of goods in commerce; and

(I) in many instances, may deprive workers of equal protection on the basis of sex in violation of the 5th and 14th amendments.

(4) (A) Artificial barriers to the elimination of discrimination in the payment of wages on the basis of sex continue to exist decades after the enactment of the Fair Labor Standards Act of 1938

(29 U.S.C. 201 et seq.) and the Civil Rights Act of 1964 (42 U.S.C. 2000a et seq.).

(B) These barriers have resulted, in significant part, because the Equal Pay Act has not worked as Congress originally intended. Improvements and modifications to the law are necessary to ensure that the Act provides effective protection to those subject to pay discrimination on the basis of their sex.

(C) Elimination of such barriers would have positive effects, including—

(i) providing a solution to problems in the economy created by unfair pay disparities;

(ii) substantially reducing the number of working women earning unfairly low wages, thereby reducing the dependence on public assistance;

(iii) promoting stable families by enabling all family members to earn a fair rate of pay;

(iv) remedying the effects of past discrimination on the basis of sex and ensuring that in the future workers are afforded equal protection on the basis of sex; and

(v) ensuring equal protection pursuant to Congress' power to enforce the 5th and 14th amendments.

(5) The Department of Labor and the Equal Employment Opportunity Commission have important and unique responsibilities to help ensure that women receive equal pay for equal work.

(6) The Department of Labor is responsible for—

(A) collecting and making publicly available information about women's pay;

(B) ensuring that companies receiving Federal contracts comply with anti-discrimination affirmative action requirements of Executive Order 11246 (relating to equal employment opportunity);

(C) disseminating information about women's rights in the workplace;

(D) helping women who have been victims of pay discrimination obtain a remedy; and

(E) being proactive in investigating and prosecuting equal

pay violations, especially systemic violations, and in enforcing all of its mandates.

(7) The Equal Employment Opportunity Commission is the primary enforcement agency for claims made under the Equal Pay Act, and issues regulations and guidance on appropriate interpretations of the law.

(8) With a stronger commitment by the Department of Labor and the Equal Employment Opportunity Commission to their responsibilities, increased information as a result of the amendments made by this Act to the Equal Pay Act of 1963, wage data, and more effective remedies, women will be better able to recognize and enforce their rights.

(9) Certain employers have already made great strides in eradicating unfair pay disparities in the workplace and their achievements should be recognized.

SEC. 3. ENHANCED ENFORCEMENT OF EQUAL PAY REQUIREMENTS.

(a) BONA-FIDE FACTOR DEFENSE AND MODIFICATION OF SAME ESTABLISHMENT REQUIREMENT—Section 6(d)(1) of the Fair Labor Standards Act of 1938 (29 U.S.C. 206(d)(1)) is amended—

(1) by striking "No employer having" and inserting "(A) No employer having";

(2) by striking "any other factor other than sex" and inserting "a bona fide factor other than sex, such as education, training, or experience"; and

(3) by inserting at the end the following:

"(B) The bona fide factor defense described in subparagraph (A)(iv) shall apply only if the employer demonstrates that such factor (i) is not based upon or derived from a sex-based differential in compensation; (ii) is job-related with respect to the position in question; and (iii) is consistent with business necessity. Such defense shall not apply where the employee demonstrates that an alternative employment practice exists that would serve the same business purpose without producing such differential and that the employer has refused to adopt such alternative practice.

"(C) For purposes of subparagraph (A), employees shall be deemed to work in the same establishment if the employees work for the same employer at workplaces located in the same county or similar political subdivision of a State. The preceding sentence shall not be construed as limiting broader applications of the term 'establishment' consistent with rules prescribed or guidance issued by the Equal Opportunity Employment Commission.".

(b) Nonretaliation Provision—Section 15 of the Fair Labor Standards Act of 1938 (29 U.S.C. 215(a)(3)) is amended—

(1) in subsection (a)(3), by striking "employee has filed" and all that follows and inserting "employee—

"(A) has made a charge or filed any complaint or instituted or caused to be instituted any investigation, proceeding, hearing, or action under or related to this Act, including an investigation conducted by the employer, or has testified or is planning to testify or has assisted or participated in any manner in any such investigation, proceeding, hearing or action, or has served or is planning to serve on an industry Committee; or

"(B) has inquired about, discussed or disclosed the wages of the employee or another employee."; and

(2) by adding at the end the following:

"(c) Subsection (a)(3)(B) shall not apply to instances in which an employee who has access to the wage information of other employees as a part of such employee's essential job functions discloses the wages of such other employees to individuals who do not otherwise have access to such information, unless such disclosure is in response to a complaint or charge or in furtherance of an investigation, proceeding, hearing, or action under section 6(d), including an investigation conducted by the employer. Nothing in this subsection shall be construed to limit the rights of an employee provided under any other provision of law.".

(c) Enhanced Penalties—Section 16(b) of the Fair Labor Standards Act of 1938 (29 U.S.C. 216(b)) is amended—

(1) by inserting after the first sentence the following: "Any employer who violates section 6(d) shall additionally be liable for such compensatory damages, or, where the employee demonstrates that the employer acted with malice or reckless indifference, punitive damages as may be appropriate, except that the United States shall not be liable for punitive damages.";

(2) in the sentence beginning "An action to", by striking "either of the preceding sentences" and inserting "any of the preceding sentences of this subsection";

(3) in the sentence beginning 'No employees shall', by striking "No employees" and inserting "Except with respect to class actions brought to enforce section 6(d), no employee";

(4) by inserting after the sentence referred to in paragraph (3), the following: 'Notwithstanding any other provision of Federal law, any action brought to enforce section 6(d) may be maintained as a class action as provided by the Federal Rules of Civil Procedure.'; and

(5) in the sentence beginning "The court in"—

(A) by striking "in such action" and inserting "in any action brought to recover the liability prescribed in any of the preceding sentences of this subsection"; and

(B) by inserting before the period the following: ", including expert fees".

(d) ACTION BY SECRETARY—Section 16(c) of the Fair Labor Standards Act of 1938 (29 U.S.C. 216(c)) is amended—

(1) in the first sentence—

(A) by inserting "or, in the case of a violation of section 6(d), additional compensatory or punitive damages, as described in subsection (b)," before "and the agreement"; and

(B) by inserting before the period the following: "or such compensatory or punitive damages, as appropriate";

(2) in the second sentence, by inserting before the period the following: "and, in the case of a violation of section 6(d), additional compensatory or punitive damages, as described in subsection (b)";

(3) in the third sentence, by striking "the first sentence" and inserting "the first or second sentence"; and

(4) in the last sentence—

(A) by striking "commenced in the case" and inserting "commenced—

"(1) in the case";

(B) by striking the period and inserting "; or"; and

(C) by adding at the end the following:

"(2) in the case of a class action brought to enforce section 6(d), on the date on which the individual becomes a party plaintiff to the class action.".

SEC. 4. TRAINING.

The Equal Employment Opportunity Commission and the Office

of Federal Contract Compliance Programs, subject to the availability of funds appropriated under section 10, shall provide training to Commission employees and affected individuals and entities on matters involving discrimination in the payment of wages.

SEC. 5. NEGOTIATION SKILLS TRAINING FOR GIRLS AND WOMEN.

(a) PROGRAM AUTHORIZED—

(1) IN GENERAL—The Secretary of Labor, after consultation with the Secretary of Education, is authorized to establish and carry out a grant program.

(2) GRANTS—In carrying out the program, the Secretary of Labor may make grants on a competitive basis to eligible entities, to carry out negotiation skills training programs for girls and women.

(3) ELIGIBLE ENTITIES—To be eligible to receive a grant under this subsection, an entity shall be a public agency, such as a State, a local government in a metropolitan statistical area (as defined by the Office of Management and Budget), a State educational agency, or a local educational agency, a private nonprofit organization, or a community-based organization.

(4) APPLICATION—To be eligible to receive a grant under this subsection, an entity shall submit an application to the Secretary of Labor at such time, in such manner, and containing such information as the Secretary of Labor may require.

(5) USE OF FUNDS—An entity that receives a grant under this subsection shall use the funds made available through the grant to carry out an effective negotiation skills training program that empowers girls and women. The training provided through the program shall help girls and women strengthen their negotiation skills to allow the girls and women to obtain higher salaries and rates of compensation that are equal to those paid to similarly-situated male employees.

(b) INCORPORATING TRAINING INTO EXISTING PROGRAMS—The Secretary of Labor and the Secretary of Education shall issue regulations or policy guidance that provides for integrating the negotiation skills training, to the extent practicable, into programs authorized under—

(1) in the case of the Secretary of Education, the Elementary and Secondary Education Act of 1965 (20 U.S.C. 6301 et seq.), the

Carl D. Perkins Vocational and Technical Education Act of 1998 (20 U.S.C. 2301 et seq.), the Higher Education Act of 1965 (20 U.S.C. 1001 et seq.), and other programs carried out by the Department of Education that the Secretary of Education determines to be appropriate; and

(2) in the case of the Secretary of Labor, the Workforce Investment Act of 1998 (29 U.S.C. 2801 et seq.), and other programs carried out by the Department of Labor that the Secretary of Labor determines to be appropriate.

(c) REPORT—Not later than 1 year after the date of enactment of this Act, and annually thereafter, the Secretary of Labor and the Secretary of Education shall prepare and submit to Congress a report describing the activities conducted under this section and evaluating the effectiveness of such activities in achieving the purposes of this Act.

SEC. 6. RESEARCH, EDUCATION, AND OUTREACH.

The Secretary of Labor shall conduct studies and provide information to employers, labor organizations, and the general public concerning the means available to eliminate pay disparities between men and women, including—

(1) conducting and promoting research to develop the means to correct expeditiously the conditions leading to the pay disparities;

(2) publishing and otherwise making available to employers, labor organizations, professional associations, educational institutions, the media, and the general public the findings resulting from studies and other materials, relating to eliminating the pay disparities;

(3) sponsoring and assisting State and community informational and educational programs;

(4) providing information to employers, labor organizations, professional associations, and other interested persons on the means of eliminating the pay disparities;

(5) recognizing and promoting the achievements of employers, labor organizations, and professional associations that have worked to eliminate the pay disparities; and

(6) convening a national summit to discuss, and consider approaches for rectifying, the pay disparities.

SEC. 7. ESTABLISHMENT OF THE NATIONAL AWARD FOR PAY EQUITY IN THE WORKPLACE.

(a) In General—There is established the Secretary of Labor's National Award for Pay Equity in the Workplace, which shall be awarded, as appropriate, to encourage proactive efforts to comply with section 6(d) of the Fair Labor Standards Act of 1938 (29 U.S.C. 206(d)).

(b) Criteria for Qualification—The Secretary of Labor shall set criteria for receipt of the award, including a requirement that an employer has made substantial effort to eliminate pay disparities between men and women, and deserves special recognition as a consequence of such effort. The Secretary shall establish procedures for the application and presentation of the award.

(c) Employer—In this section, the term "employer" includes—

(1) (A) a corporation, including a nonprofit corporation;

(B) a partnership;

(C) a professional association;

(D) a labor organization; and

(E) a business entity similar to an entity described in any of subparagraphs (A) through (D);

(2) an entity carrying out an education referral program, a training program, such as an apprenticeship or management training program, or a similar program; and

(3) an entity carrying out a joint program, formed by a combination of any entities described in paragraph (1) or (2).

SEC. 8. COLLECTION OF PAY INFORMATION BY THE EQUAL EMPLOYMENT OPPORTUNITY COMMISSION.

Section 709 of the Civil Rights Act of 1964 (42 U.S.C. 2000e-8) is amended by adding at the end the following:

"(f) (1) Not later than 18 months after the date of enactment of this subsection, the Commission shall—

"(A) complete a survey of the data that is currently available to the Federal Government relating to employee pay information for use in the enforcement of Federal laws prohibiting pay discrimination and, in consultation with other relevant Federal agencies, identify additional data collections that will enhance the enforcement of such laws; and

"(B) based on the results of the survey and consultations under subparagraph (A), issue regulations to provide for the collection of pay information data from employers as described by the sex, race, and national origin of employees.

"(2) In implementing paragraph (1), the Commission shall have as its primary consideration the most effective and efficient means for enhancing the enforcement of Federal laws prohibiting pay discrimination. For this purpose, the Commission shall consider factors including the imposition of burdens on employers, the frequency of required reports (including which employers should be required to prepare reports), appropriate protections for maintaining data confidentiality, and the most effective format for the data collection reports.".

SEC. 9. REINSTATEMENT OF PAY EQUITY PROGRAMS AND PAY EQUITY DATA COLLECTION.

(a) Bureau of Labor Statistics Data Collection—The Commissioner of Labor Statistics shall continue to collect data on women workers in the Current Employment Statistics survey.

(b) Office of Federal Contract Compliance Programs Initiatives—The Director of the Office of Federal Contract Compliance Programs shall ensure that employees of the Office—

(1) (A) shall use the full range of investigatory tools at the Office's disposal, including pay grade methodology;

(B) in considering evidence of possible compensation discrimination—

(i) shall not limit its consideration to a small number of types of evidence; and

(ii) shall not limit its evaluation of the evidence to a small number of methods of evaluating the evidence; and

(C) shall not require a multiple regression analysis or anecdotal evidence for a compensation discrimination case;

(2) for purposes of its investigative, compliance, and enforcement activities, shall define "similarly situated employees" in a way that is consistent with and not more stringent than the definition provided in item 1 of subsection A of section 10-III of the Equal Employment Opportunity Commission Compliance Manual (2000), and shall consider only factors that the Office's investigation reveals were used in making compensation decisions; and

(3) shall reinstate the Equal Opportunity Survey, as required by section 60-2.18 of title 41, Code of Federal Regulations (as in effect on September 7, 2006), designating not less than half of all nonconstruction contractor establishments each year to prepare and file such survey, and shall review and utilize the responses to such survey to identify contractor establishments for further evaluation and for other enforcement purposes as appropriate.

(c) DEPARTMENT OF LABOR DISTRIBUTION OF WAGE DISCRIMINATION INFORMATION—The Secretary of Labor shall make readily available (in print, on the Department of Labor website, and through any other forum that the Department may use to distribute compensation discrimination information), accurate information on compensation discrimination, including statistics, explanations of employee rights, historical analyses of such discrimination, instructions for employers on compliance, and any other information that will assist the public in understanding and addressing such discrimination.

SEC. 10. AUTHORIZATION OF APPROPRIATIONS.

(a) AUTHORIZATION OF APPROPRIATIONS—There are authorized to be appropriated $15,000,000 to carry out this Act.

(b) PROHIBITION ON EARMARKS—None of the funds appropriated pursuant to subsection (a) for purposes of the grant program in section 5 of this Act may be used for a Congressional earmark as defined in clause 9(d) of rule XXI of the Rules of the House of Representatives.

SEC. 11. SMALL BUSINESS ASSISTANCE.

(a) EFFECTIVE DATE—This Act and the amendments made by this Act shall take effect on the date that is 6 months after the date of enactment of this Act.

(b) TECHNICAL ASSISTANCE MATERIALS—The Secretary of Labor and the Commissioner of the Equal Employment Opportunity Commission shall jointly develop technical assistance material to assist small businesses in complying with the requirements of this Act and the amendments made by this Act.

(c) SMALL BUSINESSES—A small business shall be exempt from the provisions of this Act to the same extent that such business is exempt from the requirements of the Fair Labor Standards Act pursuant to section 3(s)(1)(A)(i) and (ii) of such Act.

SEC. 12. RULE OF CONSTRUCTION.

Nothing in this Act, or in any amendments made by this Act, shall affect the obligation of employers and employees to fully comply with all applicable immigration laws, including any penalties, fines, or other sanctions.

RESOURCES

PROCESS FOR FILING A COMPLAINT OF
EMPLOYMENT DISCRIMINATION

THE EQUAL Employment Opportunity Commission (EEOC), established as part of the Civil Rights Act of 1964, enforces Title VII and other antidiscrimination laws such as the Age Discrimination in Employment Act (ADEA) and the Equal Pay Act. Sex-discrimination claims must use Title VII, which requires that an employee file a charge of discrimination within 180 days of the act of discrimination. Some states have their own antidiscrimination laws and give the employee 300 days from the act of discrimination to file, while federal employees have a different complaint process and must contact an EEO counselor within 45 days.

Before filing a federal lawsuit for discrimination and harassment under Title VII, you must first file a charge of discrimination with the EEOC, which then investigates the charge, requesting relevant information and documents pertaining to the charge from both the employee and employer. At the end of its investigation, the EEOC may close its file without completing the investigation, conclude that it did not find a violation of law occurred, or conclude that there is substantial evidence of a violation, otherwise known as "cause determination."

If the EEOC makes a cause determination, it will attempt to conciliate the case by achieving a settlement between the parties, as well as require the employer to take certain steps to preclude future occurrences of discrimination or sexual harassment. If this fails, the EEOC has the right to file its own case against the employer and the employee may join that case with her own attorney. If the EEOC does not pursue its own case, it will issue a right to sue and the employee has 90 days to file in federal court.

If the EEOC closes its file without completing the investigation or is unable to conclude a violation occurred, it will also issue a notice of right to sue. The employee then has 90 days to file her case in federal court, losing her opportunity to file once that 90 days has passed.

A violation under the Equal Pay Act does not require an employee to file a charge with the EEOC. The time limit for filing a case in federal court is two years within the alleged unlawful compensation practice; in the case of a willful violation, the limit is three years.

ADVOCACY

While the author has made every effort to provide accurate telephone numbers and Internet addresses at the time of publication, neither the publisher nor author assumes any responsibility for errors, or for changes that occur after publication. Further, the publisher does not have any control over and does not assume any responsibility for author or third-party websites or their contents.

**American Association of
University Women**
Phone: 800-326-AAUW
www.aauw.org

ACLU Women's Rights Project
(co-founded by Ruth Bader
Ginsburg)
Phone: 212-549-2500
www.aclu.org/womens-rights

Black Women United for Action
Phone: 703-922-5757
www.bwufa.org

**Business and Professional
Women's Foundation**
Phone: 202-293-1100
www.bpwusa.org

Coalition of Labor Union Women
Phone: 202-508-6969
www.cluw.org

Equal Employment Opportunity Center
Phone: 800-699-4000
www.eeoc.com

Equal Employment Opportunity Commission
Phone: 800-669-4000
www.eeoc.gov

Equal Rights Advocates
Advice and Counseling Hotline:
800-839-4ERA (4372).
The hotline provides advice
on differential treatment of
women and girls at work or
school, unequal pay, pregnancy
discrimination, family leave, and
sexual harassment.
www.equalrights.org

Federally Employed Women
Phone: 402-898-0994
www.few.org

Feminist Majority Foundation
Phone: 703-522-2214
www.feminist.org

General Federation of Women's Clubs
Phone: 202-347-3168
www.gfwc.org

MANA, A National Latina Organization
Phone: 202-833-0060
www.hermana.org

Moms Rising
www.momsrising.org

National Association of Commissions for Women
Phone: 505-681-8629
www.nacw.org

National Committee on Pay Equity
Phone: 703-920-2010
www.pay-equity.org

National Council of Jewish Women
Phone: 202-296-2588
(Washington, D.C., office);
212-645-4048 (New York City
headquarters)
www.ncjw.org

National Congress of Black Women
Phone: 202-678-6788
www.nationalcongressbw.org

**National Council of
Negro Women**
Phone: 202-737-0120
www.ncnw.org

**National Council of
Women's Organizations**
Phone: 202-293-4505
www.womensorganizations.org

**National Organization
for Women**
Phone: 202-628-8669
www.now.org

**National Partnership for
Women and Families**
Phone: 202-986-2600
www.nationalpartnership.org

**National Women's
Political Caucus**
Phone: 202-785-1100
www.nwpc.org

**9to5 National Association
of Working Women**
Phone: 414-274-0925; Job Survival
Helpline: 800-522-0925 and
mailto:hotline@9to5.org.
The hotline provides information
on sexual harassment, family
leave, pregnancy discrimination,
and other employment issues.
www.9to5.org

**Nontraditional Employment
for Women**
Phone: 212-627-6252
www.new-nyc.org

**OWL: The Voice of Midlife
and Older Women**
Phone: 877-653-7966
www.owl-national.org

The Wage Project
www.wageproject.org

**Wider Opportunities
for Women**
Phone: 202-464-1596
www.wowonline.com

Women Employed
Phone: 312-782-3902
Women Employed provides
telephone counseling to women
facing employment problems
Friday 10 A.M.–12 P.M. (CT).
www.womenemployed.org

**Women Work! The National
Network for Women's
Employment**
Phone: 412-281-9240;
866-PAWOMEN (729-6636)
www.womenwork.org

YWCA USA
Phone: 202-467-0801
www.ywca.org

LEGAL

National Women's Law Center
Phone: 202-588-5180
www.nwlc.org

Women's Law and Policy Project/Sargent Shriver National Center on Poverty Law
Phone: 312-263-3830
www.povertylaw.org

SUPREME COURT DECISIONS

Oyez Project
www.oyez.com

PROFESSIONAL

National Association for Female Executives
Phone: 212-351-6451
www.nafe.com

U.S. Women's Chamber of Commerce
Phone: 888-41-USWCC
www.uswcc.org

RESEARCH

Catalyst
Phone: 212-514-7600
www.catalyst.org

Cornell University Institute for Women & Work
Phone: 212-340-2836
www.ilr.cornell.edu/iww

Institute for Women's Policy Research
Phone: 202-785-5100
www.iwpr.org

National Council for Research on Women
Phone: 212-785-7335
www.ncrw.org

FURTHER READING

Brzezinski, Mika. *Knowing Your Value: Women, Money, and Getting What You're Worth*. New York: Weinstein Books, 2010.

Burk, Martha. *Cult of Power: Sex Discrimination in Corporate America and What We Can Do About It*. New York: Scribner, 2005.

———. *Your Money and Your Life: The High Stakes for Women Voters in '08 and Beyond*. Austin: A.U. Publishing, 2008.

Collins, Gail. *When Everything Changed: The Amazing Journey of American Women from 1960 to the Present*. New York: Little, Brown and Company, 2009.

Greenhouse, Linda. "Justices Limit Discrimination Suits over Pay." *New York Times*, May 29, 2007.

Murphy, Evelyn, with E. J. Graff. *Getting Even: Why Women Don't Get Paid Like Men—and What to Do About It*. New York: Simon & Schuster, 2005.

ACKNOWLEDGMENTS

I NEVER COULD have made this journey alone, a journey that began in rural Alabama in one of the poorest counties in the country and led me to the Supreme Court, on to Congress, and all the way to the White House. Countless individuals and organizations contributed to the successful passage of the Lilly Ledbetter Fair Pay Restoration Act in January 2009. Individuals committed to pay equity—both women and men, young and old, rich and poor—supported me on my long journey. Legal, political, nonprofit, business, and professional groups provided the practical guidance and financial means to sustain this endeavor I'd embarked upon. Without so many passionate people, my story would have had a very different ending. To all, I am most thankful and forever grateful.

INDEX